DOWN
the ROAD

Journeys Through Small-Town British Columbia

Rosemary Neering

whitecap

Edited by Elaine Jones
Interior design by Carolyn Deby
Cover design by Jacqui Thomas
Cover photograph by David R. Gluns/Natural Image Photography
Typset at The Vancouver Desktop Publishing Centre Ltd.

Printed and bound in Canada at Friesens

National Library of Canada Cataloguing in Publication Data
Neering, Rosemary, 1945–
     Down the road: journeys through small-town British Columbia/
Rosemary Neering.

     ISBN 1-55285-464-7

     1. Cities and towns—British Columbia.   2. British Columbia—Description
and travel.   I. Title.

FC3811.N44 2003   971.1'04   C2003–910246–7
F1087.N44 2003

The publisher acknowledges the asssistance of the Canada Council and the Cultural
Services Branch of the Government of British Columbia in making this publication
possible. We acknowledge the financial support of the Government of Canada through
the Book Publishing Industry Development Program for our publishing activities.

This book is dedicated
to all those people
who welcomed me to their towns,
who invited me home for dinner
or out for a beer,
who shared their lives with me,
who insisted I come back again some time.

Meeting you has been the greatest pleasure.

Thanks go to
Bob Turner and Bill Valgardson; to Tim Cummings,
Bryan McGill, Dan Pasemko, and Delia and John
Sansom, all of whom read all or parts of the manuscript
and commented thereon; to Colleen MacMillan, for
believing; to Elaine Jones for good ideas, *-our* and *-re;*
and especially to Joe Thompson,
for unfailing help and support.

~

The author gratefully acknowledges the assistance of
the Cultural Services Branch, through the Ministry of
Municipal Affairs, Recreation and Culture, Minister
the Honorable Graham P. Bruce.

Contents

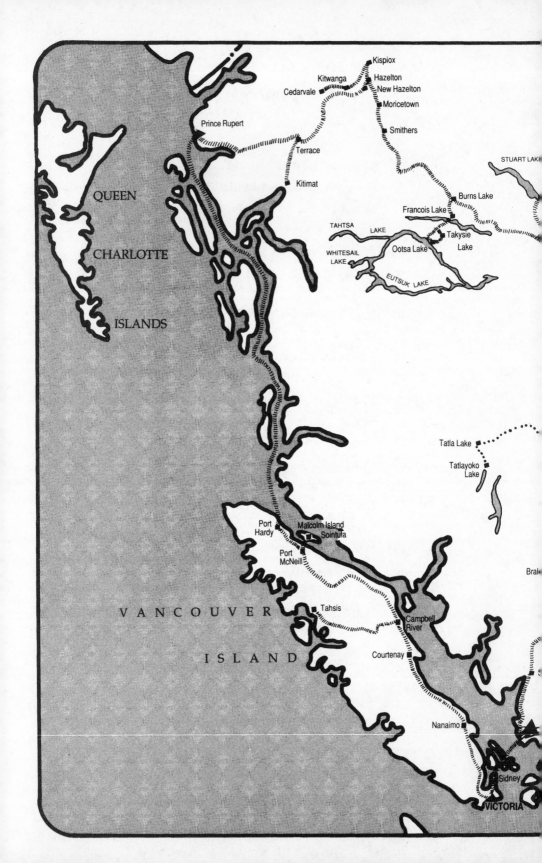

Foreword, 2003

It happens every time.

An hour or two from the city, I leave the four-lane for the two-lane, the two lane for the gravel. My speed slows, my heart leaps and I am singing—very badly—as I once more enter small-town country.

I don't know why I have this fascination with the rural world. I was born in a very large city, grew up in a smaller one. Other than a few months here and there, I have never lived in a place where there are no stoplights. I am an indifferent chopper of wood, and my version of self-reliance—a quality imperative in small towns—tends more towards paying someone to fix the plumbing or reshingle the roof than to doing it myself.

So why do I find these travels into the world of small towns so fascinating—intriguing enough that, a decade ago, I spent more than a year wandering the back roads and writing *Down the Road: Journeys through Small-Town British Columbia*?

Part of the reason is the pace of life, slower and saner than the city swiftness. Part is the closeness to nature, the forest or the mountains just outside the town. Much, though, has to do with the people and the tales they tell. When I first began visiting small towns, I was amazed by the time people took to talk and by their willingness to tell me stories (some of which were true and some of which were legends.) Sometimes, it seems as if everyone has a story to tell and the time to tell it. *Out there*, I find a much greater connection to the past, to the community and to the surrounding country.

Part of the attraction is the remarkable resilience of small-town life. Small towns are dying: we hear it all the time. The mill closes, the doctor leaves town, the school shuts its doors, and the town is doomed. Yet the towns still carry on. When I wander the byways now, I find the same mix of dreamers and realists, adventurers and lost souls, gregarious folk and loners, that I encountered a dozen years ago.

When I began the odyssey that resulted in this book, I thought I might one day be among them, lured by the community feeling, the closeness to nature and the strong self-reliance that I found. By the time I wrote the last line, I knew I was a city person. I'm too ill at ease with the small social compass of small towns and too fond of city services and amenities to make the move.

But I always return, drawn back by the friendliness, the stories, the silence and the stars so visible far from the city lights. I never can resist a chance to head down the road, journeying once more to small-town British Columbia.

CHAPTER 1

Coffee at the Red Top

JJ Frost is welded to the windshield under a starry predawn sky. A faint growl echoes from the road, as the driver of a chip truck gears down for the descent to the lumber mill. At the Red Top Cafe, the smell of fresh coffee filters out into the freezing air and Marianne turns on the grill.

At half past four, Wilma opens the door and the regulars drift in: truckers waiting for the mill to open, millworkers retired from their jobs but not from their morning coffee and conversation. They kid Wilma and Marianne and each other, easy every-morning jokes, and talk about the weather and what went on at the bar last night. Police constable Judy Dempsey, on a mid-shift break, sits drinking coffee and smoking cigarettes with grader operator Bob Tarney. She describes her recent Hawaii vacation; he brings her up to date about the fatal accident out on the highway last week, a driver killed when his car spun across pavement slick with freezing rain into the path of two giant trucks.

Small-town British Columbia, early morning. A decade ago, I spent five years wandering the province, writing stories for a tourist magazine. Now I am back on the road again, this time in Merritt, a town of sixty-five hundred people surrounded by hills in the dry interior plateau country.

The day that starts at four in the morning with the sound of trucks and the smell of coffee brings many small-town glimpses. In the late morning, I drive out along the Coldwater River, through grey rounded hills fringed with golden bunch grass, dotted with solitary pines, dusted with snow. In his studio on the Coldwater Interior Salish Indian Reserve, Opie Oppenheimer strokes the emerging curves of a stone sculpture he is creating, and talks about his life. Opie's arms are laced with scars, but they are nothing compared to the scars inside, from the bad times, when he was down and out on Vancouver's skid road, prisoner to drink and drugs, eating out of garbage cans.

"I was so angry and so bitter for so long at the man upstairs," he says, quietly. "I had reason to be angry. It was like I was dragging a big, heavy bag around, being brown and being hated. I read once there were three big risks for banks: ex-convicts, the insane—and Indians." Opie dragged that bag around for twenty years, then found a way to let it go. He became a born-again Christian —and he came home to the Coldwater. "A lot of us came home from the city about that time. It was just a nothing life. We said, 'Enough's enough. Let's be something.'" Opie points with pride at the bright houses and the school on the reserve, speaks with deep feeling about the lakes and hills of his home country. Like many other people I have met, native and non-native, he has traded the stress and the hustle of the city for what he sees as the sanity of rural life.

But small towns have their own dilemmas. An editorial in this week's Merritt paper expresses one clearly: the sawdust burners at the lumber mills spit flyash that coats the downtown cars and streets, and a permanent brown cloud hovers above the valley. Demand for wood denudes the hills in an ever-growing circle widening out from town. But the mills are the major employers, and Merritt once spent twenty long years legally bankrupt. The mine to the north has closed, the ranches employ only a few hundred people, and tourism pays poorly. Without the mills, fear the people of Merritt, the town would die. Like other small-town people, they are between their desire to live life their own, often fiercely individualistic, way, and their need to make a living in an economy increasingly ruled by big corporations and big government.

The world of men and women is not so simple in a small town either. Out in the snowy hills that ring Merritt, I drive past a hideaway that used to belong to a man I met last time I was here, angry and maudlin because his wife had left him. "Wasn't much life for a woman out here," he confessed. "But now she's in town, having a good time with all the single guys. And what am I supposed to do? There's not even a goddammed whore in this town!"

They have their drawbacks, but small towns also have their strengths. Late in the afternoon, just off main street, the United Church men fire up Old Smoky, Merritt's peripatetic griddle that travels from one service club event to the next, and dish out pancakes, bacon, sausage and gallons of coffee to townspeople who crowd long trestle tables in the church hall for the annual pancake supper. Everyone knows everyone; greetings spill out over the noise of plates clashing and chairs scraping. The church minister, bemused by the question, says that the argument over the ordination of homosexuals hasn't affected his congregation at all. "I guess we're a little more tolerant in a small town."

Supper's over, and Alf and Carol Tessier are at the Coldwater Hotel on Merritt's main street, she with a frothy pink drink, he with a beer, ready for an evening of swapping stories. Alf drove a logging truck for years before "industrial safety"; he rolled trucks more than fifty times, five times in one particularly bad week. At the end of that week, Alf's boss picked him up and started driving. Alf figured he was being paid off, but the boss didn't stop in Merritt, and he didn't stop down the road in Ashcroft or in Hope. When they reached Vancouver, the boss dropped Alf off at the Hotel Vancouver and told him there was a room booked in his name. Alf unlocked the door—and backed off when a lovely lady emerged. "You Alf?" she asked. "Yup." "Come on in." Alf didn't leave the room for two days. "Boss figured if that didn't change my luck, nothing would." He still remembers the room number.

Of course, he chuckles, that was in the days before Carol. Now he stays closer to home, but he still loves to dance, so right away, he's up on the tiny floor, stepping to the rhythms of the country and western duo twanging away in a corner of the room, his round face getting redder and redder, sweat running into his white beard and sideburns. He rarely sits down on a dancing night, because if you dance with one of the gals, you'd better be prepared to dance with them all.

I go happy out into the frosty night, hearing in the distance the ever-present murmur of the chip trucks. As I head up the hill towards my motel, I think about how much I have missed talking to people like Opie and Alf, drinking coffee in places like the Red Top, seeing snowy hills lit by stars. And I decide it is time to escape from the clocks and complications of city life, to spend some time in the small towns and rural areas of British Columbia. I want to be back where it is a five-minute walk to the edge of town, where story-telling is still an art, and where people know their neighbours and accept them, good and bad. I want to know how the people out there are faring in these days of dish antennas and high-speed highways. Are they surviving the bottom-line thinking that devalues the independence they care about and that makes it ever harder for them to earn a living? Is living close to the lakes and mountains, never seeing a traffic jam, ample compensation for not having the conveniences of the city? Do small-town people know something about life that we in the cities have forgotten?

I decide to avoid in my wanderings officials of any stripe—chiefs and mayors, members of parliament, and designated spokespeople for any cause at all—and listen instead to people I find in coffee shops and at work, at home and in the hills. I will stay away from any place that has shopping malls or parking meters; I will spend as few miles as possible on main highways.

As I drift off to sleep, I begin to plan my route on a mind's-eye map of British Columbia.

CHAPTER 2

Spring:
Vancouver Island

JJ Three months later, I set out on the road. The dogwoods are in bloom along the island highway from Victoria north to Campbell River, 165 miles away. Pickup trucks with whip antennas play tag with lumbering mobile homes and transport trucks, pulling out to pass at thunderous speeds on curves and hills. Through winter and early spring, highways crews have dynamited and trundled away loads of rock, widening the highway so it takes four hours, not four and a half to reach the River. Such is progress.

Just north of Campbell River, Highway 28 branches west from the coast, one of only two public roads that cross Vancouver Island's mountain spine. Spindly trunks of second-growth forest stand in regimented ranks along both sides of the highway as it climbs towards the mountains; the stumps and spars drowned when Buttle Lake was dammed more than thirty years ago rise bleached and bony above the water.

Any time you mention the west coast mill village of Tahsis, people ask, "You're not going in on *that* road, are you?" True, the gravel road from Gold River north to Tahsis hairpins across mountainsides above sheer drops; sharp rocks lie large and loose on some sections, embedded and treacherous in others, and fresh gravel slides and slips. Rain, ice or snow would make the road truly interesting. But this main road seems not one-tenth as frightening as the narrow, twisting, abrupt tracks that wind up into the clouds through the logging clear-cuts.

Two hundred years ago, the Mowachaht people of the coastal Nootka, led by Chief Maquinna, wintered at the end of Tahsis Inlet, sheltered from the storms and trials of the open ocean. When the herring ran in February, they returned along the inlet to their summer villages on the coves of the coast. Fifty years ago, the only residents of Tahsis were two squatters who lived at the inlet's head, visited from time to time by wandering prospectors and trappers. Then the Gibson brothers towed in a floating logging camp and set twelve men to work felling trees at water's edge. The brothers established a permanent onshore camp in the late 1940s.

A subsidiary of the multinational Danish East Asiatic Company bought out the Gibsons in 1950, and expanded the sawmills. By 1956, the Danish company planned "an industrial empire of major import-ance to British Columbia," and though the town of eight hundred could still be reached only by boat or air, an admiring visitor wrote, "Tahsis is the largest and most progressive town on the west coast of Vancouver Island beyond Port Alberni." Ten years later, the manager of Tahsis's new, large, automated sawmill boasted that "it takes about 300 years to grow a tree and three minutes to cut it up." This was a company town, planned and regulated by its owners, who at one point even limited the maximum length of cars —ten feet, eleven and a half inches—that could be barged in to Tahsis's narrow streets. In 1970, the village was incor-porated and residents took over control from the company. Power lines and a road were built to connect Tahsis to the rest of the world and East Asiatic sold its two mills to Canadian Pacific Forest Products Limited.

Though Tahsis has changed, lines of identical mill houses still border its streets, older on the hill above the sawmill, newer on the straight-edged townsite between the inlet's curve and the river's edge. Urban British Columbia may be converting to bright, trendy pubs, but the bar out past the mill is unreservedly a working man's beer parlour, born and nurtured in the days of pickled eggs, pepperoni, and waiters who carry a dozen glasses of beer on a tray, shoulder high and one-handed.

In years past, I'm told, this bar netted the highest revenues of any bar in British Columbia. Millworkers made forty thousand dollars a year; they came here to save a stake, pay their bills, and get back to the city. Every year, as winter rains isolated the little world of Tahsis, they'd spend their savings on B-52s and other exotic drinks, or gamble them away in high-stakes card games.

At a table up by the bar, Ken Paisley orders a southern comfort and orange and talks about those raucous bunkhouse days, when employee turnover was 200 percent every year. He was eighteen and naive when he arrived in Tahsis, and he'd never seen anything like it. "There was one bunkhouse for addicts, one for East Indians, one for homosexuals. They put me in with the addicts. I didn't get any sleep, with the partying and the noise." He asked to be moved, and was bunked in with the East Indians. That didn't suit him either, so he was assigned to the gay bunkhouse. "They were all older guys, and they didn't bother me, so I stayed there for a couple of months." And then did he go to an "ordinary" bunkhouse? He looks amused. "I don't know what 'ordinary' is in this town."

Ken rarely went to the bar then: too much violence, with knife fights and broken bottles slashing through the air. The company closed the bunkhouses in 1986 and shut down the cedar mill in 1987. Tahsis's population dropped almost overnight from fifteen hundred to nine hundred. Tonight, only a few dedicated drinkers are at scattered tables, their cigarettes burning beside the draft beer that spills over onto the tatty carpet. A buddy from the mill reels by on the way back from the toilet, and does a double–take when he sees Ken, a rare patron of the bar. He slumps into a chair beside us, his head drooping almost to the table. "I need a break," he mutters. "It's a competition over there," he flips a hand towards his table of drinking companions, "and I'm losing. I used to do this before I got married. What'll I say when I get home?" He gets up with difficulty and goes back to the battle.

Every weekday, Ken cycles to his work on the booms below the mill. Every winter weekend, he dons wet suit and straps on air tanks, to sink beneath the inlet waters with his friends in the scuba-diving club. "You can pick anywhere. It's great; nobody's ever dove there." For several years, he's been searching for the remains of an American whisky trader, captured and burned by the Nootka in 1803. Diving, playing slowpitch baseball, fishing, exploring the limestone caves back along the road, bowling, watching television: Ken and his family find lots to do in and around Tahsis. But he both loves and hates this town.

"It's a safe place to raise kids. We have our share of weirdos here, but everyone knows who they are and we tell our kids to watch out for them.

"The worst thing for me is that people are always saying they're going. 'When we go, we'll . . . .' They don't want to get involved because they think they're just temporary. A small group of very active people do just about everything. Mostly, the ones who volunteer for one thing volunteer for everything." The others? "Watching TV and drinking."

Ken is one of the active people. He wants Tahsis to survive, and he's convinced that logging practices will have to change for it to do so. "We need more community involvement in the decision-making process." He submitted a brief to recent government forest resources commission hearings, and was invited to Campbell River to read it. When he talks about the forest industry, he's passionate. "The wood cut in an area should be processed in that area. We lose massive amounts of wood to sinkage. Ten percent of the hemlock handled here never reaches the mill; it's deep-sixed. I've got underwater videos to prove it. The mill could move their equipment to shallower water, break bundles in shallower water.

"If the commission listens, things will turn out well for Tahsis. If not, Tahsis will disappear." Ken sees only disaster ahead if the big corporations continue to make decisions that ignore the welfare of the towns that fuel the logging industry.

Though he's a member of the International Woodworkers of America, Ken is contemptuous of union leadership. "They're the green dinosaurs. They don't represent me, they don't represent anyone but themselves. There was a one-dollar levy on the latest vote card to fight the 'tree huggers'. Well, I'm a tree hugger."

After I talk to Ken, I call up one of the long-time managers at the mill to make an appointment to see him in the morning. But in the morning, he's off with the flu, diplomatic or real, and no one else wants to talk to me. Writers are not welcome visitors in the B.C. forest industry these days, when everyone is taking shots at clear-cutting and other logging practices. I persist. Grudgingly, a management man, in Tahsis just two years, spares half an hour to reel off statistics and optimism. But his upbeat words can't hide the malaise revealed by talk around town. In retrospect, long-time Tahsis residents see the paternalistic East Asiatic Company as a caring company, locally involved. Canadian Pacific is viewed as an uncaring, impersonal giant, concerned only with the bottom line and not at all with whether the village of Tahsis continues to exist. The East Asiatic chairman used to show up for company-sponsored Christmas parties; CPFP doesn't sponsor parties.

The manager goes off to a meeting, and long-time office workers Margaret Ross and Karen Zabinsky sit me down with a coffee and tell me about their Tahsis lives. Margaret has lived on the west coast all her life: born just around the corner at Esperanza, she sampled city life for five years in Vancouver, then came happily back to Tahsis twenty-seven years ago. She got married here, is raising kids —now nine and eleven— here, loves life here. "It's peaceful, quiet. I enjoy having the kids able to

do things— in the city, I'd be afraid to let them go." Her husband works
as a superintendent at the mill, her father-in-law and brother-in-law as
millwrights. At Easter, the family made a video, eight cousins all
playing and performing together. "In the city, cousins don't always get
to be cousins."

Karen came to Tahsis twenty years ago with her first husband, and
raised three children here. She has always been determined that her
family would not fall into the "it's raining again; let's watch TV"
couch-potato trap. She hardly ever turns her television on unless there's
something good on Knowledge Network. The family is always going
off by boat down the inlet to Friendly Cove, or Gold River, or Zeballos,
or Fair Harbour.

Remarried just last weekend, she and her new husband plan on one
day retiring to the island's east coast. They'll make the move because,
despite the clean air, the quiet, and life on a smaller scale, things aren't
the same here anymore. When the road opened in 1972, the community
began to change. "Before, we were all one big happy family. Everybody
looked after everybody else. When the road opened, a lot of people came
in just to make big bucks. People keep more to themselves now. We
don't have that small-town feeling any longer."

With regret, Margaret agrees. "The people who have come in the last
few years are just not community-minded. They're here to work.
They're not here to stay. They really don't take any responsibility in the
community."

Last night in the pub, Grant Skinner whizzed by, far too busy for
anything as frivolous as a social drink. Intense, a perpetual motion
machine, he runs between his day job for B.C. Telephone and a second
job servicing vending machines, his work as Tahsis alderman, and his
family role as single father, summoned back and forth by the pager
hooked on his belt. He wouldn't stop to talk, but suggested we "do
lunch." I demurred: I don't do lunch. I agreed to eat lunch. Grant
grinned. "I just wanted you to know I was bilingual."

"Do you know what a diode is?" he demands over sloppy joes in the
hotel restaurant today. He compares the road to Tahsis to a diode:
one-sided communication where the outside world talks, but refuses to
listen. Tahsis, he says, is a different reality.

"Those commercials on TV about drinking and driving, they say if
you drink, take a bus or a taxi home. Tahsis doesn't have a bus or a taxi.
Maybe some of the profits the liquor board makes could be used to

subsidize a taxi here.

"We have all the downside of government control but none of the resources. If the insurance agent here gets sick, that's just too bad—but don't drive without insurance, because we do have police. The punitive and enforcement side is here, but not the benefits."

He remembers arguing fiercely with a provincial government tourism representative, telling her that normal regulations couldn't apply to Tahsis. She wouldn't agree that Tahsis was any different from any place else in the province. She headed for the village, to continue the discussion, but turned back after a few miles on the dreaded road, and conducted her future conversations by phone. "How many other places," Grant demanded, "did you never make it to because of the road?"

He suspects he's fighting a losing battle, but it's a battle he won't retreat from. "Some people here speak as if they are in prison: 'When I get out of here, I'm going to . . . .' But some of us value personal freedom. That's being rapidly eroded outside. And we still escape some regulations, living here. I love the fact that we don't have a single no-smoking sign here." He has a lot of freedom in where and when and how he does his telephone company job. "This is probably the only job I'm emotionally equipped to handle," he says, quite seriously.

Grant came here fifteen years ago from the closing-down town of Ocean Falls up the coast. "Now that was truly isolated," he recalls. Some of the changes he sees in Tahsis make him angry. "We used to be able to get CBC, sort of. Now we get thirteen channels of mind-rotting garbage, and the theatre has closed down because it could no longer afford to run movies. We're as well equipped to sleep, work, and watch TV as people in New York City—probably better, because we don't have to fight the subway."

Though he wants to bring in tourists, Grant doesn't want to see a good paved road leading the world to Tahsis. That would put a permanent end to the village's isolation, and to what independence it still possesses. "At Gold River, if you give people a long coffee break, they drive to Campbell River."

When the company closed down the cedar mill and the population of Tahsis dwindled, people became increasingly uncertain about the town's future. "You can buy a house here for twenty-five thousand any day of the week, and rent it out for six hundred a month— but nobody does, because they're not sure there will be tenants here long enough to pay off the mortgage."

The uncertainty, the isolation, the two hundred inches of rain a year, the limited services, result in an unusual population distribution, with almost ninety percent of Tahsis people under fifty, no unemployed to speak of ("if you lose your job, you just leave town," says Grant) and just one or two retired. Charlotte Tasker and her husband Ken are anomalies, happily retired and with little intention of leaving town. They came here in 1956, when the only ways in and out were by sea and air. Her husband came first; she and their two young daughters arrived later aboard the *Princess of Alberni*, chugging along the inlet one day and two nights from Port Alberni, with the little girls penned up in the wheelhouse the whole trip, to keep them from tumbling overboard.

For years, Tahsis lived by the rhythm of the sea. Charlotte remembers Saturday nights when the water taxi *Merry Mead* docked with a precious cargo of drinkables from the liquor store upcoast at Zeballos. At Christmas time, "we chartered the boat and went to Zeballos, three hours there and three hours back, and that was our Christmas shopping. There was nothing here but the company store."

The *Merry Mead* was followed by the *Uchucks I, II* and *III*; the *Uchuck III*, a converted minesweeper, still comes regularly to Tahsis, bringing, now, mostly tourists and some heavy freight. For years, the steamer *Tahsis Prince*, built in 1920 in Europe and a tramp steamer since then, brought in the heavy loads, but the *Prince* ran aground in 1968. She was followed by the *Northland Prince*. When the road came through, that ship was towed north to Pendrill Sound, to end her days as a floating camp for an oyster seed farmer.

Charlotte and Ken invested their emotional capital in Tahsis. Ken was a lumber inspector, the magistrate, the coroner and the citizenship court judge—the last two, positions he still holds. "Any parties here, we had to be away by midnight," recalls Charlotte, "because after that the fights broke out, and Ken was magistrate."

As public health nurse, Charlotte dealt with all the problems brought on by isolation. "I would always tell new mothers, don't go to the neighbours for a coffee klatsch unless you want to go crazy. Go buy a loaf of bread even if you don't need one, go for a walk." Always involved, Charlotte led Girl Guides and Brownies, played the organ, joined the United Church women's group. But now the church group is down to three people and Charlotte, tired of all the infighting and gossip that go on in any small town, has backed off, content to work in her garden, among her rhododendrons. "A lot of the younger people here don't know what to do with themselves except weep—and drink. We always had to make our own fun."

But Tahsis will always be home to the Taskers. "All our spiritual and financial resources are here. These are our roots."

CHAPTER 3

Island Utopia

)) Back across the island, in Campbell River, the rain hammers down, a drum roll on the windshield, curtaining up from the roads and coursing down the gutters. Metal fishboat masts appear and disappear through the squall; the harbour is here and gone, here and gone. Despite the downpour, a dozen cars are lined up at the McDonald's drive-thru, and traffic in this city of seventeen thousand is constant.

North of town, the traffic thins, then evaporates. For decades, Kelsey Bay, fifty miles out from the River, was the end of the highway and the beginning of the Inside Passage ferry route to Prince Rupert far to the north. Until the 1950s, there was no public way to the north island by car. After the highway west opened, you could head out to Gold River, then bump and slither over logging roads to the isolated logging camps and fishing villages on the north end of the island.

In 1979, road builders completed a new highway, cutting inland from the east coast north of Campbell River through forest that had long been almost the private preserve of logging companies. South of Campbell River, the coast is crowded with condos and resorts and towns, tamed by farm fields that stretch from water's edge to mountain slope. But here, no houses exist for mile on mile; this is still a raw, new road. It passes through old logging clear-cuts, greening now, with brave new signs that announce replanting began in 1988 —or 1976, or 1922. Fir is the favoured species for replanting, with occasional cedars and hemlocks, unmistakable with their floppy tops, poking out among the alders that have taken over some of the newer cuts.

The wall that divides the restaurant from the kitchen at the Woss logging town cafe is plastered with foreign currency and silly signs; one declares, "There is no reason. It's just our policy." A slice of bumbleberry pie—peach, blueberry, rhubarb, whatever else was left over when the cook was making pies—and back on the road again.

The rain slows, then stops. A painter's sky looms overhead, pale smoky smudges brushed onto a deep charcoal base. Side roads lead off to the fishing and logging communities of Port Alice, Telegraph Cove and Port McNeill, whence a small ferry carries cars and passengers to Alert Bay, on Cormorant Island, and to the old Finnish colony of Sointula on Malcolm Island.

Down on the ferry dock, the two dozen cars and trucks that wait in line for the ferry are joined by eighty high school students making their daily return trip from Port McNeill to Alert Bay or Sointula. On board, the forward lounge is bedlam, younger boys smacking each other in mock-battle, whooping and laughing, examining the latest sports trading cards. The aft lounge, lair of senior students playing it cool, is decorous by comparison. Outside, a blonde-maned girl bends her head over her friend's lighter, straightens up with a toss of her hair and draws deeply on her cigarette.

First stop, Sointula. The ferry docks at the centre of town, where houses stack up the hill a few blocks deep behind the hotel and the two-storey frame building that houses the co-operative store and the credit union. The houses taper off in a long single line along the seafront, weathered wood or white-painted frame behind inventive driftwood fences. At the north end of town, new netlofts alternate with old shingled shacks that lean gracefully towards the water and the masts of fishing boats rise above the rock breakwater.

I park in front of the hotel and walk down the curving road. Although the Sointula library opens just eight hours a week, only librarian Linda Burrows is thumbing through books on this late afternoon. She points out a room where the stacks are lined with books in Finnish, donated by the people of Sointula, and shakes her head over the massive problem that cataloguing them properly would be. Now, they bear only a number, given to each book in sequence when it arrived at the library. "Sometimes, I don't even know whether it's the author's name or the title on the spine," she says.

The books, like the occasional Finnish words you hear spoken on the streets or in the store, like the saunas still present beside some of the houses, like the pale blonde hair of some Sointulans or the many k's and j's in the telephone book, are a legacy of Sointula's past. At the turn of the century, many Finns left home for North America or Australia, seeking freedom from their Tsarist Russian masters or from what they considered oppressive organized religion. Among them were ardent socialists who sought to establish Utopian communities that would embody their co-operative ideals. Some came to Nanaimo, where they soon rejected the boss-and-worker mentality of the capitalist coal mines. Looking for a leader who could bring into being their ideals, they wrote to Matti Kurikka, writer, socialist, firebrand, who had gone to Australia to found a community that would thrive on a "high cultural life of freedom . . . away from priests who have defiled the high morals of Christianity, away from churches that destroy peace, away from all the evils of the outside world."

Kurikka agreed to come to help establish a colony; the Nanaimo Finns sent him the fare, and he arrived full of dreams and fire. The Kalevan Kansa Colonization Company Limited was to run on a co-operative basis; work groups were organized and a townsite planned. But, as with many a Utopian experiment, the colony was long on ideals and short on practicality. Plagued by a serious lack of housing, growing debts, a disastrous fire, and the near-impossibility of making money from either logging or fishing, the colony was soon on shaky ground. Then the colonists clashed over the issue of free love. Kurikka, who favoured the concept, resigned and left the island with close to half its members. When creditors confiscated sawn lumber that was to salvage the colony's finances, the company was forced to liquidate; all its property, including the land, was sold or returned to the Crown.

Yet Sointula and its ideals did not die. As individuals, the Finnish settlers stayed or returned once they had saved enough money to buy land and build homes. For years, Finnish was the main language spoken on the island; slowly, over the past few decades, non-Finnish newcomers mingled with the descendants of the original settlers.

Denise Aleksich is one of those descendants. Ninety years ago, her great-grandmother came north from Nanaimo as one of the original Finnish Utopians. "When I was a small child," Denise recalls over tea in her seafront home, "there was a lot of Finnish spoken. My great-grandmother died when I was thirteen. She was teaching me Finnish. My parents feel badly, because they used Finnish the wrong way, to say something they didn't want us to understand." She remembers, too, when every second house in the village had a sauna; every Wednesday night, her father fired up the sauna, and she sat in the steam with her family, on benches above the alder twigs that grew up through the cracks in the floor. "When we were teenagers, we'd have saunas at parties. They were totally innocent; we had a certain lack of inhibitions. We'd have a sauna, then we'd jump in the ocean—or, once, we rolled in the snow. We don't get snow often here." That was in the days when the now-derelict old green building down near the breakwater was a public sauna with three rooms; now, only about fifteen saunas, all private, still exist in Sointula. But the tradition persists. Every Saturday night, "an old Finn lady with the vitality of a twenty-year-old" phones up Denise's dad and tells him to get on over because the sauna is ready.

Denise went fishing with her father from the time she was thirteen. "There were very few women fishing then. I cooked, then for years I worked on deck, running the drum, running the hydraulics." She also flunkied in logging camps, helping in the cookhouse, washing dishes, cleaning the loggers' rooms. "I swore I would never marry a fisherman," she grins, impishly, a happy light in her pale northern eyes, "but . . . ." She looks out the window towards the foreshore, where her husband Butch is hard at work on a new netloft. "Besides, he plays bridge." When she married Butch, the son of a Yugoslavian fishing family, they moved down the coast to Maple Bay, tied up their fishboat, and bought a house. "I knew I couldn't ask Butch to live here. Besides, to be truly happy in a small town, you have to move away for a while." They lived in Maple Bay for eight years, but when she was pregnant with their second child, Butch suggested perhaps it was time to move back to Sointula. "It was wonderful for me. I was just feeling the [closeness to my] family when I came back. Waves of emotion washed over me."

The old sense of community and co-operative effort still rides strong in Sointula. Almost everyone in town is a member of the co-operative that operates the main store—a combination food, hardware, gas station, and fishing supply store—and one of the healthiest credit unions on the coast. Beside the library/preschool/museum building rises a tennis bubble, completely unexpected in a town of eight hundred people. Denise and Butch were among sixteen Sointulans who got together to contribute half the money for the bubble. The other half came from provincial government lottery funds, and the bubble is now owned by the village.

Butch comes in and riffles through a series of photographs to show me shots taken during the recent herring fishing season. "You pay

$50,000 to $75,000 for a licence, for the privilege of fishing from fifteen minutes to four hours," he shakes his head. Only 245 herring licences are issued, and the opening ends the moment that the quota limit is reached. But Butch did well this year. His seiner *Seabound* was the high boat on the coast, with 280 tons hauled aboard in three hours. That has brought kidding, some good-natured and some not-so-good-natured from other Sointula skippers and crews, gillnetters who did less well this year. "They usually do well," says Denise. "They expect to do well. The town is not as affluent as it usually is at this time of year." That means more draft beer drawn in the bar, fewer of the vodka drinks that are the favourites of Sointulans, and no shooters—hefty drinks that demand full wallets.

Butch and Denise remember the glory days of the fisheries, back in the seventies when salmon sold off the boat for a dollar a pound, not the thirty-six cents they got last year. "I went round the world roughly three times," says Butch. "I'd get off the boat and buy an airplane ticket."

But Sointula fishermen remain prosperous. A few million dollars in drum seiners and the gillnetter-troller combinations that dominate Sointula's fleet are tied up down at the wharf behind the rock breakwater at the edge of town. "There's a lot of money here because of the fishing," says Denise. "People here love to work. This town has one of the best work ethics on the coast. One company used to wait to hire its loggers until the Sointula men came back in from fishing."

Things aren't quite like they used to be. Battles for catch quotas between commercial fishermen and sports fishermen, native and non-native fishermen, concerns about preserving fish stocks, and increasing government control, have changed fishing. Last summer, says Denise, Butch had twelve to fourteen fishing days to make the family's income for the year. Along with other coastal fishermen, he is getting political, fighting to preserve the commercial slice of the pie. "Our jobs are about to be cut," Denise says flatly, citing native claims to exclusive rights over most of the west coast fishery. "We don't mind paying our share of native land claims, but we don't want to pay all of them. But," her sunny mood returns, "I have faith that we will always make some kind of living from the sea." Then, horrified, her Sointulan heritage surfacing, "not *religious* faith."

Back along the road, hotel manager Dan is coping with the realities of a small town. One of his cooks has had an accident, the other, a death in the family. Now Dan, who came here three months ago from a big-city hotel in Burnaby, takes on the role of cook. All he knows how to do is barbecue, so tonight's special is barbecued steaks.

Dan has found his initiation into small-town life difficult. Unlike other rural areas that live on the edge of financial disaster, Sointula doesn't need tourism; it lives well from fishing and logging, and many Sointulans don't want tourists. The old temperance tradition survives. Some residents want the hotel pub closed, and if the hotel closed, that would be fine too. "I guess," says Dan, trying to be fair, "a few people have drowned in the past, trying to get back to Alert Bay with a skinful." Dan has his hands full keeping the pub under control, trying to set rules for fishermen, a notoriously independent lot. "They don't want any rules," he says, ruefully, "and they'll confront you." But he and his wife like Sointula, and delight in being away from the city, working towards their dream of owning their own small-town hotel in a year or two.

In the morning, a heavyset man in a well-used white T-shirt drinks coffee at the communal table in the hotel coffee room. May I join him? "Sure, if you can stand the smell." He has been fibreglassing his boat, and the fumes hang heavy around him. Like Dan, he is a relative newcomer to Sointula, here just three years. "I was tired of the city," where he worked as a bartender, "and I went wilderness camping with my other half for six months. Then we came over here, and my other half says, 'There's a house for rent. I want it.' Well, she has a way of getting what she wants so here we are. I miss bartending, but I make more money here, and I only work three months on the fishboats, and I got the rest of the year to work on the house, be with my kids." He and his wife and their two foster sons plan to drive along the gravel road that crosses the logged-off centre of the island to the north side tomorrow, for a barbecue picnic. He is adding on to their house, so they can take in more foster children. "This island is like a giant tranquilizer for them. You got a runner, you take him down to the ferry, show him to the crew and say, 'This kid's not allowed off the island.' Where's he gonna run to? If he wants to run into the bush, fine; he'll come back when he's hungry."

Getting work here is easy. "You wait for an opening [for commercial fishing]. You go down and stand on the dock. Somebody's bound not to show up. If you're really desperate, you go stand on the wharf at [Port] Hardy for four days, and you'll have a job."

Getting work is easier than getting accepted. "People here don't accept you for the first couple of years. With the old-timers, you have to be here for twelve years before they accept you." But this is said with good humour; it's part of becoming a Sointulan, and this man plans to stay on the island for the rest of his life.

It's Marjorie Greensides's day off from her job as assistant manager of the hotel, but she is in her office, clearing up various tasks. Though she loves Sointula, she is leaving. Six months pregnant, an about-to-be single mother, she will go back to her family and her family doctor on the Lower Mainland to have her baby. But she is almost certain she will return. In less than a year, she has gained good friends here, "people who are there for you. It would be a lot easier to be a single mother here. There are other single mothers, the cost of living is cheaper, the kids can go outside and play, and you don't have to worry. There's no more judging here than there is in the city, and people are more willing to help. People say to me, 'Don't stay down there. Come back. When you need help, I'll take care of the baby.' My job would be waiting for me, and I could bring the baby to work."

When Marjorie arrived at Sointula, she laughed at people who told her to leave now or she'd be here forever. But the place has captured her. "It's so laid-back here. My most stressful day here is nothing compared to the city. Here, you get stressed out for an hour and it's over. It's a completely different attitude."

Barely in her twenties, Marjorie knows the city. She spent six months living in Vancouver's West End, one of the world's most crowded pieces of real estate. "I loved it. It was incredible. But to live there, you have to have money. I'd walk out of the door with fifty dollars in my pocket to buy a pack of cigarettes and I'd come home broke. I was very into downtown life. I knew a lot of musicians, I was in the bar six nights a week listening to music, wearing black all the time, my hair frizzed out to here," she holds her hands a foot out past her ears. Then she laughs, and flips up a strand of straight brown hair. "I can't remember the last time I curled my hair."

When her job ended, she hung out in a billiard hall four hours a day, and got to know some of Vancouver's street people. "I had a very personal relationship with one woman there, a street vendor. But I didn't know her real name or where she lived. In the city, you just know the bits of people that relate to you. Here, you know a whole lot about people."

Maybe too much, sometimes. She grins at the memory of the guessing game that went on when she became pregnant, but didn't reveal her lover's name. "If I worried about the things people said about me, I'd have an ulcer the size of this hotel." Instead of worrying, she gains strength from the support she finds in the community.

It's business at usual at the Lesrit Convenience Store up on the hill: Les Lanqvist sits on his stool by the cash register and Rita stands by the counter, offering coffee or herbal tea to anyone who drops by, seemingly as happy to chat as to sell the hunting licences, hockey cards and groceries that are the store's stock in trade. Two touring cyclists stop by, and Les tells them how to get to the campground on the north shore. "Take some water," he urges. "There isn't any at the campsite." They want to know where they can buy cod. None available at the wharf, Rita tells them, then donates some from the Lanqvists' freezer.

Les is the grandson of one of the original Finnish colonists. His grandfather came here from Australia, defeated by the heat and back-breaking work in the quarries. He earned enough money in Nanaimo to bring his family over, then went back to collect them. He stepped off the ship in Sydney and was robbed of every penny. That trip, he didn't even see his family; he turned around and came back to Nanaimo, saved another stake, and finally managed to shepherd his wife and young son to Sointula. Les has lived here since he was born in 1932.

Some of the old, Utopian views still stay with him. Though the church that occupies an unobtrusive space on the hill is small and anonymous, even that's too much for Les. "The downfall of this island was the church. After the war, we got immigrants coming from Finland, from the cities, and they brought religion and the cops. In the old day, we had no religion here. You didn't have to throw rocks at it. Anybody who was religious had nobody to talk to, so they left. We didn't need cops. If you did wrong, you had to stand up in front of the whole group and apologize. Everyone left their keys in their boats. If you needed someone's boat, in an emergency or anything, you just took it.

"First you get the church, then you get the cops, then you get whores and whisky and the whole bit." Les shakes his big grizzled head. "What the hell do honest people need churches for? We got nothing to confess."

Rita remembers how the island used to solve its own problems. One man was suspected of being too fond of young girls and boys. "We told him, 'Be on the next ferry out.' He was."

Rita arrived at Sointula in 1959, because she had heard she might get work here. "It was midnight when I got here," she remembers. In those days, cars were transferred from the steamer to the dock in a sling, and passengers clambered up a dockside ladder. "I climbed the ladder, took one look around, and said, 'Where the hell am I and how do I get out of here?'" But she stayed, met Les, and that was that. For eighteen years, she crewed for him on his fishboat, raising their three children aboard the boat in fishing season. "I've been fishing on my own since 1948," says Les, "pulling by hand, gillnetting. It was different then. We fished five days a week, came in on the weekend for a five-night toot, then back out again. We had haywire rigging, a haywire compass, steered north all summer, and sometimes a little more north." Not like today, he says, when fishermen work a couple of weeks a year, on fancy boats with modern equipment. But he'd be fishing still if bad luck and a shipyard fire hadn't destroyed his boat and forced him to sell off his commercial fishing licence.

Rita works at the fish-processing plant down on the dock from July to October, supervising a crew on the twelve-hour night shift. These days, each worker does only one part of the fish-cleaning job, sliding the fish on to the next person on the line. In the old days, Rita could completely dress three or four fish a minute. With deft fingers, she demonstrates on empty air: cut the gill, split the belly, cut the throat, index finger down the cavity, cut the bloodline on the spine, use the spoon on the back of the knife to scrape out the guts, and you're done. Though she's a supervisor, she still works the line. "I couldn't just . . .," and she perfectly imitates a bobbing, officious supervisor, hand-wringing down the imaginary line.

The ferry appears in the gap between Malcolm Island and Vancouver Island. I go back down the hill to the car, the ferry, Port McNeill and the short trip along the island highway north to Port Hardy.

~

At the end of the highway, on the Port Hardy wharf, Bob sips coffee from an insulated mug and waits for his ship to come in. Truck driver, ex-fisherman in his early forties, belly starting to balloon out over his belt, Bob arrived yesterday from Vancouver with his young son, to load up with sea urchins raked from the sea floor. But the weather blew up and the boats couldn't get into Hardy from the bays and islands where the divers are working. So he waits in the drizzle on the wharf, entertaining tourists with stories about the spiny, brown-red sea urchins. "I can talk to you or I can listen to my truck engine," he says, resignedly, when I ask if he gets tired of telling people about sea urchins.

"I got stuck in the knee once with a spine," he relates. "Didn't worry much—it just looked like a pimple." Infection travelled up his leg—he traces a path on his thigh—but even that didn't cause him much concern. "Then it sort of vee-ed over towards my private parts," he gestures upwards, "and I headed for the doctor." He grins. "I could do without my leg but I couldn't do without those."

The three-person crew of an aluminum skiff converted to a dive boat is unloading plastic milk crates full of urchins at wharfside. Diving gear is coiled in the boat; an orange Le Creuset frypan sits, dirty, on the wheelhouse roof, and a crewman stays warm inside his fuzzy purple Patagonia jacket. At this time of year, the crew usually plies waters farther south, near Courtenay, harvesting geoduck clams. But geoducks up to the weight on their licence can be harvested anytime. The sea urchin opening is for a brief ten days, so the divers hustled north to take advantage. Every day, the two divers spend four to five hours beneath the waves, using rakes to scrape the urchins from undersea rocks and tumbling them into nets that are hauled to the surface by the boat crew.

Diving for urchins is a profitable business. An ounce of sea urchin meat, Bob says, pure protein and rich in iodine, fetches fourteen dollars from Oriental buyers in Vancouver restaurants and groceries, or aficionados in Japan, South Korea, or Hong Kong. "An ounce, that's a bite—isn't that what they say at Weight Watchers?" asks Bob.

A giant fishpacker slides alongside the dock, its holds and decks jammed with round nets of urchins, picked up from diving skiffs whose captains elected to stay offshore, raking up more urchins. The skipper, bearded, sea-capped, pipe in hand, like the seafarer in paint-by-number pictures, curses mildly and shouts insults at dock loungers as he issues the orders that will position his boat by the wharf. Bob cheers up: with the arrival of this cargo, he should have a full truck by midnight and be off in time to catch the night ferry from Nanaimo to the mainland.

At dock end, the crew of a dragger loaded with turbot chats idly with wharf workers as they wait for the boat to be connected to the shore. A compressor hums and thumps into life, and vacuum tubes that lead deep into the ship's fish-filled hold spill the flat, shiny bottom fish into crates and boxes.

Supper and sleep. But late into the night, from the hotel room window I can still see the lights on the fork-lifts as they scuttle back and forth along the wharf. And the voices of men at work and the muffled drum of the compressor still sound across the bay, in the dark.

CHAPTER 4

Kitimat, Model Town

)) In the morning, the sky over Queen Charlotte Strait has opened to blue between wedges of cloud that cling to the mainland mountains and the Vancouver Island shore. June through September, Port Hardy moves to the rhythm of the ferry that plies the Inside Passage to and from Prince Rupert fifteen hours to the north. Last night, the hotels and restaurants were busy with travellers booked onto this morning's ship departure. Late at night, passengers arriving on the *Queen of Prince Rupert* filled every remaining hotel room. Tonight, with the ship away, the town will be quiet.

Six A.M. loading, seven o'clock sailing. Groggily, at half past five, I fall in with the line of traffic that struggles from the motels to the ferry dock. We roll aboard, and stumble up the stairs to the passenger decks. A good shipboard breakfast, eavesdropping on conversations in accents American, English, German; a stroll around the decks; then a settling down to watch the islands and coves, inlets and mountains, slip by. I read an 1892 description of the coast:

> Free from the cares and conventionalities of everyday life, and breathing in the very air of heaven itself, you burst, like the Ancient Mariner, into an unknown sea filled with untold beauties, and sail over a bosom of waters unruffled as glass; among myriads of islands; through deep, rugged, rock-walled channels; past ancient Indian villages, medieval glaciers, dark, solemn, pine-clothed shores, snow-capped peaks, dashing cataracts, yawning mountain gorges, spouting monsters and sea-whelps —away to the north a thousand miles, almost, to mix with the icebergs that once floated under the sovereignty of the Czar of all the Russias, but now drop peacefully from ancient glaciers over which the American eagle holds watchful guard—a continuous panorama, in which the truest, the

rarest, the wildest, the most beautiful and the grandest forms of nature are revealed.

Though our taste in prose style may have changed, the coast is as filled with beauty as ever.

For fifteen hours, the ship is a small town, where passengers meet and remeet in the restaurant, on the decks, in the bar, in the washrooms, and talk about the weather, the scenery, where they are from, where they are going. Those conversational hurdles jumped, they exchange stories of their families and their jobs.

Night falls before we reach Prince Rupert; we disembark under the glaring lights of the parking lot where giant mobile homes from California and Alaska are already parked, their occupants waiting to board the ferry in the morning. The few travellers on our sailing who have not reserved hotel rooms dash madly up the hilly Prince Rupert streets, from one hotel to the other, but they are out of luck. Every hotel and motel in the city is booked solid. In the morning, the motel manager tells me a man arrived at 2:00 A.M., exhausted after fifteen hours and seven hundred miles on the road, willing to pay five hundred dollars for a room, anyone's room. She refused to wake any of her tucked-in guests, to ask if they would take the money and give up their room, but did find a disused space, little more than a closet, where he could sleep—for less than five hundred dollars, I assume but do not ask.

I am a little nervous about setting out this morning along the Skeena highway inland from the coast. Every news and weather report speaks gloomily of the rising waters of the province's rivers, swollen by two weeks of constant rain. A ferry crewman cursed this stretch of road, a highway he hated in good weather or bad. "They're always fixing it," he growled, "but I swear this year I hit the same potholes I hit ten years ago." Watch out for the Car Wash, he warned; water crashes down the cliffs onto the road below. Then he tells stories of motorists killed by falling rock or ice, and washouts that carry road and rail into the river, gulping down unsuspecting travellers.

But the weather and the river refuse to co-operate with the pessimists. Though the mile-wide Skeena runs heavy, fast and brown, lipping at its banks, nowhere has the water chewed away the road. The sun shines hot and bright, the Car Wash is gentle enough to be a novelty, not a danger, and rocks that tumbled down onto the road during the rains have been cleared away by road crews. I drive east along the skinny strip of land where road and rail are squashed close together by the river

on one side, abrupt cliffs on the other. Eighty years ago, railway promoters chose this route to the coast as much to line their own pockets
as to fit engineering requirements. The track builders needed ten million
pounds of explosive to bull through rock between Prince Rupert and
Terrace, a distance of just ninety miles. The road was built alongside the
tracks during the Second World War, when the American and Canadian
governments decided the railway needed protection against possible
infiltration or attack by the Japanese.

Just beyond Terrace, I turn south for Kitimat, Canada's first "City
Planned for the Twentieth Century." Many a traveller has followed this
trail, beginning with the Gitksan Indians who wore the first path from
the Skeena forty miles down the wide valley through forests of cedar,
pine and spruce, to tidewater at the head of Douglas Channel. The
Gitksan visited and traded with the Haisla, who lived beside the channel
for hundreds of years before the Aluminum Company of Canada
transformed the inlet head by building a smelter and a town here in
1952.

Kitamaat, the Haisla village, curls along the east shore of Kitimat
Arm, the neat houses set, haphazard and attractive, in gentle parabola
beside the shingle beach. The thrum of skiff engines resonates up from
the water as fishermen tie up at the dock. On the forested hill above the
cove, a Haisla woman slices open the coral flesh of a salmon, ready for
smoking. Two men heft a massive salmon along the road, past wild
roses and salmonberry in bloom.

Sammy Robinson lives almost at the end of the village, in a house
cunningly constructed from weathered driftwood and logs. Fisherman
and artist, he stands in his workroom, staring down, not at cedar
carvings, but at the manifold from his boat. He waves at a friend down
by the dock, to come in and take a look: fixing or replacing the manifold
is going to take a lot of cash.

Born here in 1934, Sammy has lived here all his life. When he was
young, the Haisla were almost alone on the inlet. "There were a few
farmers out there, they supplied us with dairy products, and we supplied them with flour, sugar, beans, and all that, my Dad got from
fishing down at Rivers Inlet. It was good. You were real isolated. We
had all the cheese, all the eggs, all the meat, we had every food we
needed, we didn't have to pay for it. We had so much milk, Mum used
it for fertilizer." He smiles. "Now you have to pay a lot of money for
milk at the grocery store."

Sammy looks out his window, at Alcan's huge smelter directly across the arm. He was sixteen years old when Alcan arrived. He still has mixed feelings. The company provided work for band members, "a good living. You can see the difference between here and other villages. I worked at Alcan for eight and a half years, while my kids were growing up. I couldn't make money at fishing; Alcan was a steady income. They were real nice to me. I made enough money to start my own business." But the arrival of Alcan meant more and more people coming into the valley. "They're pushing us out of all our places," he says, and falls silent.

For twenty-two years, Sammy ran a commercial fishing boat, fishing the arm and the coast for salmon, crab, halibut, bottom fish. Now, when the fishing is good, he takes charter parties, fishermen from Canada, the United States, Europe, to the places he knows from all his years on the water. In the winter, he carves. Unfinished pieces take shape on the workbench in his studio; in the small showroom, the walls are crowded with leaping cedar whales, their abalone eyes gleaming, with totemic figures, bears, and ravens. "I grew up with carving, I didn't learn at a vocational school or anything. My uncle was an artist. He had only one arm. I have two arms, and I can't carve as good as him." Others might disagree. Sammy points out a piece on the wall; someone, he says, offered him ten thousand dollar for it last week.

"I'm putting it up for bids," he smiles. "If there's another guy bidding more than that, he'll get it. I learned fast. I learned how the white people operate."

Unlike Kitamaat, the town of Kitimat across the inlet sits well back from tidewater, intentionally protected by the town planners from sight, feel or sound of waves and wind. On my right as I come down the hill into town, neat crescents curve off the main residential streets: Partridge, Petrel, Pintail and Plover; Gander, Gannet, Grebe, Grouse, Gyrfalcon and Gull. Below the houses, at City Centre, government buildings and retail stores are tidily grouped together with motels and restaurants. Kitimat was planned as a 1950s model town, all its functions segregated.

I follow the road across the Kitimat River, down past Service Centre, where auto services, a lumber yard, a nursery, a working man's coffee shop, a working man's hotel and beer parlour, are planted along streets serviceably numbered or with names like Commercial, Enterprise, Railway and Industrial. Farther down the road, well removed from town, are the Alcan smelter, a pulp mill, and a plant that produces chemical gases.

The Alcan buildings stretch out, long and low, beside the road behind a high fence. I pull into the parking lot by the information centre, the only building that escapes from the fence. Neatly attired in uniform shorts and blouse, Donna Trach waits for the people who have phoned in for this afternoon's plant tour. A vacationing family comes in, then a group of teenagers from Hazelton, up on the Skeena. We all sit down to watch a film on Alcan and the story of Kitimat.

Back in the 1950s, that story was told around the world, a postwar example of man and technology hand in hand creating something magnificent. Almost two hundred miles away, the Nechako River spilled out of lakes that lay beyond the Coast Mountains, flowing eastward to join the Fraser River at Prince George, in the centre of the province. Engineers built a stubby earth-filled dam where the Nechako left the lakes, to hold back the waters that would have emptied into the river. The huge reservoirs behind the dam overspilled the existing banks of the lakes, and turned the water flow of a dozen lakes westward, towards the mountains and the Pacific. At the westernmost end of the lakes, engineers channelled the water underground through the Coast Mountains, to a powerhouse at Kemano, forty miles south of Kitimat. Writers were overwhelmed; "the harvest of water finally garnered would fill 359 billion beer glasses," wrote one journalist in a suitably blue-collar analogy.

The purpose of all this effort was the smelting of aluminum, a job that takes enormous amounts of electricity. Kitimat, at the head of a protected channel navigable by ocean freighter, was chosen as the smelter site. Power lines were tracked across the mountains where more than thirty feet of snow fell every winter. "This is a saga of power in the wilderness," wrote that journalist, "potential power long unused and wasting but now put to service so that North America and all the free world have another major source of aluminum." The powerhouse, the writer noted, was underground to safeguard it from enemy air attack.

"And nature stood defiant," intones the narrator of the film we are watching. And man was the victor. The movie's promotional phrases sound odd in a decade where conquering nature is no longer something to crow about.

The tour group climbs aboard a bus that takes us in sanitized fashion past the anode paste plant, the switch yards, the fields of emerald green generators, the docks where alumina from bauxite ore arrives from refineries in Jamaica, Australia, and Japan. Even the harmless ingots are viewed from a hundred yards away. We learn that one potline—or was it all of them?—uses as much electricity in a day as Vancouver in a week—or was it a month? Donna builds vertical chains of paper clips to show the strength of the electromagnetic field near the potlines where the alumina is refined into shiny, silver aluminum. One of the Hazelton boys, a natural clown, balances a string of paper clips atop his broad, flat nose, like a trained seal, and is immediately imitated by the rest of the group.

The rest of the tour group wanders on its way, and Donna talks about life in Kitimat. She grew up here, then went away to university. Each summer she returns for this job; Alcan pays well and gives hiring preference to sons and daughters of long-time employees. But she will not come back once she graduates. "I was here for eighteen years and I really felt isolated. There are so many things you don't have an opportunity to do here. You couldn't go to a dance and meet new people, it was always the same people. It just felt stifling sometimes."

Outgoing, adventuresome, Donna immediately liked Vancouver and university there. Though she speaks of her family with obvious love, coming back to Kitimat opens old wounds, brings back unhappy memories. "When you're in school here, you're in a certain kind of crowd. Like, just because you play sports, you're a jock. You can't talk with anybody else, you can't be with anybody else." Donna felt squeezed into somebody else's mold. She broke the mold when she went away; when she returns, she finds old friends hostile.

"They get really angry with me because I like to be on my own here now. These past couple of summers, I have been really rebellious, because I'm not a bar kind of person, and that's what they do here, drinking and dancing. I like drawing and biking and being outside —and they get really upset. They think I'm trying to be more than them.

"When we come back to town, people put their noses in the air and say," she sniffs, "'Oh, the university students are back.' They're sort of, what's the word? Condescending. Because we've gone out and done something with ourselves, and they haven't. Because they find it easier to stay here instead of taking a chance."

Her words would seem strange to those who came to Kitimat in the 1950s. Taking a chance was what Kitimat was all about then. When Alcan built its smelter, the company recruited workers from across

Europe. Thirty-five-year-old photographs show Scandinavians with ill-cropped blonde hair and narrow, bony foreheads; square-faced Dutch and Germans; plump Portuguese and Greeks; Italians with pencil moustaches and slick, black hair. In the mid-fifties, 70 percent of Kitimat's people spoke little or no English.

Frank Tavares was one of those recruits. He gestures around at his good home in Whitesail Neighbourhood, his fine furniture, the food and drink he has in abundance. For him, Kitimat was a dream come true. The stony land of his home islands, the Azores, offered little for a boy with ambition. He tried to join an uncle who had emigrated to South America, but his mother said no. He applied to come to Canada in 1953, but Canada that year accepted only seventeen boys from the Azores. At last, in 1954, he was accepted, one of twelve hundred young men who left the islands that year for Canada. "Portuguese have always gone around the world," he says, his serious manner sitting oddly on his Groucho Marx face.

He worked in a sawmill and on the railway in northern Ontario. "We worked in Port Arthur, then we moved way up north, I don't know where. May the 9th, 1954, it snowed like hell. There were fifty or sixty guys in one gang, all Portuguese, so there was no problem to get together in the evening, play a game of cards, talk about what you had seen in the day. We were all so happy. We were young, we didn't feel stress or anything."

One day he got a letter from a Portuguese friend who had gone to Kitimat, working for $1.65 an hour. "So we start to think, 'Oh boy, that's lots of money.'" Frank and a friend headed for Kitimat, along with five or six hundred other men who had heard the same stories. Frank was lucky: he got a job at a small sawmill, then in construction, until he was hired on at Alcan in 1959.

One element was missing from his life: a wife. There were no unmarried Portuguese women in Kitimat. "You know, we were all young kids, we bring pictures of our families, sisters, brothers, uncles, aunts." Frank liked the looks of one woman shown in a friend's photographs. "I ask is she married or has she got a boyfriend or anything, and he says no. So I write to her, and we wrote to each other, and I asked her to marry me, and she accepted."

Frank booked off work one afternoon and went to church in Kitimat; Maria went to church in Sao Miguel, in the Azores, at the same time. They were married by proxy, and Frank began preparing a house for

Maria's arrival. "I spent about seven thousand dollars in one week's time, on furniture and everything. The Hudson's Bay, they deliver on Saturday, I slept from Saturday to Sunday, and on Monday, I got laid off. The town went ghost town. To be honest with you, when my wife came, I was completely broke."

That was the year aluminum prices nose-dived. Alcan stopped expansion and cut production. Hundreds of men lost their jobs and Kitimat's population dropped from fifteen thousand to eight thousand. Frank's landlord let him postpone his rent payments; finally, Frank got a job helping to build the big new hospital, planned to serve the community of fifty thousand that never materialized. Alcan geared up again and he was hired back. He has worked there ever since.

"Kitimat for me, it's Canada as a whole. Raising a family here is so beautiful, and the company is good. I've been here thirty-two years, it's a twelve-month-a-year job, five days a week, a pay cheque every two weeks, never fail. You got everything."

Now the kids are grown up, and he's getting on to retirement, Frank hopes he and his wife can spend six months of the year in the Azores, which he still calls home, and six months in Kitimat. "There's no reason to leave here. You build your life here, you got your friends here. You leave, you miss those friends, no matter what."

It's evening now. The clouds pile into the valley and a misty rain begins to fall. Down at the bottom of the hill between the town and the smelter, the railroad tracks, laid down before the road from Terrace south was opened, are rusty from disuse. The wall tiles of the empty station have slipped and shattered onto the cement platform, and an abandoned passenger car waits on a weed-grown siding.

The women and children of this town were to be spared the sight of drunks weaving down the street: the beer parlour is in the hotel here in Service Centre. But no drunk, no one at all, is to be seen on Commercial Street tonight. Boarded-up windows and blank doors front the hotel; a multicoloured pickup truck is anchored in the taxi zone outside the lone open door. One car parked behind the hotel has a flat tire and a patina of dust; a second is missing a wheel.

If there is sinning going on in Kitimat tonight, it's going on in private. Two dozen cars are decorously parked at the Legion, six at Wee Geordie's pub, another few at the pub in City Centre by the shopping mall. Two glossy new pickups crowded with teenage boys play tag down the hill and squeal into the parking lot to check out the lone nightclub, sometimes open, sometimes not. Their shouts are as high-spirited as and not much noisier than the happy squeals of two children protesting as their sari-clad mother and turbanned father, both carrying groceries, urge them into the car.

A dozen or two players make desultory bets at a charity casino in the echoing hall of the Portuguese-Canadian club, to a background of music and laughter from the bar in the room next door. Those of Portuguese descent in Kitimat number thirty-five hundred, almost a third of the town. Three years ago, a half-dozen of the women decided to start a catering business, with any profits going to the Portuguese-Canadian Association. Now most of them are relaxing on stools or chairs near the kitchen, drinking cold coffee and chattering about their work. Crammed into the cooler is the food they have prepared for two weekend banquets, eight hundred people to be served: whole cold salmon coiled onto trays and decorated; roasts of beef deep in a marinade of white wine, red pepper, seasoning salt and garlic; ham, chicken, spareribs, crabs, bowls and trays of assorted salads and cold meats.

The women slang back and forth, easy with each other. Cecilia runs the show, and everyone gives her a bad time for being bossy. Odilia loves to chat; Ursula, Lucinda, Marilia, Rosa and Maria lean up against the counters and make an occasional comment. "It's a good thing our husbands don't get mad with us," smiles one; in June and December, their busiest months, what with high-school graduation, weddings and parties, they are rarely home except to sleep, and they spend more time with each other than with their families.

Cecilia remembers well the day she arrived in Kitimat from Portugal, thirty-five years ago: "I wrote to my Mum when I arrived, 'Everything is so beautiful.' It was all white and I had never seen snow before." Two weeks later, overcome with isolation and loneliness, "I just sat down and cried."

Odilia had no mixed feelings. She was eight months pregnant when she arrived back in the fifties, but "as soon as I put my feet in Kitimat, I knew this was the place for me. Now, we go to Toronto, we go to Winnipeg, after a week, I want to go home."

Next morning, the clouds have thinned and the sky is patchy blue. At Tina's Place, down in Service Centre, breakfast all day, open 6:00 A.M. to 6:00 P.M., a dozen men in work clothes and muddy boots drink coffee and talk jobs. "Money makes money," declares one. Another, in his fifties, wearing an Esso cap over a balding scalp, lays down the law about how much truckers deserve to be paid, considering the cost of inflation, repairs, gas, insurance. Two heavyset women in jeans and T-shirts come in together; they sit at a separate table from the men.

Eating a big breakfast was a mistake. At Sylvia Mitchell's, up in Nechako Neighbourhood, coffee cake fresh from the oven fills the air with the smells of oranges and brown sugar, and the coffee is on. Magnets pin pictures of the Mitchells' children and other neighbourhood kids to the fridge door beside notes and reminders of appointments. Casual, enthusiastic, contentedly plump, Sylvia has a full schedule that includes acting as a sort of Welcome Wagon for Alcan, taking around the wives of prospective employees and assessing how well they might fit into the town; almost always, candidates for senior jobs are male. Sylvia senses immediately whether the woman will like Kitimat: if she wants a job of her own, problems will probably develop. Both high-paid industrial or service jobs and low-paid work in stores or offices are hard to come by. Someone like a recent prospect, with her own good job in Montreal and a love of big-city life, is going to have trouble adapting to Kitimat.

Thirty-five years ago, wives were glad if their husbands could get a job. Mitchell's husband, an engineer, was laid off in the 1950s, and ended up picking potatoes in the Lower Mainland to support his wife and baby. In time, he was offered two jobs: one with the provincial government in Victoria, one with Alcan in Kitimat. "Someone said the government wasn't such a good employer and Kitimat paid ten dollars more a month, so we thought we'd come to Kitimat for a few years."

During those first few years, living in company apartments with paper-thin walls, surrounded six months of the year by ten feet of snow, Sylvia kept thinking, "For ten dollars a month, we did this?" Now, she looks back on those first years of striving with pride and affection. "We were all broke. Most of us had little children. We did things together.

"My friend's specialty was fresh buns and mine was French fries. I'd chop up potatoes and make French fries and everybody left their doors open, and we'd all sit in the hallway and eat our French fries. If I wanted to go to a show, I'd just tell my neighbour. I'd leave my door open and she'd leave her door open, and the baby was in his own crib, and he was looked after." Not long after the Mitchells arrived, Sylvia fell ill. "There was no question about people stepping in and taking care of the baby. It was just automatically done."

When the Mitchells went back to the city for a holiday, Sylvia couldn't stand it any more: the noise, the traffic, the pace, the overwhelming choice in the stores. They chose to stay in Kitimat. "What better place for children? You could walk to any of the facilities. Your children could swim, or you could get them into hockey, they could skate, there were lots of little slopes for children to ski on or go sledding. I've lived in the city, and to take your children skating was a major effort."

Those were the days when snow piled up high along the streets, and the radio broadcast warnings not to let the children play in the yards because they might trip over the power lines. "Now, these were overhead power lines, but the snow was so high and with the snowblower blowing it up, the power lines were buried in the snowbanks."

Sylvia got a job nursing at the first hospital, a little makeshift building down by the smelter with basins and bedpans under the leaks in the roof. If a high tide occurred at the same time as a storm, waves would wash in through the fire doors. But the children's ward had steps down to the beach, and one night, Sylvia woke up the patients so they could watch the northern lights reflecting down the channel. Another night, nurses bundled up the patients and took them outside to watch a fireworks show at Kitamaat village across the water. In the annex, men awaiting discharge played poker and drank potent "Coca-Cola."

In those days, everyone was young and optimistic and working hard to make the community something special. One year, the hospital dietitian decided the patients could have anything they liked for Christmas dinner. One Haisla man chose oolichans; friends brought the oily fish in and cooked them up for breakfast. Later, the patient dropped back with a gift in gratitude: an enormous salmon. "We were ready to catch the bus, and by the time it got to us, it was pretty full. Well, it didn't matter in those days, you could be nine months pregnant, and someone would try to pick you up, there was such a high percentage of men in town. You'd be all crammed in on the bus and someone would come and sit on your knee. So we hauled this big salmon to the bus and it was leaking through the newspaper—and nobody tried to sit with us. So my friend said, 'This is the secret. We'll have to carry a fish with us every day.'"

But, says Sylvia, that spirit of togetherness, of people helping people, has drained away. "Women who are having a hard time of it now, being away from their families or being in a small community, aren't turning to their neighbours. They're turning to government services."

From Sylvia's, I drive back down a curving road towards City Centre;

it passes through the woods. Here, each successive graduating class from the high school has tacked to tree trunks careful, artistic signs, most the same size and shape, to commemorate their grad. Even in this, Kitimat stays neat. I head back up the hill, out along the highway, away from a town that seems caught in a time-warp of the 1950s.

CHAPTER 5

Along the Kispiox

⅃⅃ Back on the main highway, I drive again beside the Skeena, looking for something that is no longer on the map. Less than a century ago, everyone who knew the river knew Kitselas Canyon. At high water, the full force of the current threw the steamboats that plied the river from 1891 to 1912 from bank to bank, threatening at any moment to heave them up against the rocks. When the river ran its fiercest, prudent captains tied up at the lower end to wait for safer water. To serve the steamboats, a white settlement grew up not far from the Kitselas native villages at the north end of the canyon.

But river gave way to rail, and rail to road. The Kitselas natives moved away, to other homes and villages. The white village, with its hotel, church and houses, faded back into the bush. Now the canyon is not even a whistle stop on the rail line or marked by any sign on the road, and its mention brings puzzled frowns to the faces of people I ask.

After casting back and forth along the highway, I find the trail that winds towards the river. In the space of twenty-five minutes, I walk from sunshine and heat to forest shade and welcome cool, along an old road edged with bunchberry and queen's club, past logged-off slopes and into second-growth forest. At last, the muted roar of water constricted by rocks sounds through the trees.

No one else is here. When young Charlie Morison, English, green and twenty-two, reached the canyon in 1866, times were different. One of the not always intrepid crew trying to string a telegraph line overland from the United States to Russia and Europe, Morison had been disappointed in the lack of adventure he found in New Westminster. Not so at Kitselas.

"We proceeded next day," Morison wrote in his diary, "and reached the canyon both sides of which at that time were lined with large Indian houses with a population of about five hundred inhabitants. The rocks were lined with Indians far above us, they rushed down but instead of smashing us they tackled on to our tow lines and drew us through the canyon in triumph and with much yelling . . . . It took all day to get the flotilla through and we were glad to make an early camp at the head of the canyon, and after a hearty meal we were soon asleep."

On the walk back out, I meet three taciturn natives in an old pickup truck, licence plates expired, loading firewood and long barked poles. They only shrug and stare at the forest when I ask if the canyon has any meaning in their lives.

River, road and rail snake north along the valley, now flanked by the Hazelton Mountains. The Skeena springs forth high in the valleys east of the Coast Mountains, far to the north. As it flows south, it gathers strength from its tributaries, among them the Sustut, the Babine and the Kispiox. Here, near Hazelton, it joins with the Bulkley River and becomes the dominant river of the region. For centuries, this circle of land where the Skeena, Bulkley and Kispiox join has been a fertile and a magic place, one that saw the flowering of the Gitksan culture. Today, that culture still thrives, in an arc of native villages, some shared with whites, that curve north from Hazelton. I turn north towards these villages now, from New Hazelton to Old Hazelton, 'Ksan, and the valley of the Kispiox River.

The road crosses the Bulkley River on the fourth bridge built high above Hagwilget Canyon. The natives who lived at Hagwilget built the first bridge, hung a hundred feet or more above the river, of long poles lashed together with cedar bark rope. The natives built the second bridge as well, an ingenious contraption that made use of telegraph poles and wire borrowed from the ambitious and abandoned overland telegraph project. The third and fourth followed the more routine techniques of white man's construction.

The road loops from the Bulkley back towards the Skeena, past the old Silver Standard mine and the few, spread-out houses of Two Mile. Eighty years ago, travellers coming into the Skeena country camped at Two Mile with their horses. If you wanted to buy a pack horse or an Indian cayuse, the bargaining was done in these meadows. Today, Two Mile is just another part of the valley. At Silver Standard School, a bored teenager lounges against a fuel tank, waiting for his classmates and teacher to return from town. An alternate school, Silver Standard takes native high-school students who can't or won't fit into the system. Attendance is optional on Friday afternoons: this student wants to book out and go down to work for the band office. "I help out the old people, cut grass or whatever." With the twelve dollars an hour he says he earns, he'll buy tapes and shorts and T-shirts for the summer. He has lived in Hazelton all his life, and can't imagine living in the city. "I went to visit my aunt and uncle in Seattle, but I hated it. Too busy, too many people." Last summer, he worked at the Carrier campground at Moricetown up the Skeena. "I learned a lot. You know, fishing, gaffing."

The rest of the class, met two days ago on the Alcan tour, return. Like any high-school class in mid-June, they are distracted, unresponsive, half their conversation elliptical within the group. One boy says he goes to parties; an older girl scoffs, "Your mum won't let you go to parties." They are baseball fanatics, almost voluble about their favourite sport. This weekend, teams will come from most of the north country, for a fastball tournament and salmon barbecue.

They have different goals—one wants to teach, one wants to be a band worker—but they all want to stay in Hazelton, or come back after their education "outside." Unlike a previous generation of young people, herded out to residential schools in Vancouver or Port Alberni, they have lived here all their lives and are proud of their homes and heritage. The dubious lures of the big city are not for them; they have heard too many tales of the pace and the prejudice they will find in Vancouver.

The students go off to watch a video in the main classroom. As flies and wasps buzz around the open window in the hot drowsy sun, teacher Bjorn Petursson and I sip instant coffee and talk. Bjorn has worked in this alternate program for five years; he is proud of what he and his fellow teachers have achieved, teaching their students life skills and creating a place in the school system where students "who used to sit at the back of the classroom" feel they belong. "I've learned to trust and communicate with them,"he says, "and they reciprocate. These kids really have their smarts. They know about the city. They also know about being around rivers, about trapping, about wildlife and vegetation. These kids are tough. Lots of them, fifteen, sixteen, seventeen, have spent the night in the bush. There's a fight at home or whatever, they'll just sit underneath a tree all night. They know the bush; they don't have to be afraid. If a grizzly bear comes along, they know what he's going to do. In the city, walking along the streets, you're not certain what's going to happen. I talk about the city hicks and the country slickers."

After twenty years in small towns in this area, Bjorn doubts he could survive in the city. "I've tried and it just doesn't match up. Cities are all symmetrical—go down the street, turn right at the corner, three more blocks and turn left. I've always had more of a feeling for rural things." He smiles. "I like barnyard psychology. Really, rural sociology has a lot to be said for it. You can create your own interests here. People find friends, develop a support system for themselves."

In some ways, Bjorn is an alternate teacher for an alternate school, more at home down in the old Hazelton pub than in a teachers' coffee room. Right now, he lives in a tent, beset by complications from a broken marriage and unwilling to make any immediate plans for the future. His lament is a universal one, familiar from every country and western song that sounds on every small-town radio station: "I don't understand why this break-up had to happen. I don't know if I can trust anyone again."

Bjorn goes back to his students, and I go on to stay at a lodge up the valley. Saturday arrives, and early in the morning, the native cemetery that occupies the bench overlooking Hazelton and the junction of the Skeena and Bulkley rivers is deserted, and no one walks the sunshiny streets of the town below. Heavy dark clouds press down upon the hills across the river; bees buzz among the red columbine and yellow buttercups. They say that Cataline is buried here, somewhere under the tall grass. His real name, maybe, was Jean-Jacques Caux. He came, perhaps, from Catalonia—or from Gascony, or from the Basque town of Oloron Ste. Marie in the then-independent duchy of Bearne. From the days of the Cariboo gold rush till his death at the age of ninety-two, in Hazelton, he strode the trails of the north behind horse and mule, packing hundred-pound sacks of supplies as easily as another man might carry his hat. His shoulders were broad and his muscles solid, his bushy hair smoothed back with bear grease. He bought new clothes once a year, and wore them without break until the following year.

I find no sign of his grave. But, wandering across from his campfire and his car parked on the bluff beside the cemetery, Mike finds me. Mike grew up in Hazelton, but he lives in Prince George now. Slowly, as we lean against the fences of the grave plots or walk between the waist-high stone totems that mark the graves of chiefs and the simpler stones of other Gitksan, he tells me the story of this cemetery, and of himself. He points to the few foundering grave houses that once contained the favourite possessions of the dead. "Those things used to be safe here. Now people steal them, so we don't leave them anymore."

From time to time, Mike comes back home from the city, to visit his mother and to try to renew his ties with his culture. When he is in town, he visits the cemetery most mornings. His father, his grandfather, his wife, many uncles and cousins in the intertwined extended family of his clan, lie buried here. And, in ways he cannot explain to me, his family and its traditions are important. He says he is the only one in his family who still speaks the Gitksan language well. Yet he is also an outsider, a Gitksan who lives far from his past. His younger brother and older sister are both chiefs, but when it came his turn to be named, he refused. He does not explain why. "Our traditions are important—but I don't follow them." Since he turned down chiefdom, he has no status in his clan. When he goes to a feast, he is seated last, among the least important members.

Some of his confusion stems from his father's decision in 1948, "to be a white man" by renouncing his Indian status. Mike never reconciled himself to that decision. Just a year and a half ago, Mike and his mother reclaimed the legal Indian status that his father threw away. "The letter came, and I said to my mother —I have to say this in our language —" he speaks a liquid sentence, "I said, 'Mum, you don't look any different.'"

He lifts his head from contemplation of a plot that contains all the members of one family, killed in a plane crash on their way home to Hazelton. His eye is caught by the yellow slicker worn by a man who stands with a companion at the edge of the bluff. "They're cousins of mine," he says. "They're winos. When you go, I'll be doing what they're doing, picking up bottles and cans. But not because I'm like them, not because I need the money to buy a bottle of wine." He leaves unspoken his reason, his need for companionship. Mike, the city dweller called back by his ties with his village, is an uneasy citizen of either world.

Below the bluff, at the edge of Hazelton, the first tourists of the morning arrive at 'Ksan, the re-created Gitksan village at the junction of the Bulkley and the Skeena that houses both artifacts of a traditional past and a renowned school for artists of the future. The tourists are a little bewildered: the cedar big houses are blank-faced, no signs to guide the visitor, no official guide visible. They return to read the discreet map and explanation at the entrance to the village. I sit and contemplate the houses, the totem poles, the grass, and listen to the swollen river catch the willows at the water's edge. At length, a Gitksan guide appears to take us around the buildings. She points out the fishing hooks, the ceremonial masks and robes, the tools and ornaments. But she hesitates to answer deeper questions about the culture that is represented at 'Ksan. Like most Gitksan her age, she went to school "outside," sent down to Vancouver to white man's school. She says little about the experience, except that she must now relearn native traditions and language. "I don't speak the language much," she says. "I learned it as a child, but I have forgotten most of it." Earlier this week, her clan held a feast for the death of her aunt, but she understood only a part of the rituals and chants. Behind her words is an unspoken uncertainty: though 'Ksan exists as much for white visitors as for natives, some Gitksan do not want any longer to tell the stories that form the basis of their spiritual culture, for they are private, the property of the clan to which they give meaning and sustenance.

Down the street from 'Ksan, in the big pink house where Sargents have lived for a hundred years, Polly Sargent wheels herself across the kitchen floor to heat a cup of coffee in the microwave, mounted where she can reach it from her wheelchair. Since the 1940s, Polly has been a driving force in Hazelton: mover and shaker, sometime mayor, an indomitable woman of seemingly endless energy. Her legs are swollen and crippled now, and she is unable to hide the occasional grimace of pain. But she defies you to feel sorry for her. "As a child I was never allowed to say I didn't have a good time at a party. You make it good. It's up to you."

Her deepest interest in the valley of the Hazeltons has always been the life and traditions of the Gitksan. She joined with native leaders in the mid-sixties to fight for 'Ksan, against white indifference.and the determination of some Gitksan who wanted to abandon traditions, forget the past, assimilate themselves in the white world. She cajoled, persuaded, made allies and deals, found funding. The village opened in 1967. For her work, she was awarded the Order of Canada in 1972, and named the province's top senior citizen in 1985. But for her, the honours are secondary to her friendship with the Gitksan, and their shared moments of laughter and concern. She recalls the time when the Gitksan dancers gave a performance for Governor-General Roland Michener, who dressed for the occasion in fringed buckskin clothing. The dancers, who never wear fringe and consider it ridiculous, were beside themselves: throughout the dinner, they tried, often unsuccessfully, to stifle their giggles.

She talks about her friend Mary. She was having coffee with Mary one day when the impresario who booked the 'Ksan dancers phoned. "He had this bright idea that the dance group would be interested in going to London, England, and doing a command performance for the Queen." Polly said she'd ask the group, and phone him back.

She told Mary about the offer. Polly smoothes her grey, cap-cut hair, draws her mouth down, flattens her face, becomes for an instant her short, square, impassive friend. "She said, 'London?' I said, 'Yes, London, England.' 'When?' 'Next April.' 'April? Well, if there's nothing else going on in Kispiox right then.'"

Polly's deep laugh bubbles out across the kitchen. "The queen meant nothing whatever to her. It was just not part of her world."

Polly turns serious. She pauses now before she answers questions, not because she is reluctant, but because she struggles against a failing memory to get her details right, because they are too important to be careless about. Years ago, when natives and whites were planning the opening ceremonies for 'Ksan, a white organizer worried away at the question of what they would do if it rained. "What if it rains?" asked a native, utterly incredulous. "You want to know what we'll do if it rains?" "Yes. What will we do if it rains on opening day?" "We will," said the native, "wait until it stops."

"And there," says Polly, "you have the two cultures in a nutshell."

Polly has been researching the history and traditions of the Gitksan for four decades, but is constantly frustrated by her inability to translate the concepts of native belief, because there are no English words that work. "I have devoted my entire life to understanding, and I still cannot get the right meanings," she laments. Polly is beset with the problem of translating La-x-ha, for the word does not mean god or spirit or anything personified. The closest she can come is the world, the spirit within the world. "You can't translate. Sometimes, I think I'll just go crazy with it.

"An Indian feels he is only a shell. Nobody says, 'I'm beautiful', because beauty is inside me, and I'm not smart, smartness is inside me or with me." Polly gestures, searching for words, blocked by the limitations of the English language from conveying the native world view. "Every success, every ability, is because La-x-ha wants it, has given it to them. Then along come the white people with their iron and their sailing ships, their everything, and when the Indians saw these good things that the strangers had, they obviously had these things because La-x-ha liked the strangers and liked what they did and how they behaved, because otherwise he wouldn't have given them this superior stuff. So it wasn't hard to introduce the white man's way, because as far as the Indians were concerned, the white man's way was superior because their god wanted it that way."

Though she has shared as much with the Gitksan as any white, she knows she is apart from them. "Their world is a very real world and a very lively world and a very heartbreaking world. They are so close to so many people that they have known all their lives. Tragedies are terrible tragedies because their unit is so small."

Outside, white Hazelton is awake, the gift store and the grocery store open, the hotel serving lunch in a relaxed fashion. Down by the riverbank, a man is trying to get his lawn mowed before the rain comes down. In a parking lot, I catch a glimpse of a yellow slicker, a bottle of wine, three men leaning against a wall. They do not look towards me.

For thousands of years, this has been a land dominated by the moods of its rivers. When a shaman needs a new song, he goes to the woods and to the water. Beside a waterfall or rushing river, he listens to the song the water sings and brings it home. The song the Skeena sings this season is deep and forceful, fed by the incessant rain that has fallen for a week, and by the melting snows that feed its headwaters. Once more, I follow the river, brown and swollen, north to its joining with the Kispiox, along the gravel road that runs over to Cranberry Junction, and, eventually, the Stewart-Cassiar highway on its way to the Yukon.

The Kispiox Valley isn't many years away from being pioneer country, but incongruously, Josie and Rolly Steinbach, who could call themselves pioneers but don't, live twenty miles from Hazelton in a house on a crescent in a miniature subdivision.

Rolly's a country boy from Alberta: "Down the road from us the town was so small you had to back up to find it." He left Alberta in 1948, looking for work in British Columbia, then up to the Yukon, down to the United States, back to the Yukon where he got married for the first time, down to Bella Coola, working in the woods running cats or crews for contractors. He left Bella Coola too, what with problems with the Indians, his marriage and whatever. "It got a little too civilized down there. Every time I looked around I was staring at unions. I don't care for unions that much, especially if you're in the middle like I was, eh? The employer expected me to get a day's work out of the guys, and some of the guys I worked with before figured they'd known me so long they could get around me a little bit."

Rolly heard about the Kispiox from a friend, and bought property here. Then he went back to the Yukon where he met Josie. The two of them married and moved back down to the Kispiox. Tall and rawboned, sure of himself and his opinions, Rolly still works in the woods, sometimes running a crew, but "I'd just as soon work by myself, you know. These young boys, they got to be forty of them working together before they're happy. I've been working by myself for years. I might quit this fall, I might work another ten years. It just depends. If a tree hits me in the head I might quit tomorrow. It's not that I can afford to retire, but it just depends on what happens. If I feel good, I'm gonna keep going because I enjoy the outdoors. Been in it all my life." And he enjoys his present role, preparing land for reforestation, because it gives him a chance to repay the land some of the debt he feels he owes from years of logging.

Josie chimes in. She was talking to the contractor who employs Rolly to prepare logged-off land for the tree planters who pour in here by the hundreds every spring and summer. "He says, 'Is Rolly still working for me?' I says, 'Well he leaves the house every morning and he comes home every night dirty, so he's working for someone. As far as I'm concerned, he's still working for you.' 'Well,' he says, 'I never hear from him.' I says, 'I guess everything is going right. If it wasn't, you sure would hear from him.'"

Josie, a compact bundle of energy and forthrightness, started life in Victoria, the daughter of a Hawaiian-Canadian family. She soon learned how Victorians felt about her. "It was very hard for me to get a job down there on account of my colour. They are very prejudiced in Victoria." She remembers visiting a friend in a house where an elderly English woman also lived, and being asked what she thought someone like her was doing in the house. Being Josie, she answered the question in a few short, well-chosen words, and the woman retired to her room in the best English high dudgeon.

She got married and got out, to Ontario, then "up and down the coast for quite a few years in little logging camps and little islands ... beachcombed and fished and you name it, even chimney sweeping." She liked the life, but it was unsettling with four kids to pack around, never knowing where they would be from one day to the next. "My husband would come home and say, 'Well, we're moving tonight.'"

When the oldest was fifteen and the youngest nine or ten, they moved up to the Yukon. "I think we had eight flat tires going up the Alaska highway, and I took one look at the Yukon and said, 'I'm not staying.' Oh, the place was drab in the spring . . . and the winter! We lived in a tent for the summer and we decided we were going to build a log cabin way out in the bush."

Time passed and Josie had had enough, so she and her husband split up. She met Rolly, married, and moved to the Kispiox. Now, she spends most summers cooking for crews in the woods, most falls cooking for hunters at guide-outfitters' camps. This year, she's cooking at the lodge down the road, though she swore she'd never cook in a restaurant again: too much uncertainty, never knowing whether there'll be one person or a hundred for dinner.

Though she's a tiny woman, anyone who thinks Josie is easy had better think again. Not so long ago, a man who had it in for Rolly thought he'd pick on Josie. She parked her car at the rodeo grounds; he rolled it out into the middle of the road and left it. Josie found him in the lodge bar. "Why did you leave my car in the middle of the road?" she demanded. He leaned his six-foot frame back in his chair, smirked and asked, "What do you think you're going to do about it?" Josie learned from brothers who were among the best boxers in Victoria; she hauled off and thumped the man in the stomach and had to be held back from landing a few more punches. Rolly laughs as he tells the story, proud of Josie's toughness.

Josie and Rolly are going out to a friend's place, but in this country, you don't send people away without supper. Over spareribs, jug wine and rhubarb pie, Rolly adds a few more anecdotes, telling how Josie keeps the hunters in line when they come in late for supper or want special treatment. Rolly doesn't like men who pick on women, or city boys, or single parents on welfare, or high-grading loggers, or big forest companies that drive the little guys out of business. The last time he went to the Yukon "all the old guys had died off and the younger guys and the guys my age even were starting to get big-city ideas. They figured they were living on main street Vancouver or something."

Not for Rolly or for Josie either. They're in the Kispiox because it's still close to the old guys, the ones who worked hard and did for themselves and never complained or begged or took a thing they didn't earn. When that changes on the Kispiox, they'll probably be gone from here too.

Outside, at the end of the long June day, a weakening sun still glances off the muddy river that surges around the roots of flooded aspen and alder. The people of the Kispiox held their rodeo at the rodeo grounds beside the river last week. The rain held off till late afternoon Saturday, then descended heavy and hard, turning the ring to thick, greasy mud. One steer-roping cowboy grabbed the steer's slippery horns, then, as the animal lunged forward, slid slowly, precisely, flat on his face in the mud. He got up mad, but the crowd cheered and he grinned and did a slow pratfall backwards. When he stood up again, all you could see were the whites of his eyes in the brown of the mud. When the cowboys came up to the Kispiox Sportsmen's Lodge, next door in country terms, for dinner, they had to shower off under the hose outside.

It's quiet at the lodge tonight, quiet enough that Margaret Clay has time to come back for a drink in the bar from the coffee shop where she spends most of her day. Slight, alive with energy, looking far too young to have a son in his late thirties, Margaret has managed the lodge for three years. She was a newly divorced mother of three when she came north to Smithers ("I wanted to be anywhere but Vancouver, and I got a job in Smithers") twenty years ago. She met her second husband when she was managing an apartment building in Prince Rupert. The next summer, they took over a fish barge and spent the summer anchored along the Inside Passage north of Bella Bella, waiting for fishermen to bring in their catch.

In September, the towboat that was to take them to winter anchorage off the Queen Charlotte Islands hooked on and started off. The towboat captain was an old-timer who didn't like to be bothered while he was under way, so he turned his radio off and missed the gale warnings. "We were heading out as the fishboats were heading in," Margaret recalls with a shudder. The waves were twenty feet high by the time they reached midchannel, and the green water sluiced over the barge deck. Water poured into the fish storage tanks. The barge began to tilt with the wind and the new unstable weight. The tug captain tried to manoeuvre back to level the barge. The tow rope snapped. One small boat, lashed to the bow of the barge, was inaccessible. The other skiff on board was rotten, and the lifejackets wouldn't fit even around her husband's arm. Margaret and her husband scrambled to the high edge of the barge and jumped. As they clung in the freezing water to floating fish crates, they saw their malamute rush mindlessly from one edge of the deck to the other. Then the barge slid silently under the water.

They say you can last less than twenty minutes unprotected in the cold waters of the Pacific, but it seemed twice that long before the tug retrieved the shipwrecked sailors. Once rescued, her husband got stubborn. "I'm not leaving here without the dog." "We're getting out of here," said the crew. "No, you're not." The crew yielded, the boat circled and a giant wave came towards them. On the crest, paddling as fast as his paws would move, was the dog. Hands hauled him aboard by his sodden ruff. "We got on board about 6:00 P.M.," says Margaret, "and I didn't stop shivering for twelve hours."

Maybe it was this experience that convinced them to buy the lodge up the Kispiox. A month after they arrived at the lodge, Margaret's husband died of a heart attack. With two grown-up sons and a teenage daughter, she was pregnant with her fourth child. One morning, she served breakfast to her guests, then headed to hospital in Hazelton. When her eighteen- and twenty-year-old sons heard they had a baby brother, they celebrated so hard the guests had to wake them up to get their breakfast. Margaret soldiered on for ten years, then sold the lodge. Now she's back, managing for the absentee owners.

In the summer and in the autumn steelhead season, the lodge is solidly booked. The rest of the year, it welcomes occasional travellers and serves as a social centre for the valley of the Kispiox. Messages in the big logbook are left for people passing through: it's a dating service, business guide and social diary. "Dan. Could you trim the little grey mare at Wilfred Lee's?" "Open house. Everyone invited. Come and meet Dave and Nate." "Shell. This is Christopher. I have a day off on Sunday, so I'll see you then?" "Mother arriving 3 P.M. at bus depot." "Interested in bridge night? Cribbage?" "I found another waterhole, but haven't received the water analysis yet. It is not as abundant as the original hole."

In the morning, Margaret sits over coffee and talks about a relationship that has just broken up. This country is hard on relationships, the men left bitter and uncomprehending, the women hurt and seeking a new way of life. Long winters, close quarters, that damn women's lib, a life half-pioneer, half-television via satellite dish. Smithers, down the highway, is known as the place where divorced women and single mothers congregate. Mostly, you'll find the single men in the pub or in the bush.

The sky turns from brilliant blue to milky, from milky to ominous grey. Stekyawden—known on the map by its white man's name of

Rocher de Boule—the mountain that dominates the valley, is no longer a picture-perfect tourist peak topped with white fluffy clouds. Now, with charcoal cloud lowering over it, seen through slashing rain, illuminated by streaks of lightning, it is the mountain of Temlahan.

The story of Temlahan exists in many versions and with many clans and tribes; all the versions teach that man must respect nature or die. One version is the story of young Indians from the village of Temlahan who teased and tortured a baby goat, unheeding of the young man who tried to stop them. The goat people assumed disguises and invited the people of the village to come to a feast. At the feast, they cast off their disguises and destroyed the people, sparing only the man who had tried to stop the cruelty.

I am reminded of the harshness and the violence this land can offer as I drive west from the Kispiox, along a dirt road that winds at first between the river and the daisy-spotted meadows of the valley ranches. I come up behind a slow-moving pickup truck, decide there is no place to pass and drop back. Twenty minutes farther on, as I run through logged-off hills green with alder, the truck stops suddenly in the middle of the road. I accelerate to pass, then stop, unsure. A rifle pokes out of the driver's window. A shot is fired. The driver wheels off, down a narrow track.

The dirt road meets the Stewart-Cassiar and I go north to Kitwancool, a Gitksan village where tradition and modern life meld. Silence pervades the village on this Sunday morning. Two friendly dogs push their noses into my hand as I walk through the long grass between the totem poles that stand at the edge of a field. For generations, the Gitksan raised their poles here in this village. Times changed; the traditions and arts of the Gitksan were devalued and debased and no new poles were carved. Times have changed again: a pole newly carved rests on supports in the grass, its yellow-brown cedar not yet turned to the weathered silver of the standing poles.

I turn back south again, once more heading towards the Skeena. As I round a curve, a cow and calf moose step daintily across the road, then plunge into the willows in the swamp below. At Moira's Cafe in Kitwanga, a line of baseball caps hangs on the wall, and I eat bacon and eggs at long picnic tables with locals and other travellers. Another dirt road takes me to Cedarvale, as close as I can get on this side of the Skeena to completing the circle that began across the river at Kitselas Canyon. Once Cedarvale was the Holy City, Minskinish, a non-sectarian Christian village where the Rev. Robert Tomlinson gathered his converted native charges. The residents made bricks and ran a sawmill, cleared the land, planted gardens, and tended sheep. No work was performed on Sunday, nor was any steamer permitted to land on the holy day.

The village prospered, dwindled, disappeared. Cedarvale, a white community, rose in its place. Today, it too has dwindled to a tiny store and post office and a few scattered houses at the end of the road, across the river from the highway. I walk along the railway track and eat tiny wild strawberries ripe well ahead of their season. A train rattles by: tanker cars, wheat pool cars, boxcars concealing their cargo, cars loaded with railway ties and lumber from up the line, more than a hundred in all. The train crew waves. I wave back, then drive the road again, back north for one more night at the lodge beside the Kispiox River.

CHAPTER 6

*From the River
to the Lakes*

)) Next morning, the road down the Kispiox is greasy and slick with sheeting rain. Weighted down with heavy grey cloud, Stekyawden looms large over the valley, appearing and disappearing through the downpour. Now that the Skeena angles north into almost uninhabited country, the highway follows the Bulkley River south and east, towards the centre of the province. Upriver, at Moricetovn Canyon, the rock walls narrow to create a foaming, rushing waterfall. This morning, swallows chitter and dart across the river bank, and tourists clamber down from a bus at the highway-side viewpoint to photograph the falls. For years past, the Wet'suwet'en Carrier Indians have lived and fished at Moricetown, standing on the steep, slippery rocks to gaff salmon as they batter their way upstream. Stories from generations past tell us the Carriers fled here when a vast rock slide blocked the Bulkley River near their ancestral home and flooded their village. That rock slide gives Stekyawden its official gazetteer name of Rocher de Boule, "fallen rock."

The Wet'suwet'en of Moricetown, 'Kyah Wiget in native tongue, have lived in harmony with the Gitksan for many years. Together, for almost a century, they have petitioned the government to recognize their aboriginal land claim, one of the earliest in the province. In the 1980s, they launched a court case, setting forth the legal basis to their claims, that most observers expect to reach Canada's Supreme Court.

In Smithers, a town of forty-seven hundred east of Moricetown, the shops and streets are busy, and the closest thing the town sees to a traffic jam lines up six or seven cars at a main-street stop sign. Beyond the town, the land begins to flatten out and the mountains disappear from the rear-view mirror. Slim, black-trunked jackpine and willow swamps close in on the road; I have left the coastal region and entered the interior plateau. A roadside sign warns of moose on the road ahead, and I peer assiduously into brush and swamp. But, outside of a national park, I have never seen a wild beast where signs have alerted me to watch for one, and today is no exception.

Flatcars loaded with lumber and bound for the port of Prince Rupert clack westward out of Houston, where rough, muddy roads lead from the forest to the mills. Trucks spilling over with long, skinny jackpine poles thunder by, spaced by the occasional truckload of fat coastal timber. This flat, muddy terrain isn't God's country, but it might be Mammon's; money-making goes on apace. Beyond Houston, a big-lettered sign presages road construction, "Giving you the Freedom to Move, Rita M. Johnston, Minister." But all that Rita's overseeing today are deep, muddy gouges in the swampy land below the highway and a rusty cat seemingly permanently parked beside the road.

A tour bus filled with nametag-wearing wanderers trundles away from the Burns Lake Hotel. Inside, the pace is slow: a man in a baseball cap reads a fat novel and sips cold coffee and a young woman scribbles in a notebook as cigarette smoke curls up from her ashtray. What I take to be German tourists in Stetsons and jeans turn out to be eager immigrants, new settlers in the lakes country to the south. I turn south now, towards those lakes.

The pointing digits of the Finger Lakes—Francois and Ootsa, Whitesail and Eutsuk and Tahtsa—follow the valley contours from Fraser Lake southwestward to the Coast Mountains. By 1905, most of the good farming and ranching land on the prairies and in British Columbia had been taken up by settlers. Would-be pioneers reached further and further afield. Some followed the rivers and the overland trails to this rolling, pine-covered land between the lakes; more came in with the railway and trekked overland on foot or horseback to pre-empt land for their homesteads and their farms.

The main road passes this country by; the only way in is across Francois Lake on the free government ferry, or over a long, punishing gravel road around the western end of the lake. Unappealing to those who measure life in fast food and fast cars, it is a country still inhabited by pioneers who want to live life their own way, without interference from the urban world.

I drive aboard the free ferry that traverses Francois Lake. Two long

car-trailer combinations from Washington State, bound for fishing holidays, edge gingerly aboard as the ferryman hunches down to check
that the trailers won't ground themselves where the loading ramp meets
the deck. We set out across the long, narrow lake through drifting
drizzle.

On the far side, rail fences and old log buildings, some abandoned,
some in use, mark the rolling grasslands that promised good cattle-
grazing to the homesteaders. Beyond the grasslands extends a mixed
forest of pines and poplars, wet and glimmering in the weak sun that
pokes through the overcast. A requisite broken-down pickup truck rests
beside a squared log house and sagging barn. The Washingtonians with
their trailers turn down towards Takysie Lake, where they'll settle in
for their annual two weeks of fishing.

In the Takysie cafe/general store, a sign outlines the ten minimum
requirements for ranchers:

1. A wide-brimmed hat, a pair of tight pants and a pair of $200
   boots.
2. At least 2 head of Livestock, preferably cattle, 1 male, 1 female.
3. A new air-conditioned pickup truck with automatic transmis-
   sion, power steering, a trailer hitch, and a punch-button radio for
   listening to football games.
4. A gun rack, for the rear window of the pickup, big enough to
   hold a walking stick and a rope.
5. Two leopard dogs to ride in the bed of the truck.
6. A $40 horse and a $400 saddle.
7. A gooseneck trailer, small enough to park in front of the cafe.
8. A place to keep the cows; a little land too poor to grow crops.
9. A spool of barbed wire, 3 cedar posts and a bale of prairie hay to
   haul around in the truck all the time.
10. Credit at the bank.

Stan Likkel is happy to talk about why he got out of ranching. "We
came down here seventeen years ago from Lynden, Washington. We
ran a dairy farm down there. We were thirty or a little more, and
this"—moving to Canada and running a cattle ranch— "was something
we had always wanted to do, so we decided we had better do it now.
But we're so far from anything here. The nearest good cattle market is
in Williams Lake," three hundred miles away. "Most of the time, we felt
like we were working for nothing and most of the time we were." Stan

and Lois put the ranch up for sale and bought this combination of campground, cabins, restaurant, store, and gas station beside the lake.

But the business is still just one damn thing after another. Stan pushes forward a petition to Chevron, asking the company not to cut off his gas supply. He asked gas company representatives why they were cutting him off, despite the $160,000 he turns over to them every year. "They said my tanks were 'environmentally unsound'. Didn't test them—just said any tanks in the ground more than ten years weren't safe. I offered to put in above-ground tanks, at my own expense, but they refused.

"So I asked where people were supposed to get gas, and they said," Stan imitates perfectly a toffee-nosed, supercilious city slicker, "'I suppose Burns Lake. Maybe there won't be any gas available south of the lake in a while.'

"So I said," and he's getting angry just thinking about it, "'Sure, let's close the north, screw the north. We'll all move to the Fraser Valley. Put in fifteen thousand pumps on Granville Street in Vancouver and everybody can line up there and you'll only have to deliver to one location.' But," ruefully, "those guys have no sense of humour, and you can't make them mad."

He doesn't have a good word to say about Chevron, or Canada Post, or any of the other big corporations he thinks are running small-town Canada into the ground. Chevron, says Stan, boasts on television that it's the Guardian of the North. "But you have to be a certain size, or the hell with you. And that's corporate Canada."

The growing emphasis on big corporations making money and government breaking even regardless of the human cost infuriates Stan. Everything's being centralized, maximized, mechanized—and that makes it ever harder for people in small, isolated communities to make even the meagre living they'd be satisfied with. Canada Post, for example. Last year, they "privatized" the Takysie Lake post office outlet that Lois Likkel runs for them. "They cut down on paying little stores like this one. Before the change, Lois was making maybe five hundred dollars a month; the first cheque after the switch was for ninety dollars. She's making maybe two and a half dollars an hour. They sent five people out from Vancouver, in their little white pants and their little white shoes, to explain, spent more in three days than we make in a year."

Ranching's touch-and-go, and it's hard to make any money from running services for the community. What about logging, the mainstay of half of rural B.C.? The big corporations are ruining the small operators there too. "There's lots of small logging operators wondering what the heck they're going to do five years or even three years down the line," says Stan. "For years stumpage [fees paid to the government for logging rights] was so low, then, boom, it went the other way. The big companies can bring all their big equipment in and turn a timber sale over in thirty to sixty days. A small operator goes to the bank and says he needs thirty to fifty thousand dollars and he'll need six to eight months to take the timber off, and the bank says forget it.

"I'd like to have seen, instead of the government demanding these big deposits, something smaller, maybe five or ten thousand dollars. Then the small operator would be able to compete at the same level as the big operator."

But as long as they can make even a bare living, the Likkels are here to stay. "We meet a great bunch of people. In the three years we've been running this place, we've only had one bad time — and that was with a guy from Smithers. People are great, and some come back year after year." I hear lots of grumbles about the crews of tree planters that invade the north every spring, complaints that they are raucous and irresponsible, but Likkel likes even them. His tree planters were a great bunch of kids who camped at Takysie for a couple of weeks.

"I asked Lois the other day how much they'd have to pay her to work in an office in Vancouver. She said first of all, they'd have to have a limousine to drive her to work so she didn't have to worry about traffic, then . . . . Altogether, maybe about $400,000 a year."

Stan goes off to run the till on the store side of the operation. Though it has rained hard and steadily for three days, the fishermen laugh and joke over their coffee, fingering through fishing lures, toys, T-shirts and novelties, browsing through the videos for rent. Outside, dusk is dimming the lake, and a loon slips through the water, sounding its full-throated cry. A crested black duck dips down beneath the wave.

In the morning, I trek back to the main road and the pine forest and hilly grasslands that stretch down towards Ootsa Lake. "Yoot-soo," the Carrier word meaning "very low down," was the derivation for this name, but it isn't so far down as it once was. The narrow gap between the Finger Lakes and salt water drew the engineers of Alcan towards their mighty plan to reverse the waters of the Nechako and build a dam and powerhouse to run the power-hungry production of aluminum at Kitimat. The Finger Lakes became the reservoirs for the Kenney Dam not far from here. Almost forty years after the waters rose, the shoreline of Ootsa Lake is still lined with driftwood, and drowned trees poke spears up through the shallow water. Up the lake, water thunders through the Skins Lake spillway that controls the water level—though, if Alcan has its way, not for long. A proposed, and opposed, doubling of the power capacity, a twinning of the powerlines to Kitimat, require more water, more damming. Skins Lake may soon be dry.

The issues are as unclear in my mind today as they were clear in the minds of the young engineers who turned a river in its bed and flooded acre after acre of land, displacing new settlers and long-settled native tribes without a second thought —and giving only superficial thought to any environmental problems the river reversal might cause. Thirty-five years ago, a young correspondent for *National Geographic* magazine wrote admiringly: "They [the Canadians] had dammed a river, run it backwards through a mountain, dropped it down a man-made waterfall 16 times higher than Niagara, and then returned it to the Pacific . . . . I admire them for the way they shovel up mountains and throw the map all around the place and dam up rivers to make them run through a mountain—to make aluminum."

Thirty years later, that same correspondent, now a senior writer with that same magazine, took another look at the awesome project. In his 1986 story, he quoted a Cheslatta native chief whose band was exiled from its lands, with little warning, no compensation, and no comeback. "They wiped out our Indian homes and villages," the chief said, "wrecked our fishing, ruined the river, and never responded to our plight or our complaints." Writer David Boyer, like so many of us, is no longer sure of his ground.

At the Wistaria Community Hall, in the remnants of a pioneer community half-drowned by the flooding, a cairn commemorates the pioneers of Ootsa Lake. A collapsed house, boards smoothed grey by time, an old wooden boat half-hidden in the long grass, an abandoned cabin of squared timbers, four horses in a cottonwood grove: little more remains.

Back up the hill, away from the lake, odd-shaped turrets that resemble doll-sized greenhouses break a grassy rise by the road. I wheel into the driveway of what turns out to be an underground house. Karen Angal is as welcoming as a pioneer of an earlier age, immediately offering supper and putting on the coffee pot. Her three daughters crowd around to see who the stranger is.

Karen and husband Steve built this house, backed into the hill on three sides, with a magnificent view out over the lake on the fourth. When Steve and Karen married, they moved to the far end of Francois Lake, thirty miles on rough logging roads from pavement, but the arrival of their first child persuaded them to live a little closer to facilities and services such as doctors. "Steve always wanted an underground house, so we built this one," says Karen, matter-of-factly. Eighteen inches of sod top the tar and gravel roof that has a draining slope of four inches. "There's lots of money in the roof," she notes. "The house is warm in winter, cool in summer. We use about one stoveful of wood a day in the winter, we never put on the electric heat and we go barefoot all day," in weather that can drop well below freezing for weeks at a time. "When we go out to visit in other people's houses, we're cold."

At first, a steady stream of people dropped by to satisfy their curiosity, but the locals are used to the house now. With three children, the Angals need more room, so they are selling their dream house. "The kids want a house with stairs," jokes Karen. "They have no stairs to practise on."

Eight-year-old Laura, four-year-old Jordanna and two-year-old Megan finish supper in a jumble of talking and laughing. Laura gets involved with her TV Nintendo game, Jordanna settles in to draw pictures and Megan delivers and redelivers a mellow lop-tailed cat called Stumpy a dozen or more times; each time, the cat escapes and allows himself to be recaptured. Then Laura, sunny and sociable, talks about school. "Everybody asks me, 'Do you live in an underground house?'" But she's more interested in fishing. "We catch thousands of fish. Sometimes you just drop your line in and, whoo-oo-oosh!" More than anything, she wants a horse. Then Jordanna shows me she can write the first two letters of her name, and we draw cats and people together. She's better at it than I am.

The girls trail after me to the door. "Stay," they command. But I go.

Back on the ferry across Francois Lake, a laughing four-year-old Indian child and his chortling baby brother race to see a friend they've caught sight of in a pickup truck. A German shepherd dog wags a friendly tail from the bed of another battered pickup. On the road north to Burns Lake, the dog lays its ears back against the wind and canters from side to side, bracing front paws up on alternate wheel wells. A marmalade cat appears beside the road. The dog's ears prick up, he rushes back to the tailgate and stands staring for as long as the cat is visible. Then he returns and does sentry duty all the way in to town.

Fort St. James

♩♩ Eastward along Highway 16, the rain beats down again, and the water bomber depot near Fraser Lake seems spectacularly irrelevant. At a truck stop west of Vanderhoof, the rain, falling now on the interior of the province for almost the Biblical forty days and forty nights, is all the news. Highways are closed south and east of Prince George. Mudslides and floods have stranded travellers and destroyed houses. It's the worst, they say, in fifteen years, or fifty. Decidedly too much weather this year, the waitress declares, what with this and last month's high winds and tornadoes, never seen before in living memory.

Highway 16 bisects British Columbia; Vanderhoof, considered by the majority of British Columbians, squeezed down along the forty-ninth parallel, to be in the far north, is actually the geographic centre of B.C. The single paved road that branches north from Vanderhoof goes to Fort St. James, founded almost at the very beginning of white man's history in B.C., long before Victoria or Vancouver. I had planned to stay at an isolated cottage north of the fort, to contemplate history in the long northward sweep of storm-roiled Stuart Lake. But since the trip began, I have ignored all but local weekly newspapers, left the radio silent, turned off the motel-room television. I hunger for news; I want to know what the rains have done, so I book into a Fort St. James motel that offers cable television.

The evening news shows scene after scene of flood and devastation. Close to eight inches of rain has fallen so far this month, six times the normal rainfall, close to two inches in the last three days alone. A raging creek has swept seven hundred feet of highway, houses, and half a hillside into the Fraser south of Prince George. Four young tree planters are missing after their van plummeted into a river from a blank space that just hours before was a bridge. Thousands of tons of mud have crashed across the Yellowhead 5 highway, north of Kamloops. Mud has oozed across the road east of Prince George. No road connections remain between the north and the south of the province. And the rain still beats down.

The north is used to being isolated. There's even a certain pride now, as flood stories hit the provincial and national news. Disaster, violent dissent or crime are usually the only occasions when the south listens, briefly, to the north.

Beyond the town, whitecaps break the surface of Stuart Lake, whose waters disappear, mistily, into the wilderness. Simon Fraser and the fur traders who followed him must have been familiar with this wild scene: for eighty years after Fraser founded the post in 1806, Fort St. James served as the capital of the fur trade in the beyond-the-Rockies district of New Caledonia. Carrier natives and traders came and went along the lakes and rivers that stretch north between mountain ridges that parallel the Rockies to the east, the Coast Mountains to the west. Even today, no red-line highways on the map break the vast region between the mountain ranges, and only natives, prospectors, and those few who seek the solitude of swamp, mountain, and scraggy forest make their homes beyond this last town.

White man's civilization has not been good for the Carrier natives who live near Fort St. James. For the first time on this trip, I see native men and women, old and young, gathering on street corners, sitting on benches, staring into space, throwing empty wine bottles into the street. An article in the Prince George paper shows the extent of the problem. A tribal council chief is quoted as saying, "It is not far off to say that our communities are in a state of siege." A weekend conference will try to address the problems of family violence, substance abuse and welfare.

Seventy years ago, writer Lukin Johnston, a kind man but a man of his times, passed this way. "It seems unfortunate," he wrote, "when they are trying to make this place attractive to tourists, the road must pass by these dirty, tumble-down, dog-infested shacks. When you arrive all keyed up with the romance of this northern post with pictures of the Indian braves of old in your mind— these miserable hovels come as rather a shock." His solution? "Perhaps a way will be found in the future to change the route at this point."

And here still, anger and hostility exist between the native and the white populations. "You won't solve the problem until you stop giving them things," one white woman bursts out angrily when I mention the native people. "Rights? They have no rights. They lost the war." Which war? "You don't understand," said with bitterness and frustration. "You can't understand. You don't have to live with it."

The slow death of the fur trade has not helped those native trappers who used to rely on trapping for a living. Visitors come to Fort St. James by the busloads to see the reconstructed fur fort on the edge of town, but the Hudson's Bay Company, the middle man in the trade for more than a century, no longer has a representative in Fort St. James. They still call the old store "The Bay," but The Bay, synonymous with the north for so long, sold off its northern Canadian stores three years ago. With intentional or unintentional irony, the group of Bay employees who bought the stores called their new company the North West Company Inc., reviving the name of the competitor the Bay swallowed in 1821. The stores are now called The Northern.

You can order a down-filled, coyote-fur-trimmed, black leather jacket from The Northern catalogue, or a woolen parka embroidered with polar bears and a matching fox-fur hat. Black leather is big in the north, the catalogue suggests, and so are cowboy boots and outdoor gear and hockey pads. Wood stoves can be ordered through the catalogue, as can an ice-fishing sled for fifty-three hundred dollars, a CB radio, a wide choice of rifles and snowmobiles, a racing harness for your husky, snowshoes, ice drills—or, for that matter, Nintendo games, automatic cameras, wedding dresses, compact disc players and dish antennas. And you can still get a traditional Hudson's Bay Company blanket, with its characteristic stripes of red, yellow and black on ivory.

A hundred years ago or less, these blankets were prized trade goods, their quality measured in points that cost one beaver pelt each. Today, a four-point blanket sells for $239, a prime beaver pelt for $30—if there's a market. "I still buy furs," says The Northern store manager, "but it's just about over. Between the warm winters and the antitrapping activists, there's no market anymore. Prices have dropped. A lynx used to bring a thousand dollars. This winter, I paid a hundred and fifty. Lots of people rely on trapping to make a living, but there's less and less money in it."

In the 1920s, the fur trade was still going strong, and Lukin Johnston was enthralled with the romance of it all: brilliant sashes girdling the men's waists, canny traders, expressionless native faces. Beyond the village, he found the Douglas Lake Hotel, "amazing . . . in this out-of-the-way spot, [bungalows and community house] equipped with every modern luxury—tiled bathrooms with constant hot water, well-furnished bedrooms and electric light . . . . Douglas Lodge has been established only four years, but already its beauties are becoming known."

The lodge became well enough known to survive the intervening sixty-five years: locals and tourists still make the trip along the shore of Stuart Lake, past log cabins with moose horns over the door and West Coast-style cedar houses, to dine on prawn and scallop newburg—and for desert, ice cream, "brown or white." The waitress says that President Hoover used to come here, that black tie and tails were required. But now it's jeans and shorts; "it's better now," she says. But no more friendly: the staff is harried, and no one has time to chat.

In the morning, I almost trip over a heavy husky dog who lolls like a guard in front of my motel-room door. After breakfast, I see the dog ensconced in the bed of a pickup truck between two big fuel drums. The dog's owner is down from Germansen Landing, one of fewer than a hundred people who live in the fabled Omineca, where secretive men still search for gold. This man says he's semiretired, but, oh, a man can get so bored doing nothing. So he's come to the fort, looking for work. What kind of work? "Oh, something I'd like." What would he like? "Well, something that would be interesting." He's been a roughneck in mining camps and done his time on logging crews. Right now, he's just looking around.

The land to the north is vast, its geography intimidating. Those who search for gold now, unlike those prospectors who flocked on foot to the Omineca in the 1880s, do so from the air. But they are just as close-mouthed as the prospectors of the previous century. At the airport, four young men cluster around a helicopter, fiddling with the machinery they use for electromagnetic mapping of the ground. Robert Gordon, a young geophysicist from Sault Ste. Marie in Ontario, won't say where they are bound once they get their equipment back in working order. "A couple of hours north of here," is the closest he will come: they are looking for gold and I could be a spy for a rival mining company. Even my complete ignorance of the complex technology they are using doesn't convince him of my innocence. And, he confesses, the surveying company he works for doesn't tell even him which mining company hired them.

Ahead of the helicopter snake out the cables that suspend the "bird" below the helicopter: a long torpedo-shaped container with coils at the front to transmit an electromagnetic field into the ground and coils in the middle to subtract the field and produce a picture of the subterranean geography. The geophysicists know what "normal" looks like: their interpretation of anomalies suggests to the mining companies where they should be sending their earth-bound prospectors. It's hot north of here right now, says Robert. Gold is the only mineral worth looking for, and the big players on the Vancouver Stock Exchange are buying and selling madly in companies that have staked properties between the Omineca and the Yukon/Alaska border. On the ground and in the air, mining companies try to outfox each other, seeking, as prospectors have always sought, that one big bonanza, that famed El Dorado.

In a little white building over beside the airport runway, Charlotte is marking weather observations into the record. Starting at quarter to six every morning, she checks the weather instruments, makes her observations, marks them down. This spring has kept her busy. From May 5 to 19, winds tore through the region; in mid-May, one windstorm ripped roofs off houses. Funnel clouds—tornadoes that don't touch down—were reported for the first time in the recorded history of Fort St. James. And it seems like it's been raining ever since.

Weather normal or abnormal, winter, spring, summer, fall, Charlotte likes Fort St. James. With her helicopter pilot husband Randy, she has lived here for seventeen years, raising her three kids in this town of two thousand people. "You know what your kids are doing all the time. The first day my daughter had her driver's licence, I got two phone calls saying, 'Do you know your daughter's got the truck?' Right away, you know if your kids aren't in school. Somebody sees them and tells you.

"But the kids are independent. They have had to make their own fun. They think nothing of driving to Prince George [ninety-five miles away] for lunch. There's a set of caves here they explore, they have a riot, they hike out there all the time. There's a huge sailing club, a ski hill. And when your kids have skied all day, night doesn't come at three or four in the morning. They go to bed early."

People tell me that Fort St. James, population two thousand, supported by logging and two lumber mills, is really three communities: native Indian, East Indian, white. Charlotte says that East Indian and white young people are beginning to mix, to ski together, to see each other socially. But she becomes taciturn when I ask about the native people. She doesn't want to talk about that.

Charlotte is president of the local cable television system, a community group that supplies cable TV to Fort St. James from satellite signals. The group pays fifty-six thousand dollars a year for the signals, and the town collects the money from subscribers on their tax bills. In Charlotte's book, that's what small towns are all about: local involvement, local control.

But, like Stan Likkel in Takysie Lake, she thinks the system is favouring the big, killing the small. "It's eight years since there's been a raise in the flying industry; we've had a couple of wage rollbacks. We're sinking, and we have two fairly medium-sized incomes." And if their family is having problems keeping up, what about other small-town residents with fewer resources? "When these small towns start to fold, look out. Everything from the big cities is shipped out to small towns. Where do you think all those truckers on the road are going to? And if there is no logging around Fort St. James, where will the cities get all their wood from?"

Back south from Fort St. James, through forest and farm fields to Vanderhoof. In the area newspaper, the battle against Alcan's new power project is heating up: the paper reprints an obituary run in 1952: "passed away, on Wednesday, October, 1952, at 10.27 a.m., the ageless and mighty Nechako River. The passing, which brings great sorrow to residents of the Nechako Valley, was slow and agonizing to the tens of thousands of minnows, trout and the few salmon trapped . . . . [It] has destroyed forever a thing of beauty and of divine creation." An early salvo is fired by the Rivers Defence Coalition against another such death.

The rain has stopped; the sun shines brightly on the road to Prince George. Now people are worried that the hot sunshine will melt the mountain snowpack and bring even worse floods to the region. At the city of Prince George, the Fraser River runs high, brown and fast, overflowing the trails of a riverside park, water lapping muddy and turgid at the foundations of nearby houses. Above the riverbanks, in the unfamiliar sunshine, kids and adults play in the park, tape decks blaring and Frisbees flying.

With its suburban malls and subdivisions, this city of almost seventy thousand seems to have drawn its skirts away from its boisterous, boomtown past of hard working and hard drinking. Only the downtown, where the sulphurous smell of pulp mills drifts across shabby streets, seems to connect with that past. Drifters lounge on street corners, waiting, waiting. A cadaverous middle-aged man drags his ragged pant leg up over his spindly white calf and scratches endlessly at an incurable itch. A young woman in skin-tight miniskirt and T-shirt paces the corner, narrow high heels clacking on the sidewalk.

Down the main street, a hairdresser's salon advertises tree planters' buzz cuts—shaved close, good for three months in the bush— for seven dollars. At Spruce Resale, tree planters examine second-hand shovels, aim shiny rifles at hanging lanterns, test ghetto blasters for shrieking noise level. At the Chinese cafe, you can sit all day for the price of a cup of coffee—or you can go around the corner to a California-modern restaurant listed in international good-food guides. You can buy army surplus for five dollars or high fashion for five hundred, within the same block. Above new signs and bright awnings, faded clapboard façades are reminders of a dingier past. And at a native art store, a pamphlet on the Carrier-Sekani conference to consider native violence and addiction is tacked next to a radio that broadcasts a commercial for an expensive treatment program for alcohol-dependent members of the middle class.

CHAPTER 8

Living on the Edge of History

)) Three days ago, the rain still fell in sheets and the road south from Prince George was blocked by mud slides and slashed by washouts. Today, the sun shines and traffic speeds south at its normal pace. Two days ago, politicians and press helicoptered in to console and interview those left homeless by the floods. Today, the television crews have returned to their normal city habitat, and only the desultory movement of bulldozers in the new bed cut by a rampaging creek, and shattered roofs and boards that could have been caught by the current for ten hours or ten years, testify to the water's force.

Crews are repairing a bridge across the Cottonwood River. As we halt behind a flagwoman, a red-tailed hawk sails on the thermals high above. Cottonwood leaves shimmer silver green, deeper green, birds sing, and the constant low thunder of the water sounds above the groan of truck engine brakes. The line of traffic heading north comes through: trucks and campers and trailers with Alaska licence plates, their occupants ready for an Alaskan summer after a winter in Palm Springs or San Diego.

Thirty miles north of Quesnel, a huge sign borders the highway: Cinema Second Hand. The village of Cinema used to be down the old road behind us, along the river. It was named by old Doc Champlain, a pioneer settler. Some folks say the doc was going to make movies here, the prettiest place he had ever seen. Others quote the doc as saying, "Cinema means action . . . . That's what we are, action." Or maybe he was being romantic, naming the place after he and his housekeeper returned from a trip to Hollywood in the 1920s. The doc died and the Cinema storekeeper moved up here when the new highway went through and took the name along with him. That didn't sit well with the people who stayed at the old site, but time passed and now this is Cinema and whatever remains down by the river is Old Cinema. Vic Olson can't make up his mind which wording on a new neon sign would attract more people to his second-hand store: Cinema City, with its promise of movie grandeur, or Cinema, B.C. Vic was a faller in the woods for years, but then his back went on him and he decided to retire to eighty acres in the bush. "But you can't retire on fifty dollars," sighs Vic, so he and his wife Theresa decided they had better start a business. He was working a couple of days a week for a friend who had a second-hand store in Quesnel; he decided he could open a store of his own out here on the road. "Everyone told me I couldn't make a store work out here. Well, I guess they were wrong," he says, with satisfaction. Cinema Second Hand sells enough used furniture and appliances, knick-knacks and collector's items, to pay for the Olsons' needs and two or three trips a year to the car races in Skagit, Washington, besides. Car-racing is Vic's obsession. "Now," he says, "we can go down there and if we blow five hundred dollars, that's okay."

East of the highway, along the old road towards the fabled Cariboo gold–rush creeks, orange mountain dandelion, pink wild roses, deep blue lupins, yellow buttercups, red Indian paintbrush, white oxeye daisies and feathery Queen Anne's lace flower in the meadows and along the grassy banks, backed by the deep green spruce and jackpine of the forest. The cemetery at the ghost town of Stanley looks smaller and more run-down than it used to, the carefully placed stepping stones leading up the hill from the gravel side road to scattered graves among the trees. Farther on, the wooden cabins of the old town darken in the sunshine, and equipment from a placer mining operation stands idle. The tiny mountain creeks of spring splash down from snow patches still visible on the hillsides.

At her souvenir shop in Wells, Marion is back in shape after a bad winter. She took sick and refused to get help until she almost died in the middle of one snow-deep night. Her handyman rushed her out the fifty miles to hospital in Quesnel, where she recalls seeing six blonde angels in green velvet clustered around her bedside. "I heard someone talking. They were saying Jesus this and Jesus that, and I decided not to go along with them." Later, she found out that a Catholic priest had administered last rites to her. But Marion, at seventy-nine, auburn-haired and looking fifty-nine, still makes her own decisions.

She was born in Wales and came to Saskatchewan in 1925, her parents lured to Canada by immigration posters showing tractors in golden wheat fields. Marion didn't get on with her mother too well, and ran away on the train when she was nineteen. The police found her and sent her back; her mother married her off to a neighbouring farmer. "I didn't know the facts of life," she recalls wryly. "I thought you got married to keep house."

Sex came as a nasty surprise. So did the brutality of her husband. After he chased her through a wheat field with a knife, she decided it was time to leave. She was in Blind River, Ontario, at the time of the big uranium strike in the 1950s. She took prospecting classes so she could learn to identify minerals and where to find them. Then she headed to Vancouver, saw an ad for a housekeeper on the north coast at Alice Arm, and got the job. She arrived to find her prospective employer missing, leaving her alone in the wilderness. That suited her just fine: she discovered the owner owed seventy-five dollars in back taxes, paid the money and got the land. She ran a trapline, went prospecting for silver, and sold out her claims for a good price.

She might have stayed there, but she found a new husband on a trip to Ontario, and Adam didn't care for the isolation on Alice Arm. They moved to Wells and went prospecting. In the old days, some say, Adam and Marion held open their cabin door with tin cans filled with gold—but then, "they" say a lot of things. One day, a customer found Adam sitting, dead, in his chair in the store. Marion still ventures out prospecting, then sells her claims to those who seek their fabulous fortune. She owns this building, runs the store, and gets lonely. "Can't find another husband," she complains. "They all want to know how much money I've got."

Wells's main street curves up a knoll from the highway, flanked by buildings, some derelict, some renovated, that date from the 1930s. Like Tahsis, like Kitimat, Wells was born as a company town. By the mid-1930s, Pooley Street was lined with commercial buildings: a moving picture theatre showing talkies, a hotel, a church, a butcher shop, a garage for the few cars, a livery stable, a billiard hall, stores. Four to five thousand people lived in town through the worst of the Depression; it was Wells's heyday, and almost every building in Wells today dates from that decade.

Across the street from the refurbished Wells Hotel, now a lovingly restored bed and breakfast inn, Eleanor Vincent presides over a garage sale. She and her husband came here from Arizona twenty years ago, lured by an advertisement in a mining journal that offered what seemed like half of Wells for sale. "I said, if you want to go, don't even write them, send them a telegram," recalls Eleanor. They bought a mining property and worked it until 1980. Eleanor, once an engineering technician for Motorola, became justice of the peace and postmistress. She ran the post office on the main street until this year, when Canada Post closed it down. The new "office" is down on the highway, a rank of post office boxes in the gas station, and you know how Eleanor and most of Wells feel about that. Eleanor believes in gold: she says she's seen a claim with "hunks of gold that big around"—she clenches her fist—"and they'd already taken out the big stuff." One woman who worked that claim set up a sluice in a bathtub, sold nuggets to the tourists all one summer, and made a good living from it.

I wander up Nob Hill past five- and six-room houses built for mine management in the thirties, then down onto the flat, past four-room miners' cottages, the community hall, the school. Some of the cottages are bright and friendly; some subside into the ground behind tattered *For Sale* signs.

Every year, another five or six are torn down—or fall down. The residents of Wells are fighting to preserve their town, with no guarantee that they will win. Cariboo Gold Quartz closed its last shaft in 1967. When the price of gold fell a few years back, the last hard rock mine in the area closed down. There's work to be had at Barkerville, the restored gold-rush town up the road, but more and more of the Barkerville workers live in Quesnel, where they can find reliable schools, services and stores. About two hundred people live in Wells year-round, a hundred more in summer. As the substitute school teacher says when I ask her if she is in Wells to stay, "Until three o'clock this afternoon anyway. No one makes long-term plans in Wells."

Some would like to, but the uncertainty that underlies the town's existence makes planning difficult. A few years ago, faced with a dwindling school population, the regional school board refused to promise that grades four to seven would be offered in the fall. Because they feared their children would face a fifty-mile school bus trip into Quesnel twice a day, parents of children in that age group moved to Quesnel. Because the parents and their children moved, the school could no longer justify the higher grades. It was the kind of self-fulfilling prophecy small-towners rail against, and in this case, managed to do something about. Wells residents mounted a campaign to have the decision reversed, and this year, the big school building had two classes in its eight rooms, one for kindergarten to grade three, one for grades four to seven. But next year, who knows?

Every year, some buildings founder. Fifteen years ago, I played a game that faintly resembled snooker in the old billiard hall, under a shaded hanging light, on a felt-topped table with visible hills and valleys, then leaned up against the old wooden wall in the sunshine to talk to old-timers passing by. I ate in the triangular Good Eats Cafe and had a beer or two at the Jack of Clubs. But the billiard hall, once canted up against the Jack of Clubs, was torn down in 1986 as a fire hazard. The Good Eats still stands, but it is closed now, paint peeling, the latest casualty of time. Its owners are gone, and no one else wants to run what was a town tradition.

The Jack of Clubs looks much the same, but its beer parlour has changed in the fifteen years since I last saw it, and in my mind, what used to be gets in the way of what now is. The Jack of Clubs I drank in then didn't have Miami Vice on a wide screen or acid rock pouring out of ceiling-mounted speakers. No one in here looks a day over twenty-one. No long-haired hippies linger over glasses of beer, suspect hand-rolled cigarettes emitting thin plumes of fragrant smoke. No grizzled prospectors, either, in flannel shirts and battered hats: most of the men who worked here in the thirties are gone now, in the city, the cemetery or the seniors' homes. Then the bartender saves me: he points out Knut.

Knut Martinson is sitting over a beer with his stepson Jack. "He taught every young buck in the business," Jack says proudly; the bartender adds that Knut is still regarded as the best mine timberman around. Knut ducks his head shyly and grins a bashful grin. "I helped to build Wells. Then I worked in the mine and I was the best mucker they ever had." Eighty-two, his head creased by some past accident, Knut looks a dozen years younger, his arms still hard with muscle, straw hat twisting in his hands.

Knut grins again when I ask him if he knew Cold-Ass Marie. "My first job here, I built the . . . ," mumble, mumble. The what? "The mumble-mumble." What? "The whorehouse. They had three cathouses here, but the girls were good, they went to the doctor every week." He remembers Forty-Below, the Chinese laundry man; beer ten cents a glass, whiskey fifty cents a shot. "You could live on fifty cents a day, if you had a cabin. Five or six of us lived together. Breakfast was fifteen cents: bacon, eggs, cereal, toast. Lunch we never ate. Thirty-five cents for supper: beef, pork. You shot your own meat, moose or caribou. There was fish winter and summer; you salted them down."

Knut sailed from Norway for Canada in 1928. He walked out of Halifax with his pack and frying pan, and walked and rode the freights all the way to British Columbia. "There were hundreds like me. I never paid for a train ticket for ten years. We kept away from the cities. We lived off the bush where we could, shooting porcupine, grouse, deer. We stole vegetables from farms, and stewed up everything in a big mulligan pot."

Knut worked building the railway from Kootenay Landing to Nelson in southern B.C. for a while, then went north, working farms for $1.50 a day. He rode the Please Go Easy up to Quesnel, and walked in to gold rush country to start a new life. "I got a contract cleaning hydraulic dishes, made ten dollars a day and I was rich. I bought a 1929 Chevy. It was eight hours from Barkerville to Quesnel and you had to put brush on the road once in a while to get through. But we had everything, five or six grocery stores, we could buy everything here."

In 1940, he headed for Pincher Lake, Alberta, to work in the mercury mine; "that pretty near killed me." Then it was up to the Omineca, over to work on building the Bennett Dam in Peace River country, on to Kemano, road construction, logging. But he always loved mining best. "You were never out of work. Outside, it could snow, it could rain. Inside, it was always warm, always fifty-five degrees. If you want to sit down and have a smoke, nobody bothers you.

"I came back to Wells because of the mine and the people. You couldn't go no place here you weren't all dressed up. There was a dance every Saturday night. You could be drunk all night, but you had the right clothes on. If a guy was having trouble, you'd help him. If a fight started, there'd be ten guys stopping it. If a policeman got into trouble, the miners would be there helping him."

There was a down side. "There were six of us always stuck together. All of them got dusted"—died of silicosis, from breathing quartz dust in the mine. Stepson Jack worked in the mine from 1949 to 1955; he quit when his weight dropped from 165 to 135 pounds. He lives in the Okanagan, but is back for a visit, to see the man he's proud to call Dad.

Knut's not too happy about the way things are run these days. "Those guys are mining the public, selling stocks and keeping the gold themselves." He quit mining when he turned seventy-five, though men still come to town to consult him on mine timbering. But he's got the work habit, so he has barely slowed down. "I help the kids here, painting houses and whatever. I put linoleum in my house, changed the whole bathroom the way I want it. When you're old and retired, as long as you have something to do, you're okay. Otherwise, you get disgusted with it all."

He grins that shy grin and raises his glass. "And have a few schnapps every day."

Back down the street, the parlour of the Wells Hotel is empty, though all the rooms are rented. I settle down in front of the fire to browse through a copy of "The Report of the Task Force on Community Involvement in Resource-Use Decision Making." The report summarizes submissions from native councils, community groups and foresters. All demand that decisions be made at the community level, not by someone in Victoria or in some distant corporate office.

Perhaps someone is listening. This weekend, politicians and civil servants from the Cariboo and Victoria are meeting in Wells to talk about economic development in the area. A civil servant and his wife pull up chairs in front of the fire. We chat—but not about economic development. What these New Agers really want to talk about is Regression Therapy. Naively, I ask, "What's that?" "Do you believe in reincarnation?" "No." "That's all right. You don't have to." And they overwhelm me with earnest explanations of Shirley MacLaine, memories hidden in the unconscious mind, and people they have helped by guiding them back through previous lives.

Bemused, I take myself back up the stairs to my cuddly quilt, giggling quietly over the thought of a New Age in the gold rush country of the Cariboo. But maybe I'm the one who's out of step. Maybe behind the clapboard walls of Wells tonight, loggers delve anxiously into their past(s), while out on the hills, beside their lonely campfires, prospectors consider the meanings of their many lives. And maybe not.

In the morning, somnolent shopkeepers in nineteenth-century costume sun themselves on benches outside shop doors. On this first dry weekend in a month or more, householders run their lawnmowers across blooming dandelions. On the far side of the highway, beside the other hotel, a worker picks rocks, tossing them, clanging, into the hopper of a bulldozer. A tin roof creaks and clatters. Children chase up and down the street through dust devils whipped up by the wind that blows off Jack of Clubs Lake.

Between the town and the lake, multicoloured crushed car bodies anchor a gravel dike built to hold back the creek that flows past the old mine site. I throw a board across the creek and climb towards the mine.

Less than a dozen years ago, a nervous Cariboo Gold Quartz care-taker, fearful of accidents and lawsuits, torched the disused mine build-ings. Now rusting remains of mine machinery bleed orange-red into pools of water, beside charred timbers that mark the deep, abandoned shafts. Gophers poke their noses out of collapsed wooden walls and run across the decades-old core samples that spill from crazy-angled trays onto the grass. Among the pile of mine records left to solidify down to a sodden mass, some legible papers remain. "I am a flunky man waiting on tables," reads one 1948 letter, "and I would like to get a job. If you need a flunky just call for me and please write the wages. I am clean do not smoke don't drink any liquor and would like to get a job, I mean a steady job for at least one year. Please wire me back or write." But he was to be disappointed. "We regret we have no opening for a flunky," wrote back the mine accountant, "as we employ girls in our dining room, and we have no difficulty getting them locally."

The wind blows through the fir trees, ruffling the remaining papers. The sun wavers on the core samples, on the broken timbers, and on more than one man's dreams.

Down the road a few miles, Barkerville has opened for the season today. Costumed players wander the streets of the old gold-rush town, involving tourists in their nineteenth-century dramas. But at the Chi-nese cafe, the waiter is completely twentieth century. He arrived in Canada from Hong Kong ten years ago, couldn't find a job in Vancouver last year, so came on up to Barkerville. In two weeks, he was so bored that he could hardly stand it. "In Vancouver, you can go to a movie any time you want. Here, it's an hour's drive to Quesnel, an hour's drive back." And his opinion of the big city of Quesnel isn't much higher than his opinion of Barkerville and Wells. But spring came around again, and a job's a job, so he talked a friend into coming up to cook at the cafe while he waited tables. He works every night till the cafe closes at eight o'clock, cleans up, and gets home to a rented room in Wells by nine or ten. He seems to have no time for anything else. "What's it like there?" he asks of Richfield, scarcely a mile's walk beyond Barkerville. "I haven't had time to go."

Saturday night at Barkerville, opening night at the Theatre Royale. The audience stamps, hisses, cheers, and whistles at the deliberately corny performance. The provincial politician whose department administers Barkerville jumps to his feet first, turning to the crowd, to lead the first standing ovation—and the second.

Outside, it's dusk of a long June day. Along the road that leads to the Bowron Lakes, a dozen or more rabbits sit at intervals, sniffing and licking at the salts in the road surface. Ahead is a familiar lumbering silhouette: a porcupine without the speed or sense to get out of the way of traffic. A pair of deer stand poised by the roadside, then leap away into the trees. The fading light touches the rusting machinery of placer claims, abandoned, along the gravel benches by the creek.

Cariboo Trails,
Cariboo Tales

𝄢 The first trail into what would become Barkerville, the gold-rush capital of the Cariboo, wound north from Quesnel Forks and Keithley Creek, following each new creek where eager prospectors tested pans of gravel for telltale colours. A road still follows that prospectors' route, but the mud stands deep and gluelike on back roads and the locals say at least one bridge is out. Even at the best of times the road is posted for four-wheel drive only, and I'm a coward about taking two-wheel drive cars on dubious roads.

So I backtrack from Wells to Quesnel, west again from the shadow of the Cariboo Mountains to the benchlands of the Fraser and the Cariboo Highway south. The roads are almost empty and silent on this Sunday morning. The gravel road signposted to Likely and Horsefly curves round the rolling hills of the Cariboo parkland, past lupins of a startling blue, wild roses, old truck bodies and new houses. Between the aspens and the pines, a few cattle graze; a road-killed muffler lies in the dust.

Split-rail Russell fences crisscross the scraggy fields. The fences serve to keep the cattle out by the roadside, where they turn incurious eyes on the few vehicles that pass by. Near Big Lake, I turn north on a paved road that follows the original gold-rush trail towards Likely and the Bullion Pit, a deep crater gouged from the earth by fifty years of hydraulic mining.

Biggest, deepest, widest, oldest: what do the words really mean? Some claim that this deep hole that drops three hundred feet and measures a mile and a half long is the largest gold-mining pit in the world—and some may well be right. Between 1892 and 1898, the first company in to Bullion took out more than a million dollars in gold in seven years, then departed. The careful methods of industrious Chinese miners produced another million dollars worth of gold. Then, in the 1930s, a new company set up hydraulic operations and water wore away a deeper, bigger hole. Bullion's story isn't over: the locals say a prospector found a ten-thousand-dollar nugget here two years ago.

Three miles down the road, beside the Quesnel River, lies the little village of Likely, named for Plato John Likely, a bush philosopher who prospected this area and opined widely about the meaning of life in the 1920s. A cross-cut saw, a magic lantern, washboards, miners' picks, decorate the Likely hotel pub. On the wall, a painted bear leaps fearsomely from a snowy mountain peak onto the back of a startled horse, whose rider casually examines his gun, with a view, it seems, to discovering what might be inside. A runty teenager in oversize shorts and down-at-the-heels high tops runs the pool table and racks up the balls for another game. Alone at a tiny table in the near darkness, an old-timer downs, slowly, three glasses of beer. The waitress brings each new one without being asked; she knows to stop at three. Still silent, the man gets up and walks out into the sunshine, where tree planters toss Frisbees by the riverside.

A sign in the washroom pleads, "To our guests and friends: Once again the spring run-off is here (the water table rises) filling the septic tanks, so please,/ if it's yellow/ let it mellow/ if it's brown/ flush it down."

I order a beer and *poutin*, a Québécois dish of French fries and melted cheese, just because it seems so odd to see it on the menu of a back-of-beyond Cariboo bar. Nick, prospector and teller of tales, says it was introduced by an owner who was from Quebec. Bearded, gravel-voiced, his ample belly wedged against the table, Nick recounts the story of his life. He came to this country, though he doesn't say where from, in 1950, working here and there, in the woods, in the mountains, logging, guiding. "Other people had trouble finding the horses. I always found them. The other people went where the horses had been. I'd go where they were going."

Nick never had much trouble feeding himself. "I knew where the freezer was," he says, pointing outside. Then one day an old fellow got him into prospecting, looking for minerals in the mountains. "I used to guide up there—swore at all the rocks because they made the horses throw a shoe. But I was bored, so one day I ran a cat in." The gravel the bulldozer turned over looked shiny, so Nick staked a claim. Now he says a big mining company has bought him out, and wants to start a zinc mine. But that "goddamned Greenpeace" and all the environmental regulations make it tough to start a mine these days and, besides, the whole property's under thirty feet of snow right now.

Nick lived in the mountains off and on for years. One day, he says, he met a grizzly and two cubs on the trail, and it was "die or do." He shot the mother and took the cubs back along to his cabin. "All I had to feed them was powdered milk. One of them died on me." The other one lived happily ever after with Nick—at least until the day they had an argument over the cabin. "I sawed off the door and gave the place to him. Last time I went up, he was still living there."

Then a wolf adopted Nick. One morning the wolf was there "with his chin on the doorstep"; the next day, he was sitting up to the table. "He wanted company. I'd say, 'Are you hungry?' He'd say," Nick gives a soft growl. "Are you sure?" Nick growls again. "Then I'd feed him." Now the wolf is gone too, out there loping the forests and the mountains, and Nick is living down in town. "I'd do it again, only I'd do it better next time. I learned so much from them."

Up from the hotel, at the gas station, the attendant is Sunday surly and quarrelling with his family. He points in the direction of the ghost town of Quesnel Forks and says, "There's no way you can get stuck on that road . . . . unless you drive right off of it." I hope he's right: last time I drove this road, I got firmly mired in mud at the bottom of a U-shaped dip.

This time, the road has dried out and I make it easily to the Forks. Grass grows long around the abandoned buildings of this one-time boom town, fleetingly in the 1860s "the largest city on the mainland." A gold-rush town rarely lasts for long, and the life of this one was shorter than most. Though it was one of the first to draw thousands of prospectors and their hangers-on, its creeks and gravel benches yielded gold for just a few years. Then the hungry miners moved on, east and north, to the El Dorado of Williams Creek and Barkerville. Barkerville prospered; Quesnel Forks died. Only the patient Chinese remained, sifting gravel on rafts they anchored in the fast-flowing river.

Today, horses belonging to a local rancher mill restlessly in and out of one of the remaining gold-rush cabins. A family lunches from a picnic box and mosquitoes lunch on them. A taciturn man arrives in a van with a gun rack and rifle in the back, and pulls into a camping spot where ore samples are lined up on a picnic table. He's not hostile, just making it clear that his business is his own.

I've never yet made it on the road from Likely along Quesnel Lake straight across to Horsefly, and I won't this time either: the closed sign is up and bridges are out. I backtrack again, to Big Lake, and follow the Beaver Valley down along the creek, through prosperous-looking ranches, past old log barns and green hayfields, over cattleguards and along rail fences. Where the road hooks up with the paved road from Williams Lake to Horsefly, pickups, vans, horse trailers, cars line the shoulder a mile up and down from the Horsefly rodeo grounds. Spectators sit on bleachers and on the knoll rising up behind the ring. From the ring back to the road, Stetsons bob, dust flies, and cowboys load horses back onto trailers. The annual Horsefly rodeo is coming to an end.

Down at the general store, I pick up a slim pamphlet on Horsefly history ("Horsefly may take its proper place in the history of British Columbia as it was there that the first gold was discovered in the Cariboo and the year was 1859!") But I'm more intrigued by a locally produced cookbook that tells you with sly humour all the things that you can do with rhubarb. "When you think about it," considers the Horsefly Fall Fair Committee, "rhubarb shares many of the qualities that make the people of the Cariboo a special breed." It is not finicky, it is a survivor, "all it asks is a little piece of ground it can call its own," it is versatile, and it is neighbourly. What more can one ask of a plant? From "Drink Your Rhubarb, Dear," through "Let Them Eat Rhubarb," to "Rhubarb Goes to Hollywood," the fall fair committee leaves the reader prepared to make the best of their favourite peasant plant. Another little volume promises recipes for bear, beaver, porcupine and moose. It also tells how to trap and tan the beasts, and how to make bear soup and a rabbit comforter. I must be tired: I think at once of a different comforter, a tiny plastic soother, just the right size to fit between a rabbit's two front teeth.

On a sunny Sunday afternoon, Horsefly residents laze around their backyard barbecues. It seems like a good idea. I head for Williams Lake, the house of friends, and Sunday dinner, thinking all the way of rabbits and rhubarb pie.

~

Monday morning and a short jog west from Williams Lake, then almost due south on the ranch roads that follow, roughly, along the east bank of the Fraser River on the edge of the Cariboo. Fifteen miles on, the road turns to dirt, packed as hard as iron, that shows no evidence at all of the past month's rain. The Shuswap native village of Alkali Lake is quiet and morning lazy; most of the men are off spacing or planting trees, picking fruit, ranching or fighting fires, somewhere off reserve. The woman in the store shows me the Secwepemc band newsletter, with a jovial Don Quixote figure in braids and feathered Stetson, riding on a pinto pony, on the front. Inside are reports of personal growth and development training seminars. The tenth annual A.A. rodeo will be held in Alkali Lake in July: this band is known for its successful fight against alcohol abuse. "Life is so short—why do we like to waste it by drinking then regretting it later?" asks a column in the paper. "There are so many things a person can do with their life, might as well learn now."

Band members are working on a history of Alkali Lake. "Writing our history is enlightening and frustrating," writes Tommy Johnson. "Enlightening in terms of discovery, who we are, where we come from, where we are headed for. Frustrating because outside forces that decided to 'play god' were rational people and through their bureaucracy 'put' us where we are today. Thank the person upstairs for our Shuswap resilience and fortitude. We still fish, hunt, pick berries, dig roots, make sweat houses etc."

An older man sitting outside a door raises a friendly hand in greeting. Children smile and scatter. "Alkali Lake is Heaven to us. Don't drive like hell," requests a sign. I ask a woman for directions to Dog Creek; "turn to the driver's side, don't go up the mountain," she instructs.

Below the village, rain has swollen the creek and the current undercuts the road that passes Alkali Lake itself. I phoned once to the band office to find out where the lake was in relation to the village. "North a couple of miles," said the woman on the phone, giggling. "No, west. No, wait, south." Pause. "But it doesn't matter anyway. The lake's all dried up." Not in this year of heavy rain, though. A dozen white pelicans sail on or glide over the lake just south of the village, their only nesting place in British Columbia. From time to time, they rise on their black-tipped wings, then sink calmly back to the water. Loons call; black and white ducks dive underwater and reappear.

Beyond Alkali Lake, deeply incised rolling hills, bright green then shadowed grey as the clouds roll across the sky, take over the landscape.

Pioneers who homesteaded here waxed rhapsodic about the awakening of the land in spring; I can see why. In the length of a few feet, yellow-headed ragwort, sweet-smelling purple penstemon, and a dozen other wildflowers colour the hillside. Sagebrush is sometimes pungent on the warm June air; more often, its look-alike, rabbitbush, raises wiry stems. Ground squirrels appear and vanish, up and back down through the parallel metal bars of the cattleguards. Cattle plod slowly across the range, chewing methodically on spring grasses. Three mongrel dogs at one farm guard jars of honey set out for sale. The jars are in a rickety cardboard box; seeing no container for the money, I tuck it under the remaining jars, wondering what the person who buys the last jar will do.

Just before Dog Creek, I turn to the driver's side and don't go up the mountain. But I asked the wrong question. This road bisects the community of Dog Creek, past bright blue and green houses, the elementary school, and a lone tourist sunning himself full length on the bench outside a trailer that serves as the general store. I want to go south to Gang Ranch. I turn back, go up the mountain. Through wide-spaced spruce and pine, the road cuts a dramatic descent down to the Fraser River, between cliffs and cuts that score down from the benchlands to the river.

In a normal year, little rain falls on this Fraser Plateau. Jackpines and red-barked Ponderosa pines are sparse; grass and short bush lightly clothe the hills. Without a forest covering, the land here reveals its history. Lava flowing from shield volcanoes to the west set the base. The land then lifted, but the rivers stayed low, and benchlands and gorges were created. Glacial ice eight thousand feet thick bulled its way across the land and retreated, scouring, smoothing, leaving behind glacial debris. Rain fell and ice melted into the glacial depressions; without outlets, these lakes became more alkaline with each succeeding year. "The glaciers left a higgledy-piggledy mess," is how one geographer describes it; that mess of sandy-ridged eskers, mounded drumlins, boulders, and clays still litters the landscape. Relieved of its icy weight, the land lifted again, and the streams and rivers cut ever deeper courses through the land. Where wind and water found irregularities, they wore away the land, sculpting crenellations and pillars from the hillsides. Here, hoodoos stand sentry along a long switchback that curls down the side of the bench to a narrow suspension bridge of wooden girders and steel cables that spans the swollen, muddy Fraser River. The

Chilcotin begins on the west bank of the Fraser and stretches to the Coast Mountains, across soft hills, lakes, and jackpine forest. Up the hill along roads without signposts lie the headquarters of the famed Gang Ranch.

Americans Jerome and Thaddeus Harper ranched this land in the 1860s; the ranch is named for the double-furrowed gang plow that they used to break the land. Over the next hundred years, succeeding owners added to the ranch, and grazed their cattle on ever-increasing spreads of land leased from the Crown. Proud of their achievements, they boasted that the ranch was the largest in North America.

Manager Larry Ramstead, in the office, among the red-painted barns and houses that form the centre of the ranch, would just as soon not talk about "biggest" or "best." "We're just another ranch trying to get on its feet," he declares, and reels off a list of Cariboo or Chilcotin ranches that are just as big or bigger. "Sure it's eighty miles to the back end of the ranch where the last of the cow camps are, but most of that is Crown land."

A couple of weeks ago, a Japanese tourist came roaring up on a motorbike to the Gang from Vancouver, just to see what he'd been told was the largest ranch in the world. He climbed off his bike and took a look around at the neat cluster of ranch buildings and the bunch grass hills and hayfields stretching to the horizon. "Why so famous this ranch?" he asked, rhetorically, climbed back on his bike and roared away. Wonders of the world aren't always all they're cracked up to be.

The Gang fell on hard times in the 1980s, beset by banks and near-bankruptcy, charges and counter-charges, that took five years to sort out in court. Larry is employed by a management company that runs the ranch for current owner, Saudi Sheik Ibrahim Afandi. As far as Larry's concerned, the penchant of previous owners for publicity and grandiose statements just hurt the ranch. "I think they used to have press conferences out here." For a few years, the ranch took in dudes, but that's over now. "We're not set up to handle them, and we would only get a bad name." He doesn't need the hassle of feeding and housing cowboy wannabes, and finding them saddlehorses that they can ride without falling off. Now, he spends his time with real ranch jobs: haying, irrigation ("though," wryly, "we haven't had to worry about that much lately"), trying to get along with the timber people and the fish and wildlife people. New regulations and procedures on multiple use of the land haven't made a rancher's job any easier. "They're all easy to get along with, but it takes time. Before, we just turned the cows into the forest and brought them home again." Like every rancher you'll ever meet, he is unhappy over the distance cattle have to travel to get to market: the Gang ships north through the Chilcotin and out through Williams Lake, because the big cattle trucks can't negotiate the narrow switchbacks down to the nearby bridge across the Fraser.

I drive back to the bridge, behind a grader that is scraping down the dried mud of spring ruts and filling winter potholes, and recross the river. The road runs, a narrow brown line, along the edge of hills towards the mountains that rise now in the south. The pale spring green of the hills looks soft as velvet. Time elongates on this backroad: I seem to have driven far too long to be where I am. I turn eastward, between mineral lakes now ruffled turquoise; a month from now, they will be shrunken and salt-edged. A bluebird wings across the road in a flash of brilliant blue against a sky that has darkened almost to black. The storm comes quickly. The wind picks up, huge raindrops slash down, overpowering the windshield wipers, then hailstones rattle on the car roof and bounce up from the road ahead. Within minutes, the smoky mountains reappear; the storm is over as quickly as it began. The soft and lonely hills of the Chilcotin's verges give way to pine forest and campgrounds: the back road ends abruptly at the Cariboo Highway.

CHAPTER 10

Lillooet and Beyond

)) On every main street of every small town in British Columbia is a Chinese restaurant. Here in Lillooet, where the Fraser rides out of the dry country into the shadow of the mountains, main street is called Main Street and three Chinese restaurants sit side by side. I choose the one in the middle—mainly because the last time I was here, it was dim and raunchy, and the washrooms were labelled "Gals" and (they know their menfolk) "Duds."

The washroom labels remain, but other than that, I barely recognize the place. Pinstripe paper in fashionable tones of grey and pink clothes the walls, patrons sit at stylish tables in chairs and on carpet subtly shaded in blue-grey, mauve and burgundy, surrounded by walls and low dividers painted deep turquoise. I'm a little reassured by the salad bar: iceberg lettuce and red Jell-o. The final irony: deep-fried boneless pork and beef and broccoli are now served up by a cheerful family of East Indian Canadians.

I ask waitress Baljinder where I can buy the local cherries I see people eating on the streets and she promises to bring me some tomorrow, a whole bag if she can get over to her uncle's, but definitely half a bag from her own tree. Baljinder's father has worked in the Lillooet lumber mill for eighteen years; she and her mother came from India when Baljinder was three years old. She graduated from high school here and thinks Lillooet isn't too bad a place to live, though it has some drawbacks.

"We go to Kamloops or Vancouver for clothes. If you buy something here—well, I bought these pants here," she gestures to her boldly striped red and white trousers, "and before I could even wear them, I saw someone else wearing the same thing." Vancouver is the only place she can get silk or cotton for the traditional Indian saris she likes to wear on weekends and special occasions.

Outside the restaurant, Main Street is stately and wide enough to turn a double freight wagon hauled by twenty oxen. A hundred and thirty years ago, that width was necessary: Lillooet was the first major stopping place on the way to the 1860s Cariboo gold rush, the point from which every milepost on the Cariboo Road was measured. Today, 100 Mile House, 150 Mile House, and all the rest, keep names that tell how far they are from Lillooet. A government report published in 1902 tells what happened: "Lillooet, when the trail went that way, was a place of some commercial importance, but since the present Cariboo Road was built, much of its early prosperity has been taken away from it."

Now, as then, Lillooet has a truly spectacular setting. Bordered on three sides by dry hills clad in Ponderosa pines, it is backed to the south and west by mountains of the Coast Range, still snow-capped in late June. To the south, seen through a narrow defile, the Fraser is constricted into the beginnings of its famous canyon. Lillooet's long main street doglegs along a bench that parallels the Fraser a hundred feet above the turbulent brown river. Above Main Street, successive ranks of houses hug the benches that staircase the hill. On both sides of the river, the benches closest to the river bank are green with spring alfalfa; higher up, pines, yellow spring sunflowers and bunch grass clothe the hills.

Early in the morning, the sun streams down onto Main Street businesses. Jeff den Biesen is already in the office of the *Bridge River-Lillooet News*, folding newspapers and pushing them into the labelling machine. He seems bright and alert, though you couldn't blame him if he were sleepy. Most Tuesday nights, the newspaper flats, camera-ready, leave Lillooet by bus for the printer in Williams Lake and the press run is shipped back down for distribution early Wednesday morning. This week, Jeff was late finishing up a special supplement on the high-school graduating class and had to jump into his car and drive the 160 miles to the printer. He got back at midnight, got up again early; now he and his wife, Willy, are addressing the papers so they can get them to the post office in time for delivery today.

Two decades ago, the Lillooet paper was probably the best-known small-town newspaper in Canada. Every time its then editor-publisher, Margaret "Ma" Murray, let loose another "and that's fer damshur," she was quoted as the quintessential voice of rural Canada—and she loved the role of straight-talking, plain-dealing, professional curmudgeon.

One day twenty years ago, Jeff heard Ma say on the radio that she wouldn't be able to carry on with the newspaper forever. He was working for a printer in Vancouver, tired of the cities and their traffic jams. He wrote Ma, asking if she wanted someone who would come and learn from her, one day taking over the paper. "I worked with her, and then," he says with restraint, "we agreed to disagree."

But Lillooet had taken hold of him. "When I got here, Lillooet looked to me like a hole in the wall, gravel roads, a small, hot, dusty place you could have pulled out of any John Wayne cowboy movie." But it was small and sunny and dry, slower and friendlier than Vancouver. Jeff and Willy bought a printing company and stayed in town. Six months later, Ma Murray sold him the *News,* and the den Biesens have been running the paper ever since. Until about three years ago, they still thought of Vancouver as home, and supposed they would move back south again one day. But then Lower Mainland house prices sky-rocketed, and they looked at the city lifestyle and realized they couldn't live at that pace anymore. Without their realizing it, Lillooet had become home.

Most mornings now, Jeff wanders into the local coffee spot to gossip with "the boys" and find out what's going on in business and politics. Then it's into the office, where he sells ads, develops film, prints photographs, works on page makeup and fixes equipment. There's no definite quitting time: he and Willy, who does the accounting and other jobs around the office, go home when the work's done.

How do they deal with the fact that, in a small town, the people the paper writes about are also its advertisers and the den Biesens' friends? "I've always said that 50 percent of the population are my friends and 50 percent are my enemies, and no two days are they the same people." What makes people mad at him? "When you spell their names wrong. Politics. Religion. Especially when they know you were right and they were wrong. How do you compensate for someone's ego being hurt? That's a real tough one."

Jeff won't get into trouble for knocking Lillooet. He keeps the paper positive, because he thinks the town needs lots of encouragement. "The economics of this town, that's a strange phenomenon. In the early seventies, the economics were absolutely terrible. The sawmill had closed down for eight months, and there were no good prospects at all.

What kept us going was a healthy welfare roll, and the loyalty of the native Indians. They are very loyal to shopping in this area."

The mill reopened, then expanded, and the town picked back up. "It has always been that if the economy in other parts of the province is really bad, in Lillooet, it's not so bad. If the economy is really good in other parts of B.C., then the economy in Lillooet is not as good. That's because the economy here is very stable." He refuses to get discouraged because one of the town's main employers announced this week that it is closing down one of Lillooet's two sawmills. "Now, we might slow down a bit, but the town has enough resilience to pull itself out. Lillooet will just keep on going."

At midmorning down at the train station, senior citizens from Calgary, most of them women, climb down from a tour bus and walk out to the station platform to wait for the train that will take them north to Prince George. They came from Calgary by bus, then took the gravel Gold Bridge road to a resort for a two-day stay spent riding around in floatplanes, relaxing, eating well, fishing for trout. Last year they went to Whistler by bus, took the train north through Lillooet to the Cariboo, and spent the rest of their holiday at a resort in the Cariboo. Most of them liked that trip so much that there was a big waiting list for this year's trip.

A mud-encrusted bus with only the driver aboard pulls into the parking lot. He brought his tour group in from the United States to Whistler, put them on the train to Lillooet and drove on up over the back road to meet them here. "They say they're fixing that road, and every time they fix it, it gets worse." It wouldn't have been impossible, he grumbles, just three or four stops of five or six minutes each, except for The Flagman. "I was trying to take a run at a bad section, and the flagman—he don't get out of the house much—put up his stop sign, and down I went, twenty tons of bus into the mud." He had to get the road crew to pull him out with a bulldozer.

The train—just a couple of self-propelled passenger cars — pulls in, and natives in braids and cowboy hats and tourists wearing baseball caps and T-shirts imprinted with funny sayings crowd off. The train crew hangs around the platform speaking train arcane and handing out hints to a new man on how to get to know pretty girl passengers. Then the train whistles slowly out of the station, bumping north across the level crossing.

Arnold Malm drove trains for thirty-five years. He retired from the railway a few years ago, but he had no intention of retiring from life. "I decided I could do this when I retired, instead of running around after little white balls or fishing or chasing rabbits or some dumb thing. I have to have something to do. Nobody can sit on their butt and do nothing."

"This" is farming the benchland across the Fraser from Lillooet. Thick, wet earth clings to our shoes as we walk and talk between rows of fruit trees; along the way, Malm pinches out some of the embryo fruit that crowd the branches of his apple, peach, pear and plum trees in what looks to be a bumper year.

"There's a degree of satisfaction in growing something. It's a lot of work, but it's better than what you find in cities. In the cities, you retire, and your life is centred around institutions—the doctor's office, the government office. They get sick. Out here, I don't have time to get sick."

Lillooet's long hot days of summer and water carried up from deep wells produce fine fruit. That 1902 government report deemed this region "admirably adapted for the production of the finest quality of fruits; indeed, it is difficult to imagine that a better quality of apple, or more luscious pears, cherries, grapes, peaches, melons or other varieties of semi-hardy fruits can be grown." Malm and the few other farmers who grow fruit here sell most of their produce at roadside stands: someone in Williams Lake told me about his fine, juicy melons. Other Lillooet-area farmers concentrate on hay or alfalfa or on crops like the oriental root ginseng—or, in remoter valleys, marijuana. A year or two ago, a minor war broke out between marijuana growers and some Lillooet boys who went in to get a little grass the easy way.

But, like any farmer, Malm dismisses the idea of making money from farming. "There's not many farms around that can carry themselves. It's like having a relative around: you have to subsidize it to some degree." Malm and his wife, Aggie, did most of the early work on his farm when he was still working for the railway. "I cleared land when I had the money to spend." But, he says, if you have to borrow to buy equipment or drill a well, you're in trouble: raising food doesn't bring in enough money to pay the costs of a loan.

Beyond the neat rows of fruit trees and vegetables, Malm has lined up a collection of old farm equipment that he and his son have restored: flail mower, ditchdigger, potato planter, rototiller, specialty planter that pokes holes through plastic, a cultivator for hilling spuds or corn, a machine to lay plastic. "You have to be able to cut and weld. If you don't do your own work, you won't have a chance."

B.C. Rail treated him well, paid him well. But this is better. "The railway got me where I was going, wherever the hell that was. But working for the man is still working for the man. I don't consider what I do as work. If I did, I'd quit and go get a real job."

I cross the Fraser on the "Bridge of the 23 Camels," named to commemorate the camels brought up during the gold rush as beasts of burden. Their tender feet, antisocial habits and unwestern smell doomed them and their owner's get-rich-quick scheme. Just downstream from here, where the Bridge River enters the Fraser, enterprising men built a toll bridge at the start of the gold rush in 1859, and charged prospectors twenty-five or fifty cents to cross. Two prospectors lacked the money; stuck on the south side of the river, they set themselves to panning gold and made thirty thousand dollars—or so the story goes.

Back down on Main Street, three rockhounds are hanging out at the rock shop, drinking coffee and talking rocks. "What do we find most of here?" asks one innocently. "Leaverite and dog rocks. 'Leave 'er right there, and throw 'em for the dogs to chase.'" In her sixties, she is addicted to rockhounding; her car is full of rocks, she confesses, her house and her garden are full of rocks. She's not alone: there are enough rockhounds in town for three clubs, whose members haunt the hills, looking for jade, jasper, agates, and other precious finds.

Behind the counter in the gift store, Karen Vanderwolf declares she's had enough of rocks. Her dad arrived here in the 1930s, and staked a gold claim out along the Bridge River. Wife and family were expected to help on the claim. In the mornings, Karen worked on her correspondence lessons; in the afternoon, she hauled buckets of pay dirt from the trailhead above the river down to the sluice box her father operated beside the river. "I have never hated anything so much in my life. I vowed if I could ever quit, I'd never have anything to do with gold again. When I went to high school in White Rock, I was never so happy in my whole life." But Lillooet drew her back. Ironically, she and her husband have claims out along seven miles of the Bridge River—but she won't carry buckets or sluice down dirt ever again.

Four roads cut south from Lillooet towards Vancouver. One, the paved highway, follows the Fraser to its mouth. A second, the route cursed roundly by the bus driver, runs behind the first rank of mountains along Cayoosh Creek to Duffey Lake and Pemberton. A third goes through spectacular scenery alongside the railway tracks high above Anderson and Seton lakes and down to Pemberton, but it is fit only for drivers of four-wheel drive vehicles with a good sense of direction, who are not apt to be misled by the myriad of crisscrossing logging roads.

The fourth, the one I will follow, is the long way to the coast, striking into the main ranges of the Coast Mountains, back behind Carpenter Lake and Gold Bridge, then down the Hurley River to Pemberton and pavement once again. For the first fifteen miles, the iron-hard gravel road switchbacks high above the Bridge River, cut into mountain or hill above a heart-stopping drop. I remind myself that two days ago, thirty-five grey-haired and enthusiastic seniors travelled this road by bus, and soldier on.

Writer Lukin Johnston passed this way in the 1920s, but the valley described in his book bears little resemblance to the one that unfolds below me now. Drowned trees stand white along the shoreline of Carpenter Lake, and snags still mark the ice-blue waters. Man-made by a dam and man-controlled by sluice gates, Carpenter Lake is shrunken today; it is as if the torrential rains and awesome floods that have plagued the rest of the province for a month have never happened.

Johnston was overwhelmed by the mega-project, then just beginning, that created the lake and a mighty source of hydroelectric power for the growing city of Vancouver. "It seemed unreal," he wrote, "this talk of creating lakes and tunnelling for miles through mountain ranges, damming the course of a river of considerable size—all to provide power for Vancouver, which lay 132 miles away over a sea of mountains to the south." He continued with the litany, now familiar, of thousands of men employed, tens of thousands of tons of machinery and supplies, towns built on the instant, and hundreds of thousands of horsepower harnessed.

The clearings and farms he described now lie under the lake, which reaches, curved and narrow, thirty-three miles long and half a mile wide, up the valley to Gold Bridge. Back in the thirties, the Bralco mining company cranked up operations on the old Lorne gold mine and built a company town they called Bralorne. Miners being miners, the working men founded their own town at Gold Bridge, where the road crossed the river, so they could better indulge in wine, women, and song. When the mine closed in 1971, Gold Bridge lived on, its hundred or so residents supported by logging and recreation.

Down in the Gold Bridge hotel restaurant, a government employee from the city is looking for one of the hundred. "I'm with the government," he announces, perhaps foolishly. "Has anybody seen this guy?

I was supposed to meet him some time this morning, but his place is all locked up, and there's nobody there." Heads are gravely shaken. "I think I saw him head up into the bush," volunteers one man. "Nope, he don't come back down for lunch." The government man, frustrated, sits down and orders soup and a sandwich.

Up the road, the sun shines on the empty streets of Bralorne, below snow-capped mountains and green meadows dotted with wildflowers. Bralorne houses sat empty after the mine closed, and some saw opportunity there. Up by the museum, where he is working this summer courtesy of a government grant, Dennis sits on the steps and tells his story. He was living in a big house in Vancouver's hippie district in the late sixties. "A bunch of us decided we just had to get out of the city. We heard the mine had just shut down, and we came up here." Eight, including Dennis and his sister, came to Bralorne. His sister now lives out on the road to Lillooet; Dennis and one other woman from the original group are still in Bralorne. The other five are long gone. Last year, he bought the small miner's cottage he was living in for one-tenth the price of the cheapest house in Vancouver.

With one leg amputated above the knee, he is on crutches this week, because his artificial leg has worn sores on his stump. He developed circulatory problems after he moved up here, and had to go down to Vancouver for a series of operations that ended with amputation. He still goes to Vancouver from time to time, to get a new artificial leg, but he always comes back. "I'll be here for a while," he smiles. Life is quiet in Bralorne. The long, cold, isolating winter is over; the rains of the past month have given way to warm spring sunshine. Pretty soon, Bralorne's annual baseball tournament will draw eight teams from outside the valley for a weekend of competition. Saturday night, a live band will play; there will be a beer garden, hamburgers grilling by the baseball field, and a whole bunch of people camping out in the field up beyond the museum. That's something to look forward to.

Close to a hundred people live in Bralorne; no one lives at Bradian. Double rows of almost identical blank-faced cottages, roofs alternately green, red, green, red, line up by the few short streets. Bradian was built to accommodate employees from the Lorne mine; now, only signs that proclaim *No Trespassing* or *For Sale* suggest that anyone cares.

Beyond Bradian, the broken roofs and weathered walls of the Lorne mine slide slowly down into Cadwallader Creek. They started the mine up for a while again a few years back, but now it's closed again, machinery removed, shafts flooded. I sit by the bridge and try to imagine: in the thirties, miners staged a bitter strike here, fifty-five of them setting up camp fourteen hundred feet below the surface of the earth, others standing watch. Hunting crews brought game to a cook and two helpers, who fed the men underground. But too many winters have ground down the Lorne; the ghosts are gone.

Back down at the Bralorne cafe, the waitress talks about life in the mountains. She spent the winter on unemployment insurance payments, skidooing most of the time and loving it. But everybody got a little bushed, what with snow blocking the roads out and nobody different to talk to. "By the end of March, you think somebody's gonna get killed." Then it rained all May—she rolls her eyes and shakes her head. A Bralorne family back up from Pemberton comes in for chicken strips and hamburgers, and they all wander back to the kitchen to talk life over. The waitress brings the bills and apologizes: "Sorry I didn't stay and talk longer."

That family came in over the Hurley; now I'm going out that way. I like roads with one-word names: The Hurley, said gruffly, a working road with torn T-shirt and cigarettes rolled in the sleeve. At the Bralorne museum, an uncredited newspaper clipping gives a preface: "Never treat a car kindly. If you do, it will plague you with feeble and silly ailments. Boot it around some so that it knows life is in earnest, that it must put out or else it will be nought but a bump under the snows of winter on some roadside." Then the writer headed for the Hurley.

Despite dire warnings, the road proves driveable, only occasionally springing surprises in the form of deep and lurking potholes that jar your teeth loose. Brawny streams and waterfalls thunder down the logged-off hills towards the pale turquoise, glacier-fed Hurley River. Logging clear-cuts show brown and burnt before the deep green of forested mountain slopes and the silver-white of high and distant glaciers.

Everyone I talked to about the Hurley said to gear down and inch along the switchbacks that curl down from the mountains to the Pemberton Valley and the coast. They didn't quite tell the truth. Low gear, yes; slow speed, definitely. Switchbacks? Apart from three or four snaky curves, the road barrels straight down without a pause, nine miles into the valley.

After the rawness of the Hurley, the paved road to Pemberton, through hay meadows, past long-established farms and grazing cattle, is oddly gentle. The long thin spires of jackpine, companions for so many miles, have given way to massive cedars and hemlocks. I drive past Pemberton to Whistler, a ski resort village with time-share condominiums, luxury hotels, sky-high real estate prices, sushi and import beer. The next morning, an elderly home-owner in Squamish, at the head of Howe Sound, regards the muddy car I have parked in front of his house and suggests I should get it washed. "Make it feel better," he says. At Horseshoe Bay, traffic waiting for the ferry to Vancouver Island backs well up the highway approaches to the terminal; I'll have to wait through several sailings before I can catch a boat bound homewards to Victoria. Suddenly, it seems essential to rush pell-mell across Vancouver, through traffic lights and traffic jams, to save time by catching the ferry on the southern route to the island.

I am back in the city.

Autumn:
The Road Eastward

⟩⟩ A smell that calls to mind wet dogs or old books drifts across the freeway out of Vancouver in the warm sunshine of a day in early September. But no driver wavers, no one turns off to investigate the source of the smell. We are all Going Somewhere on a freeway that leads to a Destination. Getting there is the important thing; going there is just to be endured. So we pass each other at eighty miles an hour, exit to familiar tastes at McDonalds, get back on the freeway and pass each other all over again. I know a Greek restaurant in Chilliwack that serves an excellent lunch. But if I take a side road to it, I will Lose Time. So, caught in the four-lane, high-speed trap, I don't.

At Hope, the freeway ends. Traffic has been light since Chilliwack. What there is now splits into three streams, north up the Fraser Canyon on the old Trans-Canada, northeast along the Coquihalla towards Kamloops, east towards the Okanagan. I go east.

As my underpowered car struggles up that first long hill, I find myself singing, tunelessly but gleefully, a new composition: *Escape from the Freeway.* A few miles up the highway, I stop for pie and coffee. Pointillist lino covers the coffee shop floor, dark brown vinyl the metal-framed chairs. The complete wine list is, "Glass, $2.65. Bottle, $9.75." The murals of mountain and lake painted on the wall are bluer and greener than life. But the pie is perfect, the coffee hot and happily refilled, and over the grill, beside the blackened cast-iron frying pans, hangs a sign: "This isn't Burger King. You do it my way."

Though it's barely September, the leaves of the poplars are thinning from green into gold. East of the summit where the highway crosses the Cascade Mountains, the country changes. West coast lush—cedars, firs, moss, bracken on steep mountainsides traced with streams—has been replaced by Ponderosa and jackpine dotted on the dry golden and grey hillsides.

Down the long hill past the mine into the town of Princeton, population three thousand. On the main street, high-school boys in football pants and a girl in spandex are arguing over the right thing to do when the hockey coach tells you to get in there and start a fight. "You should tell him no," says the girl. "Yeah, but then you're off the team maybe," says one of the boys. The woman who runs the collectibles store stands out on the sidewalk, yelling after her son to get a video and some pop, because she is *not* canning fruit again tonight. "Imagine," she says, shaking her head at me and the street, "imagine not even remembering your sister's name."

Today was the first day back to school, and in the Chinese and Canadian, Canadian and Chinese, restaurants on main street, teenage girls chatter over coffee and chips doused in ketchup. Who's been dating whom, what did everybody do all summer? Down the street, a grey-haired woman leaves Fields, the variety store, with a shopping bag swinging over her arm and goes into Overwaitea for groceries. Another woman startles me by saying hello; for a moment, I try to think who she is, but in a small town, you don't have to know a person to say hello.

At dinner, Bernie, a waitress whose lilting southern Irish accent does battle with flat Canadian, calls me "love" three times in two sentences, both of which end in "eh?" Dinner arrives so fast I think I'm getting someone else's order, but with a baked potato from the microwave, salad from the plastic vat and quick-cooked frozen mixed Italian vegetables, how long does it take to cook a steak? Bernie actually runs on the job, and I find I'm eating as fast as she is moving, done and ready to go in ten minutes. "It was a zoo in here last night, an absolute zoo," she says as she sweeps up my dirty dishes and delivers coffee with élan. "We had to close an hour early to get cleaned up. Kids coming back from some motor race in Vancouver." She drops my bill on the table, smiles, and dashes off to serve six other tables.

In the morning, Mike stands outside the door of his barbershop on main street, smiling broadly and greeting each person who goes by. Mike's Dad emigrated from Yugoslavia to Canada in 1923, and came to work here at the big copper mine. Mike and the rest of his family stayed behind, waiting. In 1941, the Germans took Mike away to work in a forced labour camp. When the war ended, he got a job with the Canadian army, then finally made it to Princeton in 1949. He was a a barber then, he's a barber now, serving up conversation and good cheap haircuts in a shop that has never heard the word unisex.

Faded photographs of tropical fish, mountains, castles, lakes, skiers, birds, almost cover the bright turquoise walls of the shop. A fan on the floor swivels slowly, back and forth, back and forth, lifting the pages of car magazines on the small table by the seats where patrons can wait for their turn in Mike's one chair. Glass jars and tins of tonics and talcums stand behind the chair, along the wall.

Barbershop regular J.C. sits down in the chair for his weekly trim and conversation, adding a chorus to Mike's stories. "When I first came here," says Mike, "nobody locked their doors. Our troubles started when they put that Hope-Princeton highway in." The road opened in 1949, the same year that Mike arrived in town. "Yes, yes, that's right, that's right," J.C. echoes. Clip, clip, Mike trims the eyebrows with sure little scissor strokes.

"They had a train service up the Coquihalla. They sold coffee and sandwiches, ten cents for coffee, twenty-five cents for a pillow." He smoothes cream onto J.C.'s face. "And those trestles! You'd be riding the train in the last car, going around one of those horseshoe shapes, and you could see the engine from the back. Now, that was a trip!" "Wasn't that a great engineering feat?" asks J.C. "Really, really." And indeed it was. The engineer who surveyed this route looked at the Coquihalla Canyon from a wicker basket suspended over it, and decided his men could tunnel through five separate rock faces. Though the line is long closed, railway buffs still come to marvel at the resulting tunnels.

J.C. was a logger and a builder—houses, dams, it didn't matter. "We did a lot of logging with horses. We didn't get in machinery until 1946, and that was quite a step ahead, our first bulldozer. Now, I remember we went up to a logging camp in the mountains one year on the sixteenth of April, and there was no sign of the camp. Why, we were logging on top of nine feet of snow. But," a familiar lament, "the weather's changing now. There's hardly any snow at all any more."

Mike removes the apron from around J.C.'s neck and brushes off any stray hairs. Though J.C. has retired, he is still heading off to work. "My son and I, we took over this run-down ranch. It's more work than I anticipated, building corrals and so on." He and Mike stroll out to the sunlit street, saying hello to everyone, getting change for a fifty-dollar bill from the cabbie who parks in front of the old hotel next door.

Princeton looks spruce and alive this morning, not at all like the dumpy, fraying little town of a dozen years ago. "This used to be a real dive," says one main-street businessman, "fights in the bars and beer bottles on the lawns the next morning." After the mine closed down in 1957, the region was declared an economic disaster area. Back then, the main-street buildings that dated back to the turn of the century were crumbling onto the sidewalks and the sidewalks were dissolving into the potholed streets. Now the mine has reopened and a sawmill also operates in town. Downtown, fancy façades decorate half the buildings, and carpenters are at work on the rest. The old hydro poles, and the heavy wires crisscrossing the street, have been replaced by a single row of graceful light standards. Potholes have been patched and cement sidewalks replaced with interlocking decorative bricks.

Mention the changes in downtown, and everyone sends you to see Gloria Stout. In the area since her family took over a nearby resort in the 1940s, Gloria has lived in Princeton for thirty-seven years. Once her five children were grown up, she threw herself into politics. She was an alderman for four years, until an ungrateful electorate turned her out. "That really made me mad," she says with understatement, "so I ran for mayor." Mayor for seven years, she has cajoled and bullied and over-ridden objections and convinced the townsfolk that Princeton deserved to be a better town. "I'm not really as mean and miserable as some people think I am," she chuckles, "but I fight with great enthusiasm."

She waves her heavily beringed hands at the street outside City Hall. "Sometimes, a town like this is like dragging a dead horse, businesswise. It's a marvellous community, very warm-hearted and generous, but sometimes very negative. Some people who had lived here for a long time, who didn't want anything to change, were absolutely horrified," when she dared to suggest tearing some things down, building others up, spending money. "When we put lighting down the middle of Vermilion Street, what a turmoil that was. They said we'd never be able to snowplough it." *They* said a lot of other things too, but none of it deterred Gloria. "You can't please everybody, and if you let things bother you, you never get anything done."

Though some small-town attitudes may bother her, Gloria praises highly Princeton residents' will to help others. The town raised $100,000 in six months for a series of operations for a cancer-stricken youngster who had lived in Princeton for just a brief time. Twenty mentally handicapped adults, just two of them from Princeton, live in a group–home downtown. "We restored a house for them, and even the doctors came and painted." The group-home residents, says Gloria, "are accepted here. You see them all over town. They are completely free to live an independent lifestyle that would be difficult in the city."

The new spirit in Princeton, combined with the area's proximity to Vancouver and its dry, clear climate, have started to attract attention. Though the last census nine years ago showed a drop in population, Princeton has gained three hundred new residents in the last year or so. "It's excellent here for the young retiree," says Gloria, dropping into Chamber-of-Commerce-speak. "Those bright sunny days in winter really make you feel alive. We've got people coming from the coast, for the laid-back, casual lifestyle. There's not a place to buy or rent in Princeton right now."

Northwest of Princeton lies a trio of old mining towns: Blakeburn, where miners dug coal from 1921 to 1940; Coalmont, where Blakeburn's coal was loaded aboard railway cars; and Tulameen. The railway doesn't run here anymore; the road to the old towns from Princeton cuts a wedge from rusty rock a hundred yards above the Tulameen River, named for the red earth the Thompson Indians dug from the riverbank, the source of the red ochre used for creating rock paintings.

Coalmont now is quieter than in those hectic coal-mining days, as evidenced by the sign at the beginning of town: "You are approaching the peaceful little village of Coalmont. Population: varies. Industry: none. Chief sports: sleeping and day-dreaming. Climate: hot-cold-wet-dry at various times. All clubs and lodges hold their meetings at midnight on the sixth Tuesday of each month." Why do I think Coalmont has no Chamber of Commerce? And in case you missed the point, a second sign informs you, "To all doorstep salesmen—especially those selling magazines, encyclopedias and firebells, your safe passage is not guaranteed in this village." Pity. I've never met a salesman selling firebells.

"Women beware!" the sign continues. "There is a predominance of bachelors living here." Perhaps the sleepy dog with the bicoloured face, lounging on the hotel verandah, and the only living creature visible this morning, is a bachelor. No one sits in the plush upholstered armchairs that leak stuffing onto the painted verandah boards. In the bar, the only evidence of life is the hundreds of baseball caps with assorted legends mounted on the wall, a somewhat weary snarling bear clinging to another wall, one-and two-dollar bills pasted to the ceiling, and a sign declaring, "No knives permitted in the bar."

To the casual passer-by, it seems a shame that the old hotel Gloria Stout told me about has been remodelled to meet health regulations and fire standards—not to mention lowering heating bills. Back then, the ceilings were fifteen feet high and there used to be just one bar toilet, mounted on a platform in the middle of the room, with three lockless doors. "Going to the bathroom used to be a major operation," Gloria recalled fondly, "not something you did lightly. It took four people, three to hold the doors shut, and one to . . . . "

In the next-door cafe, a tabby cat jumps down from a rickety stool; I climb up, and Gail leaves her sewing machine to serve coffee from a thermos. As we talk, she stitches one of the pale denim cowboy shirts she makes and sells in the hotel that she and her husband bought five years ago. They keep the bar open year-round, but close the coffee shop down in the winter. Like Princeton, she says, Coalmont is booming. "There were fifty places for sale around here two years ago, and now I don't think there's one." At Tulameen, up the road by Otter Lake, lots in one of two small subdivisions are selling for fifty thousand dollars each, as city folk buy their country refuges. "This is supposed to be the next hot place," says Gail.

Hot today it's not, except in temperature. I swing around the few neat blocks, past the little cottages and trailers permanently mounted on concrete pads, and still see no one. I drive back down the road to Princeton, then avoid the highway east in favour of the gravel road that winds along the north bank of the Similkameen River, a soft-flowing word for a shallow, pretty river, a word whose meaning is lost in time. Along the road, handkerchief-sized pastures are squeezed between rusty scree slopes and the water. Colonies of shiny new log houses share the river banks with old frame shacks, double-wide trailers, auto grave-yards, and satellite dishes. I meet only one car in twenty miles, and that one approaches as I lock eyes with a German shepherd dog calmly seated on the road in front of me. He wins. I wait.

At the old mining town of Hedley, I order the meat-loaf special and listen to three young men at the table behind me argue about where to put the washer and dryer if the sports car goes into the garage for the winter. Two old-timers, one in a black Stetson, running shoes and faded denim, the other in a baseball cap, old sweater and work boots, talk about the weather and how the winter's going to be.

The air now is warmer and drier, the pines sparser, the rabbit bush and sagebrush clumped along the hills. In Keremeos, on the fringe of the Okanagan Valley, rows of fruit trees lead back from stands where farmers sell apples and apricots, tomatoes and home-made jams. At the intersection of the highway north and the east-west route, the woman at the self-serve gas station snatches my money, grim-faced and rude, and I feel an attack of Okanagan dislike coming on. I'm not sure I want to stay even a night in the land of slick bronzed bodies on the lakeside, heat, noise, determined holiday-makers, hot dogs, greasy French fries. But Osoyoos, the town at the southern end of the valley, does have a restaurant that I like, and right now, Hedley's meat loaf lies none too happily atop Coalmont's coffee.

I know a motel on the quiet side of town, with a swimming pool, reasonable prices and not too much noise. But the *No Vacancy* sign is up, and I am forced back down to the lakeside strip where pastel motels crowd together under neon signs. I pull off to the side of the road. A teenage boy in a muscle car roars past in a squeal of tires, a huge thermometer by the roadside registers ninety-two degrees, and kids too young to be in school shriek ear-splittingly as they whump beach balls at their poolside parents. I make no conscious decision, but a moment later, I'm climbing the long switchback up over Anarchist Mountain, eastward to Boundary country. High above the valley, a blessed breeze cools the silent air.

The heat soon closes in again, shimmering on the highway, reflecting from the brown grass at the road verge. The road itself is pressed down upon the border with the United States by the Okanagan Highlands that ridge this part of the province. The heat and the noise and the rudeness of the Okanagan have left me edgy and restless; though I had planned to stop for the night at Midway, the next small town, my mood makes Midway seem cramped and mean, its one motel too close to the highway, its restaurant too much of a truck stop, its pub deserted and tired. I drive on.

Greenwood is narrow and stately, crowded between adjoining dry, pine-dotted hills that climb towards low mountains. In these hills, men have found the region's fortune, veins of copper that fed the Mother Lode and Phoenix mines from the turn of the century to the end of the First World War. An incorporated city by 1897, Greenwood today proudly vaunts its status as Canada's smallest city.

I can choose between the Jesus Saves-Kitchens motel and the Satellite TV! motel. Really no choice: I'm a tennis fanatic and the U.S. Open is on.

I check in and turn on—but, as the owner regrets, topography and weather are against us, and the satellite dish rarely works. Though the owners are friendly and the service good, the heat has intensified the faint odour of unwashed bodies and stale smoke that accumulates in older motels.

In the morning, I walk down the main street, looking southwards at the restored homes and public buildings that ensure Greenwood retains its Victorian flavour. So far, small-town people have welcomed me, inviting me into their homes or offices, accepting gracefully, and even eagerly, unplanned interruptions to their days. Greenwood, politely but firmly, closes its doors to me. At the restaurant last night, waitress and other customers responded to no polite comment, no attempt to start a conversation. This morning, I am gingerly passed from person to person: no, I don't think I am the right person to talk to you about that. Perhaps you should see so-and-so. But don't tell him I sent you. And don't quote me. Someone else, anyone else, would be better to talk to. Even the local history maven refuses to chat: he has to mow his lawn this morning.

Chastened, I wander into the office of a prospecting and mining company and things immediately begin to look up. Owner George Stewart's first impression of Greenwood was about as favourable as mine: when he arrived here in 1973 to look at an old mining property, he immediately hated the town. "There was nobody in the bar but a surly bartender. I got food poisoning in the little restaurant. Later, I found out it was the end of curling season, and everyone was burned out."

The lure of precious metal soon outweighed his initial impressions. He brought a crew down from Smithers and sank a shaft 290 feet into a hill. He ran the mine for two years, until "financial problems" closed him down. Six years later, he was back; together with a partner, he sank a new shaft almost five hundred feet, and operated a mine from 1981 to 1984. "Since then, I've been involved in other companies, picked up the old Phoenix property. This is a highly mineralized belt, but they haven't been very popular properties. There's a lot going on across the border. There's a couple of mines in production just across the line." It's clear he admires the energy of American mining promoters. "Some big companies are in here now, it's very hot now. The last big wave was in '81. We get one every ten years or so. Then you see ten or twenty million spent in a summer. There's prospectors in the hills all the time, always looking."

Stewart is driven by nervous energy that keeps him moving around the office, pointing out claims on the staking map on the wall, talking on the phone. Then the people he has been waiting for arrive: he's ready to take this senior man from a mining company he's "talking to" up into the hills to have a look at the claim. He doesn't say exactly where they are going or what they are looking at: like mining promoters everywhere, he's close-mouthed about these things.

Ellen Clements, whose energy more than matches Stewart's, lives with him on a farm seven miles out of town and works with him in the office. She grew up in Greenwood and has lived here all her life. "I love it here," she says. "It's beautiful. I like the quietness. I never make the trip to the office without seeing a deer or two fawns or a coyote. There's a new way of seeing things every day.

"It's really nice to live in a place where you have a choice. When I want it to be busy, I can go to Vancouver or L.A. or Kelowna." She and George spent some time in Vancouver and seven months in Los Angeles. "Here, it's your choice whether you want the hustle-bustle. You can't turn it off in Vancouver or L.A. And I can accomplish ten times as much in this office as I can in Vancouver with the FAX machine and long-distance phone. Here, I don't have to go through traffic to get to anybody, and I don't have to sit in someone's office and wait."

But she's not starry-eyed about small towns; living in one most of her life, she knows the drawbacks. "People always know more about your life than you do. They always know what you should do better than you do. But they don't tell you to your face; you always hear it from other people." She mentions one or two people in town who were good friends, but who aren't anymore. "You do what you feel it is right to do," regardless of other people's criticism, and "you put a shell around yourself. You learn to laugh when you hear from other people about the crises in your life. There are always people who do nothing but mind other people's business. If they would contribute to the community instead . . . . " But in a small town, there are always people who do things and those who take advantage. Ellen leaves no doubt about which she is.

"We have to get away from here sometimes," so every year they take their motor home south for six weeks. "You have to go do something new, but," with an undertone of still-present hurt and vulnerability, "people begrudge you that."

When copper prices plummeted and the Greenwood smelter closed in 1918, Greenwood went into decline. The four-room frame workers' cottages and the fine, bay-windowed Queen Anne houses of the city's middle class fell empty and decayed. By 1940, just a few hundred people lived in Greenwood.

In 1942, the federal government decreed that those of Japanese descent who lived on the coast were to be moved to interior B.C., to live as enemy aliens wherever empty buildings could be found for them. The mayor of Greenwood saw new settlers of any race as the town's salvation, and promptly wrote to offer the empty houses and public buildings of the almost abandoned city as housing for the deportees. The business they would bring was cited as "the biggest strike the mining town of Greenwood had ever made." Between a thousand and twelve hundred Japanese Canadians were loaded on trains and sent to Greenwood.

Some still live here. Some were among the people who, politely, smilingly, firmly, declined to talk to me earlier this morning. But Ellen is determined that Greenwood will put forward a better face for me. She takes me to see Showney Higashi.

Showney was going hunting in the hills, but he has a soft spot for Ellen, and immediately changes his plans. Of course he will act as my tour guide; he kids and teases Ellen till she protests she must go back to the office, then goes inside to change his hunting clothes for something more appropriate to his new task.

Showney was born in 1927, the second, or *ni*, year of the Showa reign of Emperor Hirohito. He was fourteen and living in Union Bay on Vancouver Island when the Japanese bombed Pearl Harbour. He was fourteen when he stopped being just one of the teenage boys in Union Bay, and became a threat to the country's security, fourteen when he was told that he alone, of all the fourteen-year-old boys in town, could not join the cadet corps. And he was fourteen when he and his family were propelled aboard a boat that would take them away from their home and to the crowded barracks full of people like him in Vancouver. "We thought we were coming back," he says, with some of the old anguish still audible in his husky voice. "We wrapped the china and the coral in newspaper and stuff, and left it behind. But we could see from the boat our house being looted."

Showney turned fifteen the day he arrived in Greenwood. "That's the day I first saw Greenwood, from the train. I thought, boy, how could I ever be dumped in a place like this? There were a thousand Japanese, and they put us in woodsheds and every bloody place. The town was awful."

Showney went to a school run by the United Church, then, in grade ten, was allowed into the regular school system. After he graduated from high school, no "real jobs" were available. He "worked like hell," in the hayfields, as a truck driver and eventually as a heavy-duty mechanic. When copper prices rose in the 1950s, and a mill started up again on the old Mother Lode mine site, he got a job there. He worked steadily as a mechanic and welder for twenty years, until he retired a year or so ago.

Showney starts up the four-wheel-drive truck he uses to explore the hills and old mining roads of Boundary country, and we head out to tour the Mother Lode property. "After the war," he tells me, "we weren't wanted on the coast. They told us, either go back to Japan or live east of the Rockies. My Dad said, they don't want us here, we'll go back to Japan. But we stayed."

Showney married a Greenwood girl. "It was the first mixed marriage in town, and my family didn't like it and neither did hers." But there is steel under Showney's gentle exterior. Over time, he and his father-in-law came to respect each other. Six years after the marriage, when the Higashis' first son was born, mixed marriages had become more acceptable.

The Mother Lode mine started producing low-grade copper ore in 1900, and set a production record of 350,000 tons in 1909 despite a four-months' miners' strike. Showney climbs out of the truck at the abandoned mine site and runs some of the crushed ore through his fingers. He points over to the deep pool where ducks swim on the water that fills the old Greyhound pit. "They figured they'd blow the top off the mountain, put in forty carloads of dynamite." He shakes his head. "It didn't work right. It never reopened."

That 1913 blast saw dynamite explode in five thousand holes drilled in the rock, perhaps the largest single blast in mining history. But the blast so diluted the ore with waste that mining it became unproductive. When the rim of the "glory hole" collapsed into the ore chutes, the Mother Lode was finished.

We climb back into the truck and drive down the gravel road to the site of the old Greenwood smelter. From 1901 to 1918, ore from the Mother Lode, from Rossland, and from other Kootenay mining towns was shovelled into the mouths of the massive blast furnaces, fuelled by coal from distant Fernie, and smelted copper emerged to fill the waiting railway cars. Today, the tall brick smelter smokestack shadows a moonscape of hardened slag and black and broken slag bells that sparkle in the sunshine. We scramble down to the smokestack; inside, we look a hundred and twenty feet skyward, to the circle of light at the smokestack top. Showney runs his hand over the pitted orange bricks, and pays tribute to the men who worked here almost a century ago. "Can you imagine the men who built this, all by hand? Can you imagine what it was like to work here then?"

Showney pilots the truck across Greenwood's main street and past the brick post office, once a showy hotel, and the fancy "Red House" with its verandah and turret and gingerbread, up the hill towards the Phoenix Mine and townsite. We cross a cattleguard and hairpin around the first of the eight switchbacks that lead towards the old mine. Showney waves at a horse logger, carrying hay to the horses that stand, collared and waiting, by the side of the road. Near the mountain top, he points out successive circular terraces worn around a deep blue pool of water; here, the ore trucks trundled round and round, moving ever deeper into the Phoenix mine pit.

That pit, a graveyard, and a monument to the men of Phoenix who died in World War I are all that remain of what was once the highest city in Canada and the largest producer of copper ore. In the graveyard, Showney points to a series of tombstones, all dating from 1918 and 1919. "Flu epidemic." Other stones carry the usual mining-town stories of women dying young in childbirth, men killed in mine accidents. "This used to be a city here," says Showney. "Someone wanted to move the war memorial down to the Kettle Valley, where more people would see it. But we said no, that's all that's left of Phoenix. It should stay here."

Before we leave, he walks to the side of the graveyard to take a leak. Catching sight of my slightly embarrassed face, he giggles. "We Japanese, we are a lot more relaxed about this sort of thing. You whites . . . ." He grins.

We drive north of town now, to Jewel Lake, where Showney has waterfront property; he spends many days on the lake, fishing. "When you come back," he tells me, "bring a friend. You can come and camp up here any time. Any time. Just call me." Back down at the restaurant, he tells me about his two sons, one a dentist in Calgary, the other a professional musician in Vancouver, his pride in their accomplishments evident.

Later, at his home, he shows me the scroll from the Canadian government, an apology for the way Japanese Canadians were treated in the war and after—a statement that means much more to him than the money that came with it. He leaves me with a final word. "I came here third class. I always told my boys, you should leave here first class. And they did. Don't forget that. They did."

CHAPTER 12

The Welcoming Land

)) From Greenwood, the highway follows the contour of creek beds that angle through the north-south range of hills and low mountains that cross the Canadian-American border. Just before it touches the border, the road circles around a rock buttress and opens suddenly into the flat and fertile valley of the Kettle River, where farm fields spread golden in the sunshine.

Though the farmers gave the town its first name of Grande Prairie, mining, not farming, directed the beginnings of Grand Forks, tucked between the Granby River and the Kettle. The early residents came here before the First World War to work in the Granby mine three miles away and in the largest non-ferrous smelter in the British Empire, or to provide services for those who mined and smelted. They seem never to have had doubts about the grandness and the permanence of their new town. Grand Forks' wide tree-lined streets lead between attractive miners' cottages, decorated with gingerbread touches and fronted by glassed-in verandahs, and the stately Victorian demesnes of turn-of-the-century newspaper editor, doctor, mine and smelter managers, and main-street businessmen. These residences bear such elegant names as Golden Heights, the House of the Seven Gables, and the Candlesnuffer House, so titled for its funnel-shaped verandah roof. Other mining towns were born in equal optimism and display, but Grand Forks survived, buoyed by a key position on the railway that led along the U.S. border, by the rich farmlands of the surrounding valley, and by a lumber industry that is now the town's major employer. Yet it did not grow too fast: its Victorian houses survive, untouched by any mania for urban renewal.

The sign outside the Winnipeg Hotel—Queen Anne revival commercial according to the guidebook—promises a neighbourhood pub. But behind the pretty, white-painted façade lies a 1950s beer parlour: a dark and smoky room where a television announcer spouts hysterically about monster truck runs and the bar is crowded with off-shift millworkers who turn to stare at the female stranger. I capture a mug of Kokanee—a close-to-local brew—and retreat to a garden outside in the sunshine. Only a pair of businessmen have chosen to drink under coloured umbrellas at the outdoor tables; their glances are slightly more subtle but no less curious than those inside.

Down the street, I find Pat Badger sitting on a stool behind a counter, surrounded by shelves of books: self-help, cooking, history, Canadian fiction. Owner of the bookstore, Pat arrived in Grand Forks six years ago, and was captivated by the valley and the town. "My husband's brother lived here. Every time we came around the mountain and saw the valley, we had an instant good feeling. Every time we visited, we thought, 'Maybe we could stay an extra day.' One day, we were walking around the seawall in Vancouver, and I said to my husband, 'I think I want to go and live there.' He said, 'Me too.' We quit our jobs the next day."

Pat and her husband Dave Matheson were quintessential Vancouver yuppies: two good jobs, one young child, and an expensive apartment overlooking English Bay. "But in our apartment building, we knew the woman next door and that's all." They moved to Grand Forks, found a 1913 CPR house for thirty thousand dollars—a fraction of the cost of any house in Vancouver—and started fixing it up. Dave, who had been in the furniture business, tried working for a radio station, did this and that, ended up back in the furniture business. Pat worked in health care for three years, then quit and started the bookstore. "I needed a job. I read about starting a business, then put together a program and went to the credit union. I convinced them, and they lent me the money." I sense that Pat can be very convincing, maybe like a bulldog is convincing. She and a woman friend did the carpentry—"You can see where we got worn out," she points to a protruding screw—borrowed a truck and hauled in shelves and books. Now she talks like any other small businessperson, heaping scorn on governments that make it tough for businesses like hers.

The family has put down roots in Grand Forks. "We've decided that this is where we will live for the rest of our lives. It's been the most dramatic experience, meeting friends who feel like family. If I lost everything, they'd take me in and feed me and look after me until I got back on my feet." Equally dramatic has been the transformation in three-year-old Sarah. "I'd say to Sarah, 'Go out and play.' She'd ask, 'By myself? In the yard?' She freaked. In Vancouver, any time we went anywhere, to the zoo, to the park, to an event, it was An Entertainment. Here—she found this tree, it has a bench under it, and it branches down to the ground. That's her secret place. And there's a field where cats go to catch their prey. We can let her just go out and play here. It's crazy." But what she really means is that the city is crazy.

The one drawback for most people, the fishbowl nature of small-town life, bothers her not at all. "I'm not a private person," she states flatly. "I want people to know me and my family. I did have a friend who left for the city. She didn't want people to know anything about her."

That evening, I forget to take a book, my usual camouflage, to the steak house to read during dinner. John, whose belly overflows his belt, and whose plate is covered with a pile of gnawed spare-rib bones, provides entertainment. For fifteen minutes, he bargains with a farmer from somewhere down the road. John wants four pounds of blueberries, but he can't get up to the farm for them. Could the farmer put them on the bus? Blueberries on the bus? Well, now, we did that once before, but I don't know. In the end, after much cautious thinking, John has his way. Outside, dusk drops swiftly on the valley, and a huge harvest moon takes over the sky.

In the morning, I head south across the border, just to see what the Amurrican towns are like. The narrow road runs beside the winding Kettle River, through irrigated hayfields, sausage-roll–shaped haystacks and dry summer pastures. The first town, Curlew, is, I've been told, home to Alberta rednecks looking for good mining properties, ageing salt-of-the-earth farmers, sixties hippies who went back to the land, and Vietnam veterans who gave up on the cities in disgust. It's a spur-of-the-moment trip, and it never crosses my mind that I might need American money to pay for breakfast. And I don't. The waitress at the cavernous barn of a restaurant, with an equally cavernous and dim tavern right beside it, says sure, they'll take Canadian dollars, they'll take charge cards, they'll take just about anything. She dishes up huge plates of bacon and eggs, hash browns, toast, pancakes, to the men who sit at the booths, thermoses of coffee to those who sit on stools at the counter. Most are over fifty, wearing work, not designer, jeans, and baseball caps carrying the usual heavy equipment names—though one says simply, "Hat," and another leaves no doubt about its owner's stand on the current save-the-owls/log-the-forest controversy: "Eat an Owl."

A seventy-six-year-old (he informs me immediately) retired millworker-logger hefts himself painfully onto the stool next to me, looks approvingly at my overflowing breakfast platter and ventures a comment or two about the weather. "That field of alfalfa up the hill, it got frosted last night." He drinks his coffee, fidgets stiffly. His hip aches today, reminding him of the operation he had a month ago. "They had me four days in the hospital, four days in the convalescent home. They said I went home too fast, but they can't keep me in no hospital. Guess I had no business using my leg like that," he says, talking about the work he did around the house yesterday.

At the phone, a severely plain woman in her thirties with startling blue eyes and lank brown hair argues with a government official somewhere in the city about money and housing, while her children play quietly in a booth. Seeing them reminds my neighbour of the problem with kids these days. "These kids today, they don't learn concentration in school. You have to tell them every damn thing twice. I grounded my kid if he didn't do what he was told, if he did what I told him not to do. Kids, they need to be hit once in a while, kept in line, shown how to work." He looks at the good food, half a breakfast, I have left on my plate and turns away.

Old Curlew is off the highway, over a narrow bridge by the river. The sign at the Curlew Saloon warns, "No public restroom. No wet clothes." Coors Lite and Budweiser signs glow in the windows of the store, behind the wagon wheels set out on the verandah, below the kind of false front you've seen in a hundred Western movies. Election posters urge voters to re-elect candidates for senator, accountant, sheriff. In the morning sunshine, Curlew is a hot, dusty, American western town.

Less than twenty miles north, I am a century and a continent away from the present-day American west. Just outside Grand Forks, on a bench beside the river, below the bare brown hills, three generations of Russian Doukhobors lie buried. The Doukhobors, a Russian peasant group whose name translates as "the spirit wrestlers," came to Saskatchewan in 1898 and 1899, fleeing persecution in their native Russia. They sought toil and a peaceful life, the freedom to live communally, unhindered by any laws but those of God. They found frustration and fear: their fear of government attempts to change them, Canadian fears of this strange sect that renounced the Bible and followed the sung and spoken teachings of their psalms. That fear and frustration drove many Doukhobors from Saskatchewan to southeastern British Columbia, where they established new colonies and tried to live according to the dictates of their faith.

On simple stone markers in the unmanicured graveyard are etched the names—Verigin, Popoff, Polotnikoff—of men and women who traded a life of persecution in Russia for a life in Canada whose turnings they could not foresee. No grave marker is ornate, for the Doukhobors believe in simplicity. Most are plain stone rectangles, engraved in Cyrillic lettering "Vechnaya Pamyat," the Russian words for "in eternal memory." On some stones are a sheaf of wheat, a jug and a salt-cellar, symbolic of bread, water and salt, the essentials of Doukhobor life. Grasshoppers whir between clumps of dry grass and tiny, bright butterflies skim from grave to grave. Some graves, simple, unmarked mounds of earth or stones, are slowly collapsing back into the earth. Above the graveyard, a flight of geese vees, honking, southward across the river. The burr of highway traffic fades in a soft breeze that barely stirs the branches of the nearby pines.

A mile or two away, in a big old brick house that stands on the hillside overlooking the valley, Peter Gritchen is pleased that I have spent an hour at the cemetery. "Other people say that the cemetery is neglected, but that is our way. We believe that when you're gone, you're gone." He strokes a carved wooden stand beside him. "This is my father's memory here, in what he made."

Fifty years ago, these soft red, two-storey brick houses were familiar sights in the valley. Each was the centre of a Doukhobor community; each housed several families in its plain rooms. For thirty years, the Doukhobors lived co-operatively, owning their lands, their houses and their tools together. But by the 1930s, complex financial troubles beset them, and people outside their faith became increasingly hostile, envious of their seeming financial success in the midst of the Depression, and suspicious of their foreign customs and communal living. When their co-operative reached the edge of bankruptcy, no one reached out a hand to save them. The financial institution foreclosed and the government offered no help—at least until their farm implements, machinery and animals had been sold off at a derisory price. The lands they had owned communally for decades went back to the government, which allowed the Doukhobors to stay in their houses, on their lands, on payment of a nominal rent. The bankruptcy effectively destroyed their communal way of life. The Doukhobor story would now become one of gradual, painful, and sometimes violent integration into the individualistic society that surrounded them.

This brick house on the hill above Grand Forks was built in 1909, one of seven in the colony, the colony one of three on this hill. In 1964, the homestead was abandoned. Eight years later, Peter and a group of Doukhobor friends took it over, to create a simple museum and a memorial to a way of life that no longer existed. The house might be called shabby, compared to the bright model tourist village built by Doukhobors near Castlegar. The whitewashed walls are streaky, the ceilings watermarked, and the orange-painted floor boards hollowed by the imprint of the feet that trod them for fifty-five years. But the light that shines through dusty windowpanes on sleepy hornets clustered in the window corners, on worn rugs and clothing, and on faded sepia photographs, conjures up the ghosts of yesterday: women spinning flax by flickering lamplight, men carving wooden spoons, children playing with simple wooden toys.

Peter smooths through his hands a hooked rug that he found in an abandoned brick house just such as this. His slow Russian bass voice resonant with reverence for his forefathers, he holds the rug up to the light. "They made each stitch by hand, by the light of a kerosene lamp. Everything they had, they made themselves."

When it came time to turn this house into a museum, Peter and his friends abjured government help. "We didn't want the red tape. We did it ourselves. When you get commercial . . . ." He sighs, and talks about the inevitable cycle of getting grants, of expanding, of having to cater more and more to tourists, of having to fill out more and more forms, follow more and more regulations. They wanted none of that. Instead, they fixed the leaking roof themselves, washed the walls with blueing, collected used and treasured artifacts from ageing Doukhobors and from sales.

Upstairs, he points out a stamping mill, used to separate millet from its chaff, for *kasha*, a traditional Russian porridge. A Russian suit with high-collared shirt hangs on one wall; the suit is made from flax grown here, and spun and woven with wooden carding combs, spinning wheels and looms like those down the hall. A photograph shows a long line of women, in head shawls and ankle-length skirts, waiting to catch a glimpse of the tomb of Peter Lordly Verigin, the leader of the

Doukhobors who died in 1924, in a still-unexplained explosion that blew apart the railway coach he was travelling in between Grand Forks and the Doukhobor settlement of Brilliant. In the background, a classic steam engine exhales a snowy cloud of steam.

Though Peter Gritchen is third-generation Canadian, the rhythms of the Russian he learned as a child underlie his English words. He sings and records Russian folk songs; I buy a record. As I drive away, the strong, haunting cadences of the songs echo in my mind.

The communal way of life is gone, but Russian traditions live on in this valley. In Grand Forks, I pass up a restaurant that offers borscht and bread, three kinds of vereniki, Chinese pork bun, and fillet of salmon as its lunchtime specials. For anyone who travels through British Columbia knows that you may not pass through Grand Forks without stopping at the Yale Hotel, famed for the best borscht and banana cream pie in British Columbia.

The borscht, the Yale's own recipe, not even a distant relation of the watery cabbage and beet soup served up in restaurants that know borscht only from a cookbook, blends tomato, cabbage, celery, dill, butter, cream. Cholesterol thoughts set aside, I also order nasleniki, a crêpe filled with cottage cheese, topped with sour cream, swimming in melted butter, with home-made strawberry jam on the side.

The Doukhobors came to Grand Forks from the east; the highway loops back along their path through a range of low mountains to the valley where the Columbia River meets the Kootenay at the town of Castlegar. Ootischenia, the Valley of Consolation, near the joining of the rivers, was one of the earliest Doukhobor settlements. From her home on the old Doukhobor lands, Polly Samoyloff takes me on a tour through her childhood.

From Ootischenia, we drive to the Kootenay River, then cross over on an eight-car cable ferry that is the only link to Glade, where once fourteen Doukhobor villages lined up along the riverbank. Polly bumps her old blue Thunderbird along a rutted road towards a waterfall where she used to play as a child. In those days, she and the other children in the villages walked from their houses to the waterfall. But the ruts in the road are too high, the car's clearance too low, for us to drive there, and we turn back, towards the place where Polly grew up, fed the chickens, brought home the cows, helped separate the milk.

In the forties and early fifties, the six hundred Doukhobors who lived here got their water from the stream that tumbled down the hillside behind the bench, towards the river. "We were the last village on the system, and sometimes it would freeze up," Polly recalls. "We would get the horses and the sleigh and bring barrels of water from the river." We drive along the gravel road that parallels the river. "Our village was right here," she points towards a dry grassy field. "It was a beautiful place to grow up. We went fishing and swimming; our village's swimming hole was where everybody else came. Everything we did was a happy occasion. Nothing was organized, but everything seemed right. It was such a simple life. We never felt we had any hardships. Not that we had much, but what we had we appreciated."

She points out where the one-room Russian school was, and I ask if she went to school there. But, inadvertently, I have intruded into the one part of Polly's growing up that has left scars. Entwined inextricably with Doukhobor beliefs was an ingrained suspicion of all state control or state infiltration of any aspect of Doukhobor life. The state sanctioned militarism, aggression, and a type of integration that the Doukhobors could not accept. And what the state sanctioned, the schools taught. For some Doukhobors, even the Russian schools run by their fellow believers were suspect, for Doukhobor belief was based on oral traditions and literacy might lead true believers astray. When Polly was very young, her mother took her out of school and refused to let her return. "I could understand the government school, but why the Russian school?" Polly questions, still anguished by a decision that she could not change, but that has left her ever afterwards bewildered. "My sisters went to school. Why couldn't I?" Today, she reads voraciously, trying to make up for that early neglect.

The inadequacy she felt was for many years hidden by her joyful marriage to the man she met the night she turned seventeen. A group of young Doukhobors from across the river came one night to Glade for a meeting of the Doukhobor Youth Council. A laughing, beautiful teenager with an impish spirit, Polly went to the boat landing to meet the visitors. One dared her to shine the light in his face as he balanced on the board that led from the boathouse to the shore. She did so anyway; he chased and caught her. Meeting forgotten, they sat together and talked for two hours. Three months later, Polly met Peter Samoyloff again in the Okanagan. "That's when I fell in love with him," she remembers, joyously. "I didn't want to eat or anything." But she was too young at seventeen to marry a man eight years her senior. "He courted me for three years, and then we were married."

For thirty years, Polly's world was her husband and their four sons. She adored Pete, he her. He went out into the world as a high-school teacher. He founded and conducted the famous Doukhobor youth choir, started the first Russian classes at the Castlegar high school, and became a youth leader who could combine formal education with Doukhobor ideals. Polly stayed at home, his support and sustenance. Then, quite suddenly, without warning, he died of a heart attack. Now, a year later, she struggles towards a new life without Pete. "He was a fine gentleman, a very loving person," she says, tears threatening to break through. "I miss him terribly."

In the year after her husband died, two of her sons were married in Doukhobor ceremonies. "The whole community came through. My son was their son. There was so much loving and caring." And that caring is part of the Doukhobor tradition. "Our culture is based on our closeness to each other, not on some compulsion to do things. Ours is a way of life where people learned by co-operation to survive in the best way they could. That co-operation comes from a deep religious belief, by being Christians, by believing in God. Everything that the Doukhobors accomplished came because people sacrificed themselves so that everyone could benefit. The community always comes through. It's instilled in everybody. This is not something you are made to do. It is a part of your life."

Just twenty-five years ago, the lands once owned communally by the Doukhobors were put up for sale by the government, with the Doukhobors given first chance to buy. Perhaps 30 per cent were bought by Doukhobors. The new owners built houses on the hill where Doukhobors once grew the potatoes, beets, carrots, onions, the tomatoes, corn, peas and beans that were the basis of their vegetarian meals. We drive up the hill away from the river, to the house of Polly's nephew and his wife. This is Polly's first visit to the house: she blooms with delight when she sees the traditional Doukhobor hooked rugs that brighten the oak chest and the wooden floors. "This reminds me so much of our old house," she says. Michael and Tyanna are melding old Doukhobor traditions with their modern life. Each piece of furniture they have brought to their new house comes from the house of someone's father, someone's grandmother. Carved into the back of each carefully crafted chair is a simple flower whose design dates back to eighteenth-century Russian peasant art. Tyanna, who has chosen to stay home with her small children, nurtures a garden overflowing with fruits and vegetables; she serves fresh raspberry juice on the cool patio, shaded from the hot September sunshine. "Somehow," muses Polly, if you are born a Doukhobor, a garden comes with it. It is part of your culture. This year, I neglected my garden, and I thought, 'Oh, no. I can't do that next year.'"

The tiny ferry takes us back across the river to the highway, and we drive to Polly's brother's house. Supper at Bill and Lovette Nichvolodoff's is wonderfully vegetarian, in the tradition of the longest-lasting of the Doukhobor prohibitions against tobacco, alcohol and meat: potatoes herbed with rosemary, corn fresh from the garden, Greek salad, green beans, bread. A minor crisis erupts: no cream for the fruit tarts. Five years ago, there would have been no crisis. But five years ago, the Nichvolodoffs got rid of their cow, so now have no more home-made butter and cheese, no more fresh milk and cream. And no more being tied down by milking times: with Lovette working in Castlegar ten miles away, and Bill at the mill at Slocan City thirty miles north, that freedom is appreciated. "Not having a cow has changed our lives," Lovette declares.

In the morning, Polly feeds me an enormous breakfast of French toast, cereal, fruit, cream and coffee, as she talks about Perry, her oldest son. Twenty-nine now, Perry worked at a mill for five years and saved his money. Then he went to the Soviet Union. Though other Doukhobor students have gone to Russia for a year, he and his roommate are the first to stay for a second year. "I'm very happy that I was born in Canada," says Polly, "but to me, it's wonderful that my son can be in Moscow. It's like we've waited a hundred years for this to happen, and it's happened in my son's lifetime. I am so happy for him that he can experience the whole thing, see the changes that are happening."

For Russia and the Russian language are still a living part of the Doukhobor culture. Two centuries ago, the Doukhobors forswore the Bible and the written catechisms of conventional Christianity for spoken and sung psalms that convey the tenets of their faith. The psalms are in Russian; without the Russian language, the basis of their beliefs cannot be expressed.

In the last twenty years, young Doukhobors have discovered a desire to learn about their past. "A lot of people were always self-conscious about their background," says Polly. "The publicity we got was always bad publicity. People said, 'Oh, you're the ones who are going around burning things and undressing and going to jail.'" Beginning in the

1920s, a minority group of Doukhobors expressed their hostility to all things material by throwing off their clothes and marching in nude parades, and by setting fire to schools and other buildings, many of them owned by the rest of the Doukhobor community. Outsiders took the part for the whole, identifying all Doukhobors with those Sons of Freedom. Books were written, commissions formed, and prisons filled, as neighbours and government struggled with the "problem" of the Doukhobors.

The negative publicity made many young Doukhobors shy. Then, "in the sixties," says Polly, "all of a sudden, it was okay for the young people to be Doukhobors. They could dress in their own clothes, sing in their own choir. It was accepted, by friends, by teachers, by the community."

Now Canadian Doukhobors are rejoining ties with the descendants of those who stayed in Russia a hundred years ago. When the Soviet government permitted a Doukhobor group to return to its traditional Russian home after more than a century of exile, first in the Ukraine, then in the Caucasus, eight British Columbia Doukhobors went to Russia, to help build houses for those returning from exile. When they arrived, they were greeted by Doukhobors in traditional garb carrying the Doukhobor symbols of bread, water and salt. When they departed, they left behind their precious building tools. Some in the Canadian community say that the only way the Doukhobors can retain their faith and their traditions is to return to Russia to live.

Polly changes to traditional Doukhobor clothing, a long-sleeved blouse and pleated skirt that echo Russian styles of the nineteenth century. We drive down the highway to the tomb of the Doukhobor spiritual leader Peter Verigin. This Sunday morning, Doukhobors will gather for an annual memorial service in honour of the mother of current leader John Verigin, Anna Markova, who is buried near her brother, Peter the Lordly.

In the glade where the tombs lie, the first leaves of autumn drift down through mingled sun and shade. In soft-hued dresses of turquoise and rose, blue and lavender, all cut to a common design, their heads covered by fringed lace shawls, the women greet each other, hold hands, smile, nod, take their places standing on one side in front of the tomb. The men, some in Russian tunics, some in plain suits, stand facing the women.

In chorus, their voices lift and die, lift and die. Most of the service is in song, and all is in Russian. The men recite psalms, then the women. Together, they sing their *Lord's Prayer*. To acknowledge the Lord's spirit rising in them, they bow: two deep bows, man to man, woman to woman, a kiss, another bow. As the singing dies away, I ask Polly, quietly, if many Doukhobors will return to Russia.

She translates the words as the singing rises again: "We have faith and faith shall lead us. We shall leave what we have and follow." "Maybe," she says, "maybe that answers your question."

We linger after the service, as Polly talks to a young man recently returned from Moscow. She asks the usual mother's questions about her absent son, Perry: how is he, is he happy? What she really wants to know is: does he have a girlfriend, a serious girlfriend? The young man smiles and teases. He is sworn to secrecy.

Silent and in harmony, we drive back to Polly's home. I want to take her picture, but Polly, with laugh lines creased at the corners of her eyes from her constant smile, cannot smile now. "I am always affected by the service," she says, again with a hint of tears. Though I have not the gift of faith, I am as affected as she by the simplicity, the oneness, and the love I have seen. We hug, and promise to keep in touch. It is a promise I will keep.

CHAPTER 13

Slocan Dreams

JJ Not far from Peter Verigin's tomb, in the village of Robson beside the Columbia River, a seeker of a different kind of truth tries to put into words the sense he has of the Kootenays. On the map, this region is a succession of mountain chains from the Rockies to the Okanagan, wedged apart by the north-south lengths of deep and narrow lakes and circumscribed by the valleys of the Kootenay and Columbia rivers. But the map does not convey the singular beauty of the Kootenays or the healing spirit some people ascribe to them.

"What is it about this place that attracts people who are bleeding?" Jim Terral asks. "I don't know." He searches for words that might describe the special meaning of this region; perhaps it is, he says, a *chakra*, a place of sacred healing, on the Rocky Mountains, the spine of the North American continent. "It's like a continental hospital, somehow. There are all sorts of groups that have come here because of their suffering. The Doukhobors are here, there are people here who came up during the McCarthy era from the U.S., there is a significant community of Quakers. The Japanese people are out here."

And though he has moved back and forth between the coast and the West Kootenay, Jim is here. A deserter from the American army during the Vietnam crisis, he fled to Canada and came to the West Kootenay in the early 1970s with a group of people who wanted to start a co-operative farm. That venture succeeded, and then fell apart. Jim now teaches writing at Selkirk College in Castlegar.

Jim grew up in the American midwest, and went to college and on to graduate school in Seattle. All through his university years, the peace movement in the United States and the protests against the Vietnam war were growing. During the Cuban missile crisis, Jim went with other workers for peace to a movement meeting in Chicago. "I remember being drunk out of my mind on the way back, and throwing up three or four times along the road. It was just sheer anxiety, like really believing that you weren't going to wake up the next morning, that it just all wasn't going to be there."

Berkeley, free speech, the draft, the war: they were all on young American minds during the sixties. In grad school, "I was very much aware that as soon as I got out of school, my student deferment would be up and I would be draftable." He finished his master's degree and went to a teaching job in the midwest. "Almost as soon as I started teaching, I got my notice that I would be drafted. I was not the only person who was in that jam. All my male students were in that situation, except for a handful who had already been through the service. It was really very difficult teaching in that kind of situation. Nobody was motivated. It was terrible. During that year, and in grad school too, I would wake up and it was like being obsessed with a woman or something, the first thing I would be aware of was the word Vietnam in my mind.

"It happened every day, day after day after day. Sometimes I would get ten minutes where I didn't think about it."

Part of the reaction was, of course, fear. "Nobody wants to fight a war, nobody wants to die. And yet, there are probably things I would risk my life for." Jim sighs. The American cause in Vietnam was not one of those things. The more he looked at American motives overseas and the conduct of the American government at home, the less he believed. "Still, all the way through that year, I believed that if I read the newspaper religiously enough, or studied the right book, or heard the right interview on TV, that it would change. So I went in.

"Years after I came here, that was the thing that really troubled me and made me wonder about myself." Why did he enter the army when he opposed the war? By the end of basic training, Jim knew he had made the wrong decision. Twenty years later, in a country he has adopted, every detail of basic training is as fresh in his mind as it was twenty years ago. The training exercises where some soldiers played the part of Viet Cong, where he learned that the massacre of villagers at My Lai was not an aberration but standard procedure. "That was the way it was done, and if you did it any other way, you were stupid, you'd have probably got yourself shot by your buddies." The mind-bending treatment handed out to people who declared themselves conscientious objectors. The recruiting of illiterate men, mostly blacks, teaching them to read and write and sending them to Vietnam to be killed—in a country that refused to teach them to read and write in peacetime. The men who pretended to be crazy to get their discharge, and ended up not pretending. The experience on the firing range with a soldier who spoke only Spanish. "The guy . . . gets up and starts waving his hands. There was a tarantula that was coming from the target to the guys, and he didn't know what to do. So the sergeant went over and he took the M16 and he took it off the single shot mode and put it on the automatic mode and blew the living shit out of that tarantula." Jim imitates the rat-a-tat of an automatic weapon, then laughs, the way you laugh when you cannot come to terms with an alien way of thinking. "And if that didn't get him, you call in an air strike. It was symbolic of the whole thing."

The bureaucracy considered Jim's case at its own slow speed, then rejected his request for CO status. Jim deserted from the army. He and his wife went to Seattle. Aided by the Quaker committee, they crossed the border to Vancouver. Once he got his Canadian work permit, he taught on the coast, came to the Kootenays, went back to the coast, came back to Castlegar. Now he's thinking again that he might move.

"The native people somehow had a sense of this as a place that you go to, but you don't stay. When you're finished with it [the continental hospital], and it's finished with you, you should go on. I feel as though I'm at a point with the Kootenays where I am ready to be released from the hospital." Behind that decision is a continuing desire to make a difference to a world that could countenance a Vietnam. He prepared a booklet that set out the case against uranium mining in the Kootenays, a project defeated by public outcry. Now he wants to try to influence changes in an educational system that he believes should, but now cannot, create fundamental change in the way people think about other people.

"I'm looking around for what I need to do next. It will probably involve more risk, less income, more meaning. It's kind of odd to be thinking about that as I'm approaching fifty. I'm not going to do some young person's thing. I don't know what it's going to be. I don't know."

From Robson, I head towards the Slocan, one of those narrow river-lake valleys that characterize the Kootenays. In the last twenty-five years, the Slocan has drawn hippies, American draft dodgers, back-to-the-landers, artists, writers: people who seek a lifestyle distant from what they view as the urban insanities.

If you look at the Slocan road on a map, you'll see half a dozen little white dots that indicate towns. On the road itself, only the occasional gas station or wayside cafe indicates that people live somewhere around here. The communities themselves are on the west side of the river, near gravel roads that wind between the poplars and firs along the river, in log cabins, farms, homesteads, new houses, at the ends of long drive-ways, and behind the screening trees. Off one of these gravel roads, the youngest students at the Vallican Whole alternate school are ready for a snack and swim break. We straggle through the forest, jumping roots and discussing which berries are edible and how the trail has changed since the spring, to the swimming hole next to the river. Some of the children, unself-conscious, strip off and leap gleefully naked into the water. Others, more modest, retain their underwear. Two or three, life's planners, have brought bathing suits with them. I talk, alternately, to a six-year-old about the best techniques of frog-stroking, and to Trudy, teacher and parent, about the school and the building it occupies.

"It took a few years for the building to get off the ground— they called it the 'Hole' to start with, because it was just a hole in the ground. When they put up the big beams, even the kids were out helping. It was a real community effort. Every day, different people would show up."

Completed, the Hole became the Whole, a community hall where weddings, anniversaries and birthdays are celebrated. But it also be-came the centre for the social activism that characterizes the valley. An annual women's festival that attracts women from across Canada, environmental impact meetings, and political campaign meetings all take place at the Whole.

During the day, the alternate school rents the building. Teacher-administrator Brenda Curry expresses the reasons for the school. "We want to keep the child a child longer [than is possible in the regular school system]. We want to nurture them more in their younger years. We want to have a more exciting, stimulating type of education, with more hands-on projects, more field trips where they learn counting and reading at the same time as they see what the community has to offer, what the world has to offer."

Though the school began as an alternative for students up to age sixteen, now two dozen children between the ages of four and ten attend. "They learn all the basics," says Brenda, "reading, writing, math, geography, language arts, painting, music. We hope to get a French teacher, and maybe a Japanese teacher."

We walk back to the school through the woods, and I drive away. And drive back. Unwittingly, I have kidnapped the Whole Cat. I let him out and depart again. No other cars leave dust plumes on the gravel road that leads me north along the Slocan River, its autumn waters fast and shallow over the rocky riverbed.

Close enough to the river that you can almost hear its murmur, an editor and graphic designer are at work at light tables. In Toronto, regional publishing refers to anything outside Toronto. In British Columbia, regional publishers have addresses like Ganges, Madeira Park and Winlaw. Julian Ross runs Polestar Press near Winlaw, one of those well-spread-out Slocan communities. He was a part of eight different businesses in Vancouver over a decade or so, all of which "didn't quite work out." He was the first creative writing graduate of the now defunct David Thompson University Centre in Nelson, bought land at Winlaw because he really liked the mix of creative, artistic people who had gravitated to the Slocan Valley, moved back to Vancouver and Victoria, and finally settled with his family here.

He knew that the odds against financial success were high. "A lot of people come here because it's very beautiful, but they run out of money very quickly. They want to get more training, more money, but they can't afford to leave because they have been out of the work force for so long. There are a lot of artistic people in the valley who do tree-planting and that sort of thing—until their bodies get too old." Left undescribed is the month-to-month struggle to survive, the growing frustration, and the recourse to welfare payments that is often the outcome of the struggle.

Julian and Ruth did not intend to lose the struggle. "We went back to Victoria to get more skills, because we felt we didn't have enough skills to prosper, to survive in the valley," says Julian. Then they moved to Creston, east of here, where Julian took a newspaper job as sports reporter, typesetter and layout man. A month later, the newspaper, in business for seventy-five years, folded. The Rosses moved to their property in Winlaw. "We had the land and we had an old barn and a really small cabin. We started doing some typesetting for other people, and then we did some books and some textbooks . . . ." Polestar was born. For several years, the press was housed in a small workshop—"at night, you'd be laying everything out and all the bugs would land on the light table"—before moving to their present light, airy, to them palatial, quarters.

For the first few years, Julian tried to distribute his own publications, spending half the time on the road with a trunkload of books and publicity flyers, half the time trying to get reorders out through the post office since there was no parcel service in any nearby town. Finally, Polestar threw in its lot with a Vancouver distributor who acts for several publishers. "On our own, we really weren't big enough for bookstores to bother dealing with us. Now, we have the same sales reps as the other publishers, and our books are treated the same way as theirs. It has always been delightful to me that once our books are in the stores, our book and some multimillion-dollar publisher's book have the same chance of sales."

And he has not lacked for creative talent. "We've been fortunate. We've used a local stained-glass artist to design some of our covers, and an architect, so our covers look fresh and different. We try to use as many people from this area as we can."

Nonetheless, Julian and Ruth must balance their desire to live here against the difficulties of working here. "Anyone in a rural area has to work a lot harder, because there are so many things we don't have the services for. You have to go outside for them, or you somehow have to create them here."

For them, hard work is balanced by the rewards of living in a rural area. "One of the beauties of being here is, I can go to the post office and they know us. If we are short fifteen dollars, they'll lend it to us to get our mail out. Or they'll undo their bags if we're late, and get our things off that day. They are tremendously helpful. And driving to the post office, you get to drive along the Slocan River. Even in the midst of a really crazy day, you get to enjoy the beauty of the place. That's one of the great advantages of being here. Even though it's very busy, you're in a very peaceful setting, and you draw comfort from that."

He finds the rural life they live more complete in many ways than the urban life they left behind. "You have respect for individuals according to who they are, not for what they do. You interact with people on a different level than you would in the city, where you only see people in one role. Here, you get to see people volunteering in the fire department, or involved in a political campaign, or fighting the logging of a watershed or the possibilities of pollution. Work is just something you do in relation to the many other things a person does.

"I feel very strongly that this is a wonderful place to live, but we are absolutely not retreating. We are connected to a greater world, a world outside."

Rita Moir looks up in mock shock from a book she is laying out. Retreat is not a word in her vocabulary. Feminist, journalist, dramatist, from a very conservative area of southern Alberta, she and her partner came to the West Kootenay for a conference, and tagged along with a friend on a visit to the valley and the first women's festival at the Vallican Whole. "I fell in love with the place. The hall needed caretakers; we applied and moved here five days later.

"Sometimes, there's a sign in your life that says, 'turning point', and you either do it or you regret that you didn't. A lot of women have moved here because they visit the area and find out there is a place for them here. Women have been outspoken in this community. It's an atmosphere where women have fought and made gains. You think you can have some effect. You're not the Lone Ranger. This is the place where a lot of us have chosen to make our stands."

The first year in the Slocan, Rita and her partner lived in a tent until mid-November. "We were very poor. We moved here with six hundred dollars. But we weren't in any worse shape than a whole bunch of other people. People were very generous to us. They took the time to teach us how to do stuff, to give us a hand."

Many years a journalist, Rita decided to move on to creative writing, fighting against her own impulses to continue writing newspaper stories she thought worthwhile. "I'd gone off to Alberta and worked in the legislature for four months as a press hack. I made enough money to come back and write plays." Her first was presented on CBC radio. Then, with two other women, she wrote a play for the Nelson-based group, Theatre Energy, on the topic of the persecution of women in medieval Europe.

"We wrote that play in just three weeks. The emotional effect was quite incredible." That effect was heightened by the events of the day. During the first rewrite, the federal government cut off funding to women's centres; scant days later, fourteen female engineering students were murdered in Montreal. "Because of our outrage, we moved forward fast. It was like a paradigm shift. We couldn't believe these things had happened."

Theatre Energy presented the play in a leaky tent on the shore of Kootenay Lake. "It was really like all the goddesses were stirred up.

There were huge winds and rainstorms. And the show was about survival and magic and persecution and fighting back and the elements. The play ended with a burning on the lake, and everyone came out in the rain and watched it. It was quite something."

But her own sense of energy and purpose does not blind Rita to the shortcomings of life in the Kootenays. "It depends on who you talk to. I don't happen to work in the forest industry. If you had been here after the university closed and the mills shut down and B.C. Tel workers were shut out . . . . There was a ton of unemployment. It was just a hell of a tough place to live. A lot of people had to leave. They had no choice. But a lot of people stayed, and scraped by on nothing. They built the foundations for the things you see flourishing now. There's a real strength in having gone through those hard times together.

"I don't want to romanticize it, but this place is of a size you can get a grip on. I feel like a lot of people feel about this area, that if I am ever going to do something in my life that really matters, this is the place it's going to happen. It's not going to happen when we move someplace else. We make our stand here."

I drive up the valley, towards Slocan Lake, which curls between the Valhalla and Slocan mountains. Traffic is halted at a road construction project that will widen the dreaded Cape Horn section of the highway that clings, narrow, to the edge of a cliff. Four hundred feet above the road, scalers' safety helmets glint red and silver against the blast-scarred rock and boulders bounce down the cliff to shatter on the road below. The sun blazes full above the western mountains, and the smell of hot oil invades the car, to remain for days.

Jim holds the traffic back with his stop sign. A flagman now, he used to be a scaler, working the province from North Vancouver to Terrace. Not any more. "You're supposed to have some brains by the time you're fifty, and you don't have any brains if you do that." He gestures upwards at the scalers, tiny dots on the sheer and crumbling rock. Every morning, the scalers follow an access road to the top of the cliff, clamber out to the cliff face, attach ropes, and slither down the cliff to lever away with their picks rock that has been loosened by blasting. "Do they have rock-climbing experience, training?" I ask. He looks surprised. "Nope. They're just scalers." Ten hours a day they dangle from their ropes, finding footholds where they can. Coffee breaks, lunch breaks and rest breaks come when the bulldozers push the fallen rock over the edge of the highway into the lake and the flagman waves the waiting traffic through. "When I worked the Fraser canyon, the Squamish Highway, it was better than this," says Jim. "It took half an hour for the traffic to go by. Here you got, what, three cars?"

But he insists the work is not dangerous. "Only way you can fall is if a rope breaks—some kind of a fluke." He saw a fluke happen once: a stump caught up somehow when a rope end whipped around it. The rope broke. Did the man live? Jim looks at me pityingly. "He fell a hundred and fifty feet."

Jim was pushing fifty and working out of Vancouver when he decided one day he'd never make his fiftieth birthday if he stayed in the city. "Hassle, always hassle." He was born near here; he and his wife bought a house in New Denver, north of Silverton. He worked "out" on road gangs for the first two years, and took courses in fixing furnaces, refrigerators, what-have-you, skills he thought he could sell in the Slocan. He doesn't need much to live on. And he doesn't miss at all the urban delights. "We were in Terrace, my wife and me, I was working there, and we had some time to kill. We went to the mall, and the first thing I did, I bought a hamster and a cage. The wife said, 'What did you do that for?' I didn't know. First thing I did when I got here, I gave it away."

I have phoned ahead to reserve a cabin at Silverton, just beyond Cape Horn. At the resort, a message is on a slate outside the door: "Rosemary. Cabin 2 is open for you." Hugh has gone fishing. Had I a boat, a rod, a worm, I would do likewise. Bereft, I swim, eat, ponder.

Hugh Wilson returns. His lakeside resort is the end of an odyssey for Hugh. English, he was sent to the United States when he was four years old, as a child war evacuee. Forty years later, he returned to North America, the guest of a North American corporation sponsoring a reunion of war evacuees with their foster parents. All was sweetness and light, Hugh recalls, until Hugh couldn't stand it any more. "What about," he asked, "the situations that didn't work out? What about the abusive foster parents, the ones who worked their newly acquired children half to death, the children who were unhappy?" That didn't make Hugh popular. He left, and began a trek across the continent, looking for something that would change his life.

"I was coming up to fifty. I was happy but I was miserable. I decided if I was ever going to do anything different with my life, this was the time." He ended up one August day in Banff, in the Canadian Rockies. "It was beautiful, but there were so many people." He fled the crowds, and followed his whims down into the Kootenays. At New Denver, he went for a walk in the park. "I thought the town must have been evacuated. There was no one in sight, just one canoe out on the lake." When he discovered that the Slocan was always as beautiful and often as empty of people as this, he knew he had to move here. He immigrated to Canada and began to build this log cabin resort at Silverton.

Yet a man's dream can be a woman's nightmare. After two years, his wife left him. "I was devastated," says Hugh, flatly. He stuffed the few hundred dollars he could scrape up into his pockets and left for Mexico. There, speaking almost no Spanish, with not a plan in his head, he wandered the byways, living cheap and risking danger. He loved it. He learned, he said, that he could survive hardship and find excitement. He returned to the Slocan revitalized. Now he pours his energy into battling any encroachment he thinks could destroy the beauty of his valley.

Eagerly, he thrusts a sheaf of papers into my hands. He has joined a coalition of environmentalists, tourism operators, and long-time residents of the Slocan to fight a proposed expansion of the pulp mill downstream in Castlegar. They fight on two fronts: against additional pollution they believe will result from the new mill, and against the converting of the Slocan into an industrial corridor, with chip trucks rolling ceaselessly down the narrow valley road towards the mill. Statistics roll from Hugh's lips: an average of one chip truck every seven and a half minutes, no proper guarantees of pollution control, access for the company to forests that cover half of southeastern British Columbia. The loggers, millworkers and truckers who favour the plan talk about the jobs it will create, the security it will bring. Hugh and the others who fight the expansion are convinced it will devastate the valley. "They aren't widening that road for us," says Hugh, referring to the road work at Cape Horn. "They're widening it for the pulp company." And he asks why the taxpayer should subsidize the mill by paying for road repair and maintenance instead of insisting that the company ship by lake barge or rail and shoulder the real cost.

At dusk, the small village of Silverton, wedged between the lake and a steep cliff that rises towards the mountains, is quiet. Two pyjama-clad children chase a curly-haired black dog across a side street where dish antennas sprout in tiny backyards; the sound of "60 Minutes" spills through an open window. Along the back street, up against the mountain, *For Sale* signs sprout in front of neat houses. A tree planter's shovel leans against the porch of an old miner's cottage and a row of clean diapers drips from the clothesline. On the main street, a dozen sceptical teenagers listen to a man barely older than they are talk about log books and certification and the bright future in store for those who take the training program he promotes.

Feeding fish create spreading ripples on the lake, in the shadow of the dark mountains to the west. Across the road, a man pauses in the spill of light from the hotel doorway to light a cigarette. He joins his girlfriend on the side of the road, at the edge of town; they stand forlornly by a small suitcase and hopefully stick out their thumbs. When I go to bed an hour later, the hitchhikers are still standing by the road, waiting for a car to appear on the empty highway.

Ghost Towns, Good Towns

)) At two in the morning, the dream terrifies me awake. Thirteen years ago, I crossed high above Trout Lake, on a twisting, narrow, one-lane dirt road misnamed Highway 31 that links the northern ends of Arrow and Kootenay lakes, in a car with half-bald tires and automatic gears. Part-way along, a flash Kootenay storm seared down, rain so sudden and so hard that I could not see a yard ahead or behind. The car slithered in the greasy mud, close at every moment to plummeting down the steep mountainside into the lake. I was afraid to go on, unable to turn back, unwilling to stop lest someone behind crash into my car in the blinding rain. Hands riveted to the wheel, I crept down the mountain. At the bottom, at the mining ghost town of Gerrard, I pried myself from the car, and stood in the rain by the river, thigh muscles jumping.

Since then, I have ridden buses on the high and narrow roads of the Andes, piloted by drivers who trusted more to their St. Christopher's medals than to their driving skills. I have wound up and down remote logging roads, skittered along the big hill to Bella Coola with more exhilaration than fear. Only that terrifying hour on Highway 31 still haunts me.

In the dream, storm clouds gather and darken above the mountain, lightning flashes, and the dusty brown road dissolves down the cliff in pounding rain. I wake and say to the dark and empty room, "You do not have to drive that road today. You can take the easy road."

But the morning dawns sharp and clear and frosty, the night's fears foolish in the sunshine. I set out north for Trout Lake.

At the coffee house in New Denver, I order *huevos rancheros*, in honour of Latin American roads. The server shakes her head. "I don't know why they still have that on the menu. We haven't made those for ages." I settle for cappuccino and ham, egg and cheese on a bagel. Pinned to the bulletin board is a notice offering a course for New Agers with a sense of humour: Lower Your Self-Esteem Naturally. "Small unappetizing meals will be served Saturday and Sunday mornings. Meaningful certificates from Shaman University will be issued. Do you know: some crystals have no desire to be healed? Centred and balanced auras can give off unpleasant aromas?"

New Denver is a mixture of new buildings and nineteenth-century boomtown architecture. The town was born and prospered in the heady days of the Silvery Slocan, one brief decade at the turn of the century when prospectors and promoters streamed into the Slocan mountains between here and Kootenay Lake, seeking their fortunes in silver. First named, with a fine disregard for linguistic precision, El Dorado, New Denver was renamed for Colorado's silver city; most predicted the new town would soon be as prosperous as its American precursor. And it was—for a while. Waterworks, an opera house, hotels, stores, houses fine and flimsy, all the frenzied construction of a mining rush, were thrown together in a brief few months. Eager passengers came to the head of Arrow Lake by rail, then embarked on a sternwheeler that brought them down the lake to Nakusp, whence a train bore them to New Denver and the bustling mining towns in the mountains. But New Denver shared the fate of many a town born of a mining boom. Silver prices dropped, and the prospectors moved on. Though the town's position on Slocan Lake and on the railway ensured its survival, the hotels and banks no longer lured much business. Diminished but not destroyed, New Denver now lives from logging, from a saw mill and from tourism.

East of town, deep in the valley of a mountain creek, a bulldozer drones in the frosty morning air, pushing dirt down a steep bank near Sandon. Sandon was the quintessential silver–rush town, born almost full-grown in 1896 when miners poured in to wrest silver ore from the rich claims in the hills above Carpenter Creek. Shafts were sunk into the rock for more than two dozen small mines. Two thousand people moved into the houses and hotels crowded either side of main street. So steep were the mountains that enclosed this little valley and so precious the land that, at one point, this main street was built on a boardwalk over Carpenter Creek.

Unlike New Denver, Sandon lay on no natural transportation route; the only reason for its existence, deep in the mountains, was silver. When the boom died, the town died, for decades all but abandoned. During World War II, Japanese Canadians were interned in the old buildings and planted gardens along the creek. The Japanese left as soon as they were permitted to; when Carpenter Creek flooded in the 1950s, the rising waters took with them most of the remaining buildings. Now, a few old-timers and a few newcomers live in the all but deserted town.

They called Sandon the sunless city; in winter, sunlight rarely reaches the valley floor. Even now, midmorning in September, what remains of the town lies in the shadow of the mountains. The two cafes that cater to summer tourists are empty and padlocked. A loaded logging truck brakes down the long hill from the mountains where logging roads crisscross the forests, and the bulldozer and a few trucks move in desultory fashion near the old mine buildings above the town, where yet another mining company tries once more to make a living out of Sandon's silver.

Back north of New Denver, Slocan Lake ends, and the road angles across to the Arrow Lakes. Lakes no longer: the long, narrow upper and lower Arrow Lakes that show on fifty-year-old maps are linked now in one 150-mile backwards S-curve. In 1965, under the Columbia River flood control and power project, construction workers completed dams that backed water up the lakes from Castlegar to Revelstoke, flooding farms and old mining communities that once bordered the river between the two lakes.

At Nakusp, beside Arrow Lake, a painted red mushroom and a curving arrow direct mushroom pickers to a local buyer, but no one is home this morning. The local newspaper touts mushrooms as a new growth industry for the West Kootenay, yet another attempt to find a renewable natural resource that will provide an income for some of the region's residents. "The total income just to pickers could amount to $320 million in the Upper Arrow Lake Valley based on today's prices," claims an advertisement placed by a Nakusp company that buys, sorts, dries, and packages pine mushrooms much in demand in Japan. "We believe that a local firm with a self-established market in Japan and which is operated and supported by locals . . . is different from those which are just outlets for foreign markets." At the coffee shop down the street, two men in overalls are discussing last year's mushroom harvest: some pickers made two, five, even ten thousand dollars, in one brief month, they say. This year? The voices turn doubtful. The weather was too wet earlier in the year, too hot and dry over the summer. Or maybe last year's pickers stripped the woods, leaving too few mushroom spores to ensure this year's crop. Whatever the cause, pickings are slim.

North of Nakusp, floating debris marks the lake surface, some from logging, but most of it branches and roots swept down the mountain streams in spring, deposited on the shore, washed into the water, then deposited back on the shore by the dam-regulated ebb and fill of the lake. On the mountains across the lake, new logging clear-cuts show like mange on a dog. Just south of Galena Bay and the ferry north to Revelstoke and the Trans-Canada Highway, I turn east, onto my feared Highway 31.

Paving crews are out today, working on improving the road as far as Trout Lake City, population fifty-six. Just hearing the name tells you the history: Trout Lake City, one of those evanescent cities of the mining boom that followed the usual sequence of dreams, growth, decline. At the height of the city's good fortune, grande dame Alice Elizabeth Jowett presided over the elegant dining room and foyer of the Windsor Hotel. Alice Elizabeth lasted far longer than most of the miners: she operated the Windsor for fifty years, retiring when she was ninety-two. She died in 1955, at the age of a hundred and one.

The Windsor still stands, almost a hundred years old. In the restaurant, hemmed in by trays of butter tarts, muffins, cookies, and squares fresh from the oven, Lois Lesage hulls September strawberries. Lois and her husband, Bob, came from Redwater, Alberta, two years ago to manage the run-down hotel. Lois weighed 175 pounds when she arrived here; I'd guess her at about 120 now. She went from a size 18 to a size 10 in the first fifty-three days spent trying to clean up the premises. "I'm going to sell my diet: hard work," she says, and offers me a bowl of strawberries. With whipped cream. "Lucky you," says Bob Lesage. A long-haul trucker for twenty-eight years, he quit after he had a heart attack. "Only got half a heart left," he says, "but I won't wear a pacemaker." Why not? He shrugs; you get the feeling he doesn't much hold with such inventions ticking away inside his body. But he doesn't eat whipped cream.

Lois and I go upstairs to stand on the worn boards of the second-storey verandah, looking out towards the lake. "I come out here every morning in my pyjamas and look at my view," says Lois. Even though they had twenty-three feet of snow last winter, she loves the valley. In fact, the more snow the better. She is looking forward to a good winter trade from cross-country skiers, skidooers, winter hikers. In the summer, the hotel caters to fishermen angling for the Gerrard rainbow trout that run to twenty pounds. And in between, construction workers, loggers and prospectors stay here. "They all love my cooking. Even the road workers who don't stay here want my box lunches." She waves off payment for the strawberries and insists that I come back some time.

The Windsor boasts a FAX number: though only forty people live here year-round, Trout Lake City has better telephone and FAX service than most Kootenay towns twenty times its size. Ten years ago, two giant corporations announced they would open a molybdenum mine in the mountains beyond Trout Lake. Like many a miner's dream, this one collapsed in the wreckage of the metals market, but not before the phone company strung in new lines and delivered modern communications equipment.

Like most early morning fears, my terror of the road above Trout Lake seems ridiculous in the afternoon sunshine. Narrow still, dirt still, winding around the mountainside with just the occasional stretch wide enough for two cars to pass, today it is just an afternoon jaunt. But I almost wish that clouds would hide the view across the lake: directly below the wide glacier that spans the hollows of a mountain above the lake, a massive logging clear-cut reaches almost to the lakeshore. I remember the words of a Forest Ministry employee, "They sure have made a mess up there."

The road winds down to Gerrard, then along the Lardeau River, running fast and turquoise with mountain silts into Kootenay Lake. I turn at the gravel road that cuts across the marshy flats at the head of the lake, past the sign that warns potential poachers that the Range Patrol is on the job, and along the reedy lakeshore towards Argenta.

Clouds gather now, and rain falls over the mountains I have just left behind. The old Argenta wharf, its boards grey and weathered and crooked, lifts and subsides gently with the growing waves. Before the road existed, the lake was Argenta's way in and out, the wharf its meeting place with the world. Despite its name, Argenta profitted little from the mining boom in the Silver Slocan. Though packers took goods overland through the Earl Grey pass from the head of the lake here, Argenta was remote from the main line of settlements that followed the lake's west shore and the Lardeau River. For half a century, it was home to just a handful of families who farmed the bench land and loaded their produce on the weekly steamer that brought their supplies from Kaslo and from Nelson. Why did they stay in this remote, not very fertile, place? No money to go anywhere else.

I follow the switchbacked road up the hill past an orchard and across the creek. Just off the road, a simple, cedar-shaked meeting hall stands beneath the trees. A carefully crafted stone chimney climbs through the roof; the wooden deck has been carpentered around a pine tree that grows beside the hall. In one room, rows of chairs are lined up, facing each other. In another, almost like someone's private study, are comfortable chairs, shelves of books. A sense of peace hangs over this building that is a place for contemplation, for silence, for a receiving of the divine message. It is the meeting place of the Argenta Quakers. And I can envision the members of the Argenta meeting, in the words of George Fox, who founded the Society of Friends two hundred years ago, waiting together in silence, "and if anything rose in any of their minds, that they thought savoured of a Divine spring, so they sometimes spoke."

Almost forty years ago, four Quaker families from California decided to leave the militarism and materialism of the United States behind. They needed a place with existing housing, close enough to a larger centre where they could find doctors, dentists and other services, but far enough away that they could create their own community life, in close touch with the land. They chose Argenta.

Though others who are not members of the Quaker meeting share Argenta with them, the community reflects the Quaker influence. A long report on the choosing of representatives to a committee on forestry is posted on the bulletin board at the post office/community hall. No one was elected. Instead, through long discussion, a consensus emerged to entrust certain people with the task. If, as time passed, the community senses these representatives are having difficulty, a new meeting will be held, a new consensus reached. The decision reflects, not doubt in the representatives' ability, but the community's desire not to put pressure on them to succeed.

Hand-lettered signs announce that the power will be off next Friday, that phone calls protesting the smoke from logging slash burning have been effective, that users of the communal freezer should keep their possessions out of the aisle or risk losing them, that all-ages soccer takes place three times a week in the community hall, that someone wants work baby-sitting, that everyone is invited to a birthday party for Nija and Esme, that someone wants to sells a car.

Two young women walk up the road from the hall towards their homes, three young children swirling around them and into the grass and trees on the verge. Where his driveway meets the road, Hugh Herbison leans on a spade and chats with a neighbour from up the road. The neighbour bicycles away, baby tucked in his snuggle pack, and Hugh and I go up the driveway to the garden where Agnes Herbison is hoeing between rows of vegetables.

Agnes puts on the tea kettle and talks about their life in Argenta. They moved here in 1961. Hugh had been teaching in the nearby city of Nelson for eight years and thought he needed a change. They were acquainted with the Quaker community at Argenta, and when a school about nine miles away advertised for a principal, Hugh applied for and got the job.

The type of community life the Quakers had created attracted the Herbisons. "They mostly had three or four children, so there was a great little community of youngsters and teenagers where our kids felt quite at home." And for Agnes, whose great love for music is shown in the piano and the other musical instruments in the Herbisons' house, there was a wonderful surprise: a community orchestra. "That was a great find in the middle of nowhere. Our kids were learning instruments and had no orchestra to play in, in Nelson. And here was an orchestra. It was just amazing. I couldn't believe it."

People in the community put on plays, brought in National Film Board films and had monthly folk-dancing parties. "They just did a lot of good things. They were all people with university degrees, with some cultural aspirations for their kids. At the same time, they wanted them to learn the meaning of work, meaningful work like growing food."

In time, four of the Herbisons' five children went off to the outside world. Other teenagers arrived. The Quakers ran a boarding school for young people, teaching and living by Quaker principles. The students, most of them from California, boarded with Argenta families. "The young people learned how to bake bread and chop wood and wash dishes," Agnes recalls. "Some of them had never washed dishes. They helped with the gardens, milked cows, did a lot of things that were quite foreign to their experience. I think it really built something into their lives that was pretty valuable, to learn a kind of self-sufficiency. Some of them come back every now and then. A girl who came back this summer was from the first class; she went about with tears in her eyes."

Hugh has finished his garden chores; he comes in for tea. Impishly, his eyes teasing under bushy white eyebrows, he adds: "My theory was that by having several teenage kids around . . . ." Agnes interrupts. "He's pulling your leg. Don't believe a word of it." "No, really, I thought they'd do all the work, the cooking and the cleaning, and Agnes and I could sit around and counsel them."

The Quakers closed the school in the 1970s, burned out by the constant strain on the community and by the changing nature of teenagers, who now brought with them from California standards that warred with the values of Argenta.

One Herbison daughter has recently returned from Vancouver to live in nearby Nelson. Another, a classical soprano who lives in London, England, took the stage name of Nancy Argenta, an indication of how she felt about the place where she grew up. Three offspring live with their families on the forty Herbison acres. "There is a certain amount of co-operation and sharing of equipment among them," says Agnes, "and they are available to help one another, but we're not interfering in each other's lives. We don't live in each other's pockets."

For them, as for other small-town dwellers, economic survival is the key to staying. One Herbison son runs a portable precision sawmill, moving from place to place as required. "He made a marginal living doing that, sufficient until he got married and had a child," says Hugh. Now, he also works as a school-bus driver. The Herbisons' daughter is the postmistress. A son-in-law is a geologist. He and his wife planted the orchard that borders the road as it runs up the hill to Argenta. "About ten years of their lives went into raising the money to buy the land and pay for everything, and then doing everything that was involved: raising the root stock, the irrigation, the fencing." Then they sold it. But they still run the orchard for the buyers, who have gone tree-planting to make the money to finish paying for their purchase, and to support themselves until they can bring in their first crop.

Tree-planting in the summer, unemployment insurance payments in the winter: half of Argenta seems to live this way. "This community was one of the pioneers in tree-planting," says Hugh, "and probably the first community to include women on the crew." The Society of Friends runs a small press that employs four or five people part time. Last year, the press paid out twelve thousand dollars in salaries, "half of one person's salary in many contexts," notes Agnes, "but here it is divided up among four people who have, you know, whatever else, husbands, gardens. It gives them each a bit of cash."

Some Argentans work as carpenters, some do government work, some teach school. When a family needs extra money, to put a child through university, perhaps, or to buy a new car, one or all of them may decamp for the city, to get a little ahead.

But they return; the lifestyle suits them. "There aren't any social pressures when it comes to demands by the neighbours or institutions as to what people do," Hugh suggests. "If you're living in a small place, it would seem you wouldn't have much personal freedom, because the neighbours would always know what you do and so on, but there's very little pressure to conform."

That's partly because the Quaker presence has established the mythology of Argenta. Community decisions are reached by the slow process of consensus, a process that is central to the beliefs of the Society of Friends. The majority does not overrule the minority. "So often," says Hugh, "the minority is right."

"We weren't Quakers," Agnes says, "though we were always interested. We had Quaker friends when we were students, and we certainly were in sympathy." Some years later, Hugh joined the meeting. He is now clerk, the member of the meeting who records its decisions. He struggles for a simple explanation of Quaker beliefs, not easy for someone who does not deal in simple solutions. Traditional Christian theology, he says quietly, teaches that humans inherit original sin, and that they must find a way to escape punishment for this. Unitarians, Doukhobors and Quakers have no such belief. Quakers must, basically, accept their duty to seek the truth and try to live it as best they can. "More than church, priests or cathedrals, Quakers value the inner light, the divine spark that is in every person, to be nurtured in oneself and others."

Quakers and Doukhobors have had a long association. The Society of Friends contributed money, time, and effort to get the Doukhobors out of Russia and to Canada. In the early 1950s, Hugh was the lay member of a provincial commission that examined the relationship between the Doukhobors and the rest of society, and that came up with thoughtful, humanitarian, and peaceful solutions all but ignored by a confrontation-minded Social Credit government. In this corner of the world, the two groups work together for peace, visit each other's communities, become friends.

Though she is in sympathy with Quaker belief, Agnes has not joined the meeting. She may, one day. "If I joined, I would feel a sense of commitment I might wish to be relieved of sometimes. There are other things in my life I might want to put before going to meetings. But I try to pull my weight and do whatever I can."

Agnes prepares a simple supper of beans, corn on the cob, salad, home-made biscuits: "People here bake their own bread and make their own soup and grow their own vegetables as far as possible." Hugh bends his white-haired head over a teacup that needs mending. I read *The Smallholder*, an Argenta-published magazine of simple advice, questions and answers for small farmers.

As we finish supper, a woman rushes in through the door and throws her arms around Hugh and Agnes. She has crossed over from the Slocan to spend a day or two in Argenta, a place that gives her peace and strength. Together, we drive back down to the community centre. Some nights, this simple, bright community hall rings to the shouts and sounds of indoor soccer. Tonight, a formally garbed piano trio presents works by Haydn, Ives, Mendelssohn. Most of the community is here, even one man known to dislike such social occasions. Small children listen quietly at the back of the hall, waiting for lemon tarts and tea at intermission. A Guatemalan refugee, married in Guatemala to a member of the Argenta Friends and married again last week in a Quaker ceremony here, sits with his wife and with another Argentan who has spent time in Guatemala, working to help the disadvantaged.

At the end of the concert, Agnes lingers to speak with the musicians. She taught music in Nelson for years, travels to Vancouver and Victoria for concerts, treasures evenings like these. Outside, car doors close and people say good night. The stars shine brilliantly in the moonless night. With real regret, I say goodbye and drive back down the hairpins, across the creek, along the lakeshore, and back to the road that curves south on the far shore towards Kaslo.

CHAPTER 15

Coming Home: Kaslo

)) Why are some places home? Through some magic that disappears when you try to define it, they call you back again and again. The valley of the Kispiox, Tatlayoko below the mountains of the Chilcotin, have that magic for me. And as I curve through the midnight silence down the last hill into Kaslo, between the pin-prick lights that glow deep in the forest and by the lake, I feel once more I have come home.

By morning light, the serried ranks of the Purcell Mountains slide off into the soft pearl sky above the far shore of the lake. I eat breakfast on the verandah in front of my motel unit, and read the words of a *National Geographic* correspondent, writing in the 1950s, who knew about Kaslo and home: "For many months, I searched for it, knowing neither its name or its location. In truth, I wasn't searching so much as simply hoping and waiting for the town to reveal itself, to touch me with its peaceableness, to arrest me with its beauty of setting . . . . Its name is Kaslo and the sight of it will fill you with joy." Joy over granola at eight in the morning is beyond me. Instead, I listen to the muted sounds of the town across the narrow bay: people's voices, the thud of hammers, the chatter of a saw or guttural mumble of an engine.

The hammers and saws are the tools of the crew at work on the S.S. *Moyie*, the last sternwheeler to run on Kootenay Lake, a boat that has come home to Kaslo. Almost from the moment that prospectors discovered the rich silver veins of the Slocan, sternwheel steamers tackled the high waves and storms of Kootenay Lake, bringing in prospectors, settlers and supplies, taking out silver and those who'd had enough of isolation and forlorn hope. The *Moyie* arrived in 1898, diverted from the

CPR's doomed attempt to run steamers up the Stikine River towards the gold of Klondike. For six years, she spanned the gap between the ends of two rail lines at the south end of the lake; then, replaced by a newer, faster steamer, she tramped the northern reaches of the lake for fifty years, running out her gangplank to take on and drop off mail, freight, and passengers at every way stop on either shore. But by 1957, roads led to almost every lakeside settlement, and the *Moyie* was retired. No one seemed to want the boat until Kaslo brought her home. But there was no money for restoration: year by year, the hull rotted down over the timber skids, the paint peeled, and the decks dulled in the wind and the snow.

Then, in one of those remarkable acts of will a small town can accomplish, the people of Kaslo, just eight-hundred-strong, mounted a successful campaign for funds to restore the *Moyie*. Now, carpenters, craftspeople and historians work on a painstaking restoration of the boat to her glory days in the 1930s.

Dan Pasemko is one of those carpenters. For him, the *Moyie* has been a godsend. Kaslo may be beautiful; it may be home. But it's no easier to find jobs here than in any other small community remote from the big city. In past years, Dan has gone north each summer, building and maintaining forestry lookout towers. The rest of the year, he's willing to try almost anything: cabinetwork, furniture restoration, antique repair, house-building, even making caskets. "It's really difficult living in a small town and trying to make a living, especially when every unemployed logger in town is suddenly a carpenter." But the *Moyie* has become far more than just a job. Dan cares passionately about the accuracy of the restoration; his home is littered with drawings and photographs of the old ship, and he talks about the sternwheeler's days on the lake as if she should still be trundling through the waves, sounding her deep whistle as she rounds each point, calling people to the wharves.

Now in his early forties, Dan grew up in Alberta, moved to the coast, tried life on two different communal farms. He was on his way to the Queen Charlottes sixteen years ago when he stopped to see some friends in Nelson. "I stayed a few days, then a week. It was so laid back, so easy to be here." He lived in Nelson, then in Balfour, then in Kaslo, where he built a house with stained glass and a tower overlooking the town and the lake.

Though this is home, he's not quite sure how he feels about it any more. "There was a time when you could come to Kaslo in the winter, and your tracks would be the only ones in the snow. Now, it's much busier. It's been discovered. There's a community plan. A lot of people who move out here from the city try to change it into a suburb of the city, with bylaws and rules."

Yet Kaslo and the Kootenays have a hold on him. Though sometimes the city calls, it's difficult to contemplate a different way of life. Some weekends, he and his fellow carpenters on the *Moyie*, Harry and Stick, take Dan's Jeep Cherokee up the mountains along the old mining roads, past orange and blue tapes that mark the boundaries of mining claims lapsed and now renewed, finding the hopeful shafts thrust deep into the mountainside, ten, fifty, a hundred years ago, while Harry summons up stories for every place they pass. Or he and his blue heeler Yip drive up past the logging slash and weekend loggers cutting shakes, to the tree line, to walk in the soft grass and prickly mountain heather, surrounded by blue grey slopes and glaciers. It would be hard to leave all this behind.

Across the street from the *Moyie*, Gordon Brown, thin, bearded, balding, intense, sits surrounded by black and white portraits of Kaslo people he has photographed. Once supervisor of photography at the University of Calgary, Gordon grew disenchanted with the fine-arts world and moved to Kaslo in 1979, to eke out a living as photographer, draftsman, picture framer, sign painter, and graphic artist. He is building a three-thousand-square-foot house on four levels north of town, on "Kootenay time": twice as much money and three times as long to build as the original estimate. He has no plans to leave Kaslo—ever.

"It is hard to make a living here," he says. "It took me two years to figure out that I had the capability to survive without a 'real job'. But I learned that my personal freedom was probably the most important consideration in my life. Here, I'm free to act on a given creative stimulus, to pursue it, find out where it will take me. I hit the city once in a while and have a pavement fix, but I have this"—he points out his window towards the lake and mountains —"to come back to. I'm going to stay here forever."

Gordon heads off to the credit union, for some creative negotiating that will allow him to buy a much-desired large-format camera that has just come up for sale. For fun, before Gordon leaves, I ask him to point out an old reprobate to show me the other side of town. He laughs and sends me across the street. "Dick Smith," he says. "But don't tell him I said so."

Of course, I tell Dick. He is delighted with the idea, but refuses to emit a single swear word or outrageous opinion as long as the tape recorder is running. Instead, the Scottish burr still sounding in his humorous voice, elbows resting on the kitchen table in the Smiths' combined office/house, he tells me how he and his wife Deedee came to Kaslo.

At fifteen, Dick started a five-year apprenticeship at a shipyard on Scotland's Clyde, going to night school two nights a week at his own expense. "Then I had to do my national service. I had a couple of weeks' decent good money when I finished my apprenticeship, then I was dragged into the army, right back at fifteen bob a week again. So when I got out of that, I got on a boat and came over to Canada."

He worked in Montreal, helping to design destroyer escorts, but found little enjoyment being a very small cog in a very large wheel. He moved on, here and there, ending up on the west coast as an engineer working on building the pulp mill at Crofton on Vancouver Island. He had an idea he might go to New Zealand, was waiting for a cargo boat bound that way. But somehow, his money dribbled away and Dick headed east for Calgary, where good jobs were said to be available. There he met Deedee, just arrived from Montreal with a girlfriend, "young and foolish," she says with a grin. "Then I met up with this guy . . . ."

They discovered Kaslo on their honeymoon and fell in love with the town. Nine years and three children later, they made the big move, from big-city security to small-town uncertainty. "Part of the idea," says Dick, "was, if you're going to do something, you might as well do something you like. If you're going to work for somebody, you might as well work for yourself. You work a lot harder and you have something to see for it when you're finished."

Dick wanted to build houseboats he could then rent out to tourists. But Kootenay Lake is deep and narrow and treacherous: high winds rush down the lake and huge, choppy waves build fast. The normal houseboat ("boxes with outboard engines") would be suicidal. Dick wanted to build steel-hulled boats with inboard engines— an unconventional design viewed with great suspicion by the banks they approached for financing.

The Smiths convinced one bank to help, and the great plan proceeded. They bought lakeshore land from the town council, and Dick started designing, cutting, and welding. "We had a really weird welding machine," Deedee recalls fondly, "a gas machine we had to kick every morning to get the darn thing started." Not so fondly, she recalls the first winter in Kaslo, when Dick went back to Calgary to make some money, and she coped with three children, a tiny cabin in the woods out of town, and a car that always broke down. "We had two wood stoves and I had never chopped wood in my life. I didn't know anything about country living at all. It was quite an experience." She chuckles. "But it was fun. I did get on to splitting wood finally—though I always tried to get someone else to do it if I could."

Dick reads widely, from philosophy to drama to anything else he can find. They called their first boat *Cacambo*, after a character in Voltaire's *Candide*. "They're starving to death," Dick retells the story, "and Candide is thinking this is the end of it, the game's over. But Cacambo says to him, 'No, no, don't despair. A river always leads somewhere. Let's put the coconuts in the canoe and float downstream, for the place that we come to may not be any better than this, but at least it will be different.'" He and Deedee smile at each other. "So we put our coconuts in the canoe," says Deedee, "and floated upstream," finishes Dick.

Dick and I scramble into his rattletrap pickup, with the passenger door that doesn't open, and clatter down to the dock where the four boats Dick has built are tied up. We climb aboard the *Ariadne*, his new pride and joy; he shows me the fine woodwork, but his real delight is in the walk-in engine room. We walk along the water back towards his house, and he points out the old railway tracks that he still uses and the old shed where he welded his first seam. "And," he finishes dramatically, as we ascend back up past the clothesline, "these are my pyjamas."

It's midafternoon; scenting a fellow reprobate, Dick offers me a beer. The three of us sit out on the verandah beside the home-built barbecue, in rickety lawn chairs, looking across the blue lake towards the Purcell mountains in the east. Dick and Deedee have plans to build a new house here, five storeys up from the lakeshore. "And we'll put an elevator in," says Dick, "because by that time, our legs will be falling off."

Deedee's friend Rita joins us, for the ritual Thursday afternoon beer with the girls. "The girls" used to go down to the hotel lounge every Thursday afternoon, but the group got too big, too diffuse, so now Deedee and her friends gather at the Smith house instead. Rita shows pictures of her grandchildren, from a recent visit to the Okanagan. Conversation drifts to past and future riotous houseboat trips around the lake.

Rita invites me to go with her tonight to the Legion. Founded after World War I as a service organization for veterans and their dependents, the Royal Canadian Legion had its heyday after World War II. Lately,

with the number of ex-servicemen on the decline, it has become increasingly irrelevant in Canada's cities. But it doesn't limit its membership
to veterans; all you need to join is a recommendation from someone who
is already a member. In western Canadian small towns, that means
everyone who likes a good time. For women, especially those over
thirty-five, it's a haven where you can have a drink and a dance and a
few laughs, and no one will bother you unless you want them to. You
go for the Monday night crib league, the Thursday night darts league,
and the Saturday meat draw. You go there after curling or bowling; you
go there when the country and western band plays on Saturday night.

It's quiet tonight: no one chalks cues at the billiard table or scatters
wax on the shuffleboard. Cone lights on the wall illuminate the pictures
of Queen Elizabeth and Prince Philip and the Canadian and military
flags in their holders. Some of the older members, in berets and blazers
decorated with medals and ribbons, come down to the bar after a
committee meeting, for a decorous drink. Someone asks Rita where
she's been: "I saw your curtains didn't move for a week, so I thought
you must be away." She shows them the pictures of the grandchildren.
We join a table of women, who talk about their husbands and their
children. One talks about a male friend she lived with for a while, whose
ex-wife set the welfare people on her, "and I can't tell you what I did
for those children. I put my heart into it." Being single, changing
partners: the intricacies of intimacy in Kaslo, as in any small town, are
daunting. "Spring breakup" here refers, not to the melting of the ice on
the lake, but to the number of relationships that come asunder after each
long winter. A woman from Argenta speaks delicately of the "realign-
ments" that routinely take place even in that small community. One
man says regretfully he's given up on finding someone to date among
the slender ranks of single women in the town. If he does find a date,
"before we sit down to dinner, she knows more about me than I do."

Dick and Deedee show up and bartender Winston Churchill Barclay
goes into his fawning, hand-wringing "what can I bring you, sir?" act.
Though Winston's known for histrionics, sometimes dancing on or at
least in between the tables as he makes his rounds, he's subdued tonight,
toning things down because the committee is here. But you can't keep
him completely serious; in minutes, he and Dick, Scots both, embellish
their "remember the days of the Empah" routine, recalling with Sahib
accents and mock fondness those days when "we ran all the pink bits
on the map." Winston buys me a drink and invites me out to have coffee

with him and his wife Maureen the next day.

Winston is hammering away at some new creation, sweating in the autumn sun, when I arrive in the morning. The Barclays' stone and cedar house, with its magnificent view from the bench north of Kaslo out over the lake, is distant in many ways from the condominium they used to own in Calgary. One major difference is that no one is throwing rocks or making threatening phone calls. And that is one of the reasons that the Barclays now live here.

Winston's an old railwayman. He worked in the CPR shops in Calgary for almost all his twenty-seven years in Canada, a shop-floor man who at various times held seven different union positions and who was thinking of running for full-time office, heading the machinists' union in all of western Canada. Then the troubles came. The leaders of another railway union were set on taking their men out on strike. Winston was convinced the union members had not been given a fair chance to consider the company's offer. The other union went on the picket line, and Winston did some soul-searching. Finally, he decided to cross the line, an almost unheard-of move in close union circles. The machinists followed him in.

The nasty phone calls and the rock throwing began. "I decided then that the union world was a fake world, and I wasn't going to be able to change very much," says Winston, sadly. His health suffered from the conflict. He was almost fifty; one day he was struck by severe chest pain. He hurried to his doctor. "How did you get here?" asked the doctor. "Can you get yourself to the hospital immediately?" He could. He did. How strange, said the nurse who attended to him; a man in the very next room is also named Barclay. The man was one of Winston's elder brothers, long estranged, in Canada for a visit and suffering from a stroke. That same year, a third brother decided to retire. Before he could carry out his decision, he was killed in a car accident. The tragic coincidences set Winston thinking about his own health and life.

Before the union battle erupted, the Barclays had been considering moving to the Kootenays. He had connections to Kaslo: during the bitter strike, the machinists had taken on restoration and rebuilding of the *Moyie*'s old steam whistle. "It took a lot of strain off the men, to have a project going. They knew they had to cross the picket line to come to work. Some of them were coming in at four or five in the morning. The whistle gave them something to come to work for." Inside the whistle are engraved the names of the men who worked on it.

The whistle came back to Kaslo, and so did Winston and Maureen. "I was with the CPR and Maureen was working in the computer section at the Calgary hospital. Nobody believed we were going to quit. When I left the CPR, I was making $16.50 an hour." Now he works part time at the Legion, mostly to meet people, and "this summer, I took a job flagging and I made $9.25 an hour. But we don't need any more when we are raising our own food." From the time when he was a boy in Scotland, visiting his grandmother in a small village, Winston has always wanted to have a farm. Now, he and Maureen do. He takes me, pridefully, on a tour of the rabbit hutches and pheasant pens.

Down on Kaslo's main street, a noon-time ritual takes place. Like many a small town, Kaslo has its divisions: old-timers and newcomers, back-to-the-landers and loggers, visiting civil servants and main street businesspeople. Though it's not like the old days, when "the rednecks were throwing hippies through the window in the bar," to some degree you eat with your own kind. I opt for the Treehouse, home of longhairs, artists, craftspeople, *Moyie* workers. I had plans for a quiet lunch, but the table is soon crowded with almost everyone I have met in three days in Kaslo. Ken Butler, who commutes daily from New Denver to his job as *Moyie* project manager, laughs at the idea that anyone might manage a private life in Kaslo. "We recognize you three blocks away from your walk. We know if you've bought a new shirt." We joke and laugh, and then it's time to go. And, yes, leaving is a little bit like leaving home.

CHAPTER 16

East,
in Mind and Body

JJ South of Kaslo, I take the ferry across the lake, heading east in more ways than one. Loaded with all the scepticism of my western rational mind, I drive a dusty road towards the Yashoda Ashram.

Forty years ago, a German immigrant to Canada, a dancer in her early forties, lent her Montreal apartment to a group that used it for meditation. Reluctantly, she agreed to join in one session. During that meditation, she saw an unknown face. Driven by her desire to identify the face, she searched relentlessly until, one day, she found that face in the photograph of an Indian guru. She flew to India and stayed six months under his tutelage. Then she returned to North America, to westernize and update the guru's teachings. She took vows of poverty, celibacy, obedience, accepting the traditional twelve years' renunciation of the things of this world. She took the name of Swami Sivananda Radha; with her followers, she started her first religious retreat, an ashram in Burnaby. But the city was not her answer. She wanted somewhere more remote, where life and spiritual seeking were not measured to an urban beat. In 1963, she started this ashram at Kootenay Bay on Kootenay Lake. Since then, the Yashoda Ashram has provided retreat and courses in the teachings of Swami Radha.

Though the ashram is closed to the public this month and every September, Linda Pelton meets and guides me down along a gravelled path to sit beneath the cedar trees. In her teens and early twenties, Linda was a sceptic like me, atheistic and proud of it, working hard on a career that took her north, setting up mental health programs for native peoples. "It was quite remote; we had to fly in," she recalls, in her deep, slow-paced voice. "There was quite a bit of the traditional ways left, if one was interested. Which I was. Something started to rub off. I wouldn't have called it spirituality, but a way they had of seeing the universe. I felt I was missing something. I began to ask, basically, what is the meaning of life? I was very happily married, I liked my work, I had good friends, good health, everything seemed fine, but . . .," she asked herself, "this is it?"

She tried dream therapy. She talked to psychiatrists who worked with her in the north. But western psychoanalysis couldn't help with her questions about the purpose of her life. She went to see a friend's wife, who introduced her to hatha yoga, the eastern practice of achieving mental calm through body postures that induce breath control. Linda went to a workshop led by Swami Radha.

"I barely remember the content, but there was something that just really moved me. I realized they practised what they preached, and they had learned from it. I went back for a few more workshops, because, if nothing else, I wanted to know, how come they did such good therapy? I'd been working with really good people in the north, and they did good therapy . . . but not as good."

Linda and her husband came to the Yashoda Ashram for a course, then for more courses and workshops. "I wasn't really shopping, so it was really quite startling," she says of her discovery that this was her chosen spiritual path. "It was like waking something up inside. I knew this was really what I wanted." After four years of thinking—"it's a big commitment. It's very intense, and somehow the time just wasn't right"—she and her husband moved to the ashram in 1982. They have lived here ever since.

We walk past rows of fruit trees, nod to Pumpkin the cow, go past the chickens, stroke the cat that twines itself around us as we enter the workshop where ashram residents and visitors do jobs that range from car repair to woodworking. "We try to be self-sufficient," says Linda. "What we can do depends on the skills of the people here." The workshop building includes a darkroom, a recording studio for making videotapes, and computers and typesetters used for the books and pamphlets that the ashram publishes. "Our publications have just taken off in the last few years, though our market is more in the States than here."

Down by the lakeshore, the afternoon light floods in from the west through the eight-sided skylight in the dome at the top of the ashram's new temple. The octagonal temple, with eight exterior arches, is to be a temple of all religions, each side representing one faith. "There are no images inside," says Linda, "just the light. The roundness inside is symbolic of unity. The vision of the temple came complete to Swami Radha. She drew it one day on a table napkin and took the napkin to a Nelson architect. He said, 'Yes, we can build it.'"

As we walk back towards the old log building that houses the prayer room, with its orange legless chairs, Linda tries to explain the beliefs that underlie the teachings of Swami Radha. "Her guru said to western-ize, so what she has done is to update the teachings, to use a lot of the western psychological tools and combine them with what she thought was the essence of the eastern teachings. In some ways, the ashram is like a monastery, where there is that spiritual energy and support and incredibly intense focus. It's really a mixture of two things—of spiritual practice and of reflective work."

What does this mean? Linda pauses for a long moment, trying to say in a few minutes things she is still exploring after twelve years as a follower of Swami Radha. "We write a lot of what we call papers, on whatever aspects of ourselves need to be addressed. Say we had a workshop on the senses, so we do some observing of ourselves and how our senses work and take that back to our daily lives." How, she asks herself, does the way she hears or sees affect her relationship with people, and how can she change? They keep spiritual diaries, focussing on areas where they see the need for personal change. "And most of us really work with our dreams intensively."

She describes their use of hatha yoga, "the physical type, but in a different kind of way, where we go into a posture, but if you couldn't do it, you could visualize it. And in it we ask ourselves certain questions. Like the headstand is an upside-down posture, so the kinds of questions that go with it have to do with reversing our concepts. So we say, 'What is one of my cherished beliefs about myself, about the divine, about other people?' When I go into the headstand, I turn that belief upside-down. It taps into the non–rational part of ourselves, like dreams do."

The community also chants mantra as its main form of spiritual practice, as a means of becoming a vessel for the divine light. "There would be somewhat more of a Hindu flavour in our practices, because of Swami Radha's connection. But we've had people live here who are Jewish rabbis, we have had some close connection with nuns. For me, the benefit of the spiritual path is that there has to be a commitment and that you have to dig deep. If you dig a lot of different wells, then you're tasting, testing. At some point, there has to be a commitment."

Linda mentions names of other communities, other practices, other paths, with the passion of a disciple. But there is a distance between us, for I am trying to understand with my rational mind something avowedly non-rational. And as I listen, a comparison comes to that rational mind: the Quakers, letting the divine spirit shine in them, but reaching outward to the world to work for peace. Here, the teachings demand a reaching into the self, a constant self-examination. The ashram looks inward.

Monday comes, and the morning clouds give new dimensions to the mountains, fading from charcoal to soft grey in the distant mist. Not far from the ashram lies the neat little town of Riondel. Nothing on Riondel's deserted streets this silent morning gives any clue to its violent past. More than a hundred years ago, claim jumping, two years of court trials, and two further years of growing bitterness ended in, ironically, the murder of the loser of the battle by the winner. The murderer was arrested, tried, and hanged. The Bluebell mine at Riondel was worked until the late 1920s by a French, and then a Canadian company. But, by 1941, only fifteen people lived in the town by the side of the lake. Then a mining conglomerate opened the new Bluebell in 1952, and shipped silver/lead ore down the lake. In 1971, plagued by flooding and poor ventilation in the shaft, the company closed down the mine. Jobless, the miners left too. Once more, buildings were torn down or boarded up. But this time, some residents knew the value of their little community by the lakeshore, with its school, recreation centre and shops. Retired people bought up the houses and Riondel came back to life.

This morning, a pack of yipping dogs chivy each other across the streets and empty lots. Cars with Alberta licence plates are parked beside stacks of firewood in the driveways and carports of small, neat, 1950s miners' cottages. A television glimmers bluely through lace curtains. At the nine-hole golf course, a single, broken-down car is mired in the muddy parking lot: in Riondel, no one needs to rush to the course to squeeze in a round of golf before work. And it's too early in the year for curlers to wield their brooms at the curling rink housed in the big school building, no longer needed for its original purpose.

At 9:00 A.M., the store-cum-post office-cum-liquor outlet opens to rent videos, sell farm-fresh eggs and lottery tickets, distribute mail, and dispense chat about the weekend along with stamps and three-day-old Calgary and Vancouver newspapers.

South along the lakeshore road, a wild turkey struts calmly along the centre line just where a roadside sign announces *Blacksmith's Shop, Visitors Welcome*. Inside at the forge, a blacksmith sings cheerfully and off-key, "Monday, Monday, can't trust that day," while forge owner John Smith shows a new apprentice how to shape a bar of glowing steel. "Just use the hammer in your right hand, like you would an ordinary hammer. Don't use it like a sledgehammer," he cautions. He taps the steel out into a fireplace tool handle. Then he demonstrates the heavy thud of the New Little Giant Trip Hammer, built at the turn of the century. John wants this shop to be as close to the traditional nineteenth-century blacksmith's shop as he can get; his only concessions to modernity are using steel instead of iron, and propane instead of coal. "The coal gas was affecting us," he apologizes. "It's dirty, and using it adds to acid rain."

After John emigrated to Nova Scotia from England, he took a blacksmithing course, so he could smith as a hobby. The hobby soon grew into a business. He and his wife Lorna have run Kootenay Forge here since 1981; demand has grown so steadily that they need other blacksmiths to work at the forge. That creates difficulties. "Training is always a problem, because it's an unusual occupation. According to Canada Manpower," says John, "there is no such thing as a blacksmith. I have to train anyone who works here. There are very few people in western Canada who can do this," he gestures at his forge.

In the sales section of the shop, a Mercedes driver from Alberta, whose car bears the sticker, "My other car is an airplane" picks up some custom iron work. He doesn't want a bill; he doesn't want to pay the sales tax the nasty British Columbia government imposes. As two tourist-bearing cars drive in, John returns to his anvil, hammering the glowing end of steel to fatten the taper, as the other blacksmith sings contentedly at his work.

Breakfast is now a major concern. I could have eaten at the cafe where the ferry docks, but wandered on in search of a small-town restaurant where I could eavesdrop on village business. Riondel doesn't get up this early. At Crawford Bay, just beyond the forge, a sign promises a cafe a hundred yards farther on, but the grass grows knee-high around the door and the windows are boarded up. Just past the *Caution: Turkeys on Road* sign I'd like to see posted on all highways, I spy someone drinking coffee in the cafe of a fishing resort—but he's a workman and the restaurant doesn't open for passersby till 5:00 P.M.

Finally, an encouraging sign: *Open, Homestyle Cooking*—though that could depend on just whose home we're talking about, and the battered *For Sale* sign on this motel-cafe doesn't look promising. Hunger conquers discretion. Inside, pieces of mirror tile and false brick are glued to the walls, and sections of the same carpet that cover the floor are pasted both to walls and the backs of white wooden chairs. Brilliant blue lakes and green mountains blaze forth from the pictures that hang above the brick. But the coffee is hot, I'm hungry, and the owners are friendly. Fourteen-year refugees from Calgary—does everyone on this side of the lake hail from Alberta?—they ask me where I'm from, what I'm up to, then chat with the locals who drop by for coffee. The Spokane radio announcer shouts out, "LIVE! The world's favorite entertainer! Roger Whittaker! In concert! In Spokane, October 7!"

South of the restaurant, between the road and the lake, appears one of British Columbia's more spectacular oddities: a castle, complete with moats and turrets and curving bridges, built entirely from half a million empty embalming fluid bottles. How did the glass castle happen? Was one-time undertaker David Brown sitting around in his slippers one quiet Sunday afternoon, musing on the practical properties of embalming fluid bottles? Was it a moment's sudden inspiration or the culmination of long and creative questioning that burgeoned into this strange obsession?

Imitations exist, built of soft-drink bottles, but they lack the sheer practicality and *joie de mourir* of this creation. How *very* reasonable, one thinks, to see that these hollow, brick-shaped bottles would serve so well as building material. A dozen mobile homes and cars, most with Alberta licence plates, are drawn up outside the castle, their occupants exclaiming over David Brown's feat. Brown's children learned early, I would guess, not to throw stones.

Down the lake through Sirdar, named for Field Marshall Lord Kitchener, commander-in-chief, or *sirdar*, of the Egyptian army in 1892. And who possessed that piece of arcane knowledge and thought it important enough to warrant the naming of a tiny Kootenay town?

South of the lake, the steeply ascending mountains of the last week give way to the flat bottomland of the Kootenay River, protected by dykes built seventy years ago. The thirty thousand acres thus reclaimed are golden with the stubble of harvested wheat or black with rich, ploughed earth. Swans, geese and ducks float on the ponds: the wide valley is on the flyway for thousands of migrating birds who touch down each spring and autumn. The nose-tickling smell of alfalfa from a plant where alfalfa hay is pressed into cattle feed mingles with the sour, yeasty, malty smell from the brewery on the south edge of town.

Creston, on the benchland above the wide, flat valley, has the spacious, windy feel of a prairie town. Men in plaid flannel shirts stand on street corners discussing the weather and the crops. "What are you doing these days?" "Oh, the usual." Flat-roofed and single-storey like those in any other small town, the buildings here look smaller and lonelier without enclosing mountains or forests to set their bounds. Artists have painted on main–street walls, murals of mountains, orchards, an overalled farm couple, a hawk perched on a branch of a tree that bears perfect rosy apples.

Gossip swirls around the streets and through the coffee shops about the sensational trial this week of a polygamist, member of a break-away Mormon sect that lives south of town, on various charges of sexual assault against members of his large family. Oddly, for a small town where such details are more often whispered than printed, the local newspaper report of the trial is far more sexually graphic than accounts carried in Calgary and Vancouver newspapers—which have discovered for almost the first time since Sons of Freedom nude marches that the Kootenays exist.

Eastward now towards the Rockies and the whistle stop of Yahk. Once, Yahk was a major railway depot, but that species is near death. Beside the tracks, the old board and stucco hotel and its pub show few signs of life. Through a cracked railway bunkhouse window, held together by tape and plywood, I glimpse a white-haired man slumped in an old, overstuffed chair, watching dingy images on TV. What remains of residential Yahk is across the highway, by the river. Neat white-painted cottages bordered by bright flowers and vegetable gardens alternate with sagging unpainted verandahs on houses that look the same age as the *For Sale* signs that sprout in their overgrown front yards.

Through midday, the clouds stayed hooked over the hills, and for the first time in more than a week, I could see no mountains in any direction. Now, in midafternoon, the clouds break and the first sharply etched peaks of the Rockies appear. Lulled by the rhythm of the tires on the road, I drive past a rest stop where a caravan is parked and people seem to be searching the undergrowth with metal detectors. Two miles down the road, my mind wakes and I come to a sudden stop. I swing back— but my wandering eyes have deceived me. What I thought were gypsy fortune hunters are contract sprayers, dousing roadside weeds with chemicals.

I drive towards the Rocky Mountains and Cranbrook, with more than fifteen thousand people, my first big city in ten days. Tourists out to see the Rocky Mountains are here. Cars from Utah and Manitoba, rentals from Vancouver and Calgary crowd the parking lots of motel row along the highway. Cranbrook offers malls and used-car lots, steak houses, an airport and a golf course. It's a pretty city, a friendly city—but already I want to be back in my small towns.

CHAPTER 17

Rocky Mountain Trench

)) The next day dawns in glorious sunshine, and I head out again towards St. Eugene Mission. The sun shines on the stark, sandy-white hoodoos along the St. Mary River and on the grey grass and pines scattered on the arid hillsides. Near the old mission, a work crew is slapping siding onto a building beside the St. Mary's native band office. Three men are kidding the two women working at computers in the office; one of the men agrees to talk to me about life on the St. Mary's Kutenai reserve.

Speaking so softly that I must strain to hear him, David Williams describes the changes in his own life and in the people around him. "If you had come to me ten years ago, you wouldn't have got a word out of me," he says. "I would have thrown you out. I used to drink. I couldn't sit down and talk to anybody." He wasn't alone: at that time, alcohol and drug abuse was widespread on the reserve. Then David was involved in an accident—he doesn't talk about the details—and a woman he knew told him he must face up to his responsibilities instead of running away. Something in him, and in other people around him, changed.

"I think the people were getting tired of going to the graveyard over there," he gestures towards the field outside the window. "We used to have people dying every month. I got tired of seeing people beaten up. I got tired of seeing families broken up. I come from a broken home, so I know what it's like. I've heard the fights and the arguments."

Outside, you can hear the voices of children at the Ktunaxae Kinbaskit School. "All the little kids are going back to school now," says David. Before the band opened Ktunaxae Kinbaskit, native children went to what one of the other men in the office terms, with hatred, "that place over there," the old Catholic residential school of dun-coloured stone that sits up the road from the band office. "A lot of people have a lot of stories about that place," David says, mildly. "We really got the language beaten out of us, some of us. The older people, if they talked the language, they were whipped. That wasn't very good for the older people." Unlike some other band members, he has come to terms with the treatment meted out at the school. "You can't take anything away from a person unless they give it up. If the person wants it, they'll get it back."

The new elementary school run by the band has proved one way of "getting it back." There is also a language school, where elders teach the Kutenai language and traditions to children and adults. "This is where the people come from. This is learning for ourselves, about ourselves. It makes it easier when a person knows their own background. Like the white people, they have their own background, and the Chinese, they have their own background. Everybody gets to know where they come from and it helps them to get over other obstacles. It makes it a little easier to get along with other people."

David treasures the sense of tradition he gained from band elders. Fifty years ago, they would have talked to me, he says. "They would have given you a good run-around. The Kutenai bands, we're famous for our sense of humour," and throughout the conversation, he drops deadpan one-liners, testing, to see if I'll catch on. "They would have told you good stories. The stories they told were a part of my life. They'd talk about the rabbits and the coyotes having a fight. After a while, you'd find out one of them wins, eh? And what they're saying to you is, it doesn't matter how smart or how sly—like the skinkoot, the coyote, is sly and sleazy— things can happen the other way round. What they're saying is, it doesn't matter how big you are, what you are, you can still lose."

He remembers his grandfather well. "He was probably one of the last to walk to town, to still walk in and get his groceries. Then one day, he was walking back, he just died, I think of a heart attack."

An elected band councillor, David works on education, administration and social development. It is not an easy job. "Sometimes, you have to ask people to leave a house because they're not paying the rent. You hate to do that to your own people. Like when I talk to people, they're drinking and their families are having problems, then you ask the

parents to seek help. Sometimes, it's pretty hard to make these decisions." His voice drops, almost inaudible. "At the same time, you feel
good, because your help is there."

Violence has erupted between native and white at Oka, in Quebec;
British Columbia natives have blockaded road and rail to make a
forceful point about incursions on their land. When he saw the confron-
tational images of Oka daily on television, was David emotionally
involved? "No, not emotionally. We see pain and hurt here every day,
so you have to learn to grow with it. All people want you to do is listen.
That's all the people at Oka want too, is someone to listen." He sits up
straight. "But if they did end up starting a war there, there would have
been a lot of people from here going."

The Kutenai here have filed a land claim. What do they want?
Straight-faced, "All of B.C. No, that's what the white people are afraid
of. They hear land claims and they think we want to take their houses,
their garages, everything they have. That's not what it is. If somebody
built their house on a piece of land, we want a land exchange." He tries
to explain why. "They can't understand, how come we want all this. It's
our life. This is pretty well our last stand. This is where we'll be until
the end of time." As long as the band has just its white-ordained reserve,
"I feel it's like a jail without a fence."

When the white man came, the natives were willing to share the land,
but, says David, the white man hasn't treated the land very well. "When
I was a kid going to school, I used to be so proud of our river, because
it was red. I didn't know it was poisoned, eh? I just thought, 'God, I like
the colour of that river.' Then I finally realized water wasn't supposed
to be that colour.

"One of our chiefs a long time ago, he said, the white man is welcome
to stay as long as the grass is green, the waters are clean and you can
breathe the nice air. Well, I told one white guy, I think it's time for you
guys to pack up and go home. The grass ain't green no more, with the
chemicals and everything, and the waters aren't clear." He shakes his
head, mock puzzled. "He didn't think that was very funny."

Isaac comes in from the front office, kidding, pretending I mustn't
learn his name but letting it slip anyway, trying to find out what the
white woman wants here. He turns serious. He lost a job he valued, that
he held for eleven years, because of his drinking. Now he's dry, and
celebrating "getting my dignity and my mind back." When he was a
boy, Isaac danced the traditional prairie Indian grass dances; then, the

bad parts of life intervened, and he stopped dancing for twenty-seven years. Now, he is dancing again.

"I'm starting to perform at pow-wows all over. At one, there were seventeen drums pounding, at least ten singers per drum, and I got out and danced around them. They cheered me on. I was overwhelmed." As Isaac finds pride in his dancing, so the band finds pride in its school and its projects to build agriculture and tourism on the reserve. "We're looking ahead," says Isaac. "We're getting out of the gutter."

Less than half an hour's drive away, Fort Steele stands as a reminder of the divergent realities lived by native and white. It's an odd place, this fort that never really was, named for a man who spent just a year here, called in to solve a problem that should not have arisen. Fort Steele was born as Galbraith's Ferry, named for the man who ran a ferry across the Kootenay River here when gold fever ran high in the 1880s. As elsewhere, the coming of the gold seekers brought white settlers and white law to the region. The local magistrate, Colonel Baker, fenced in and began surveying land long used by the St. Mary's band natives for grazing. At the same time, surveys began for Indian reservations to which the bands would be henceforth confined. Bad feelings flamed when Baker arrested an Indian, on the flimsiest of evidence, for the murder of two American prospectors who had gone missing in the mountains. Chief Isadore and his followers stormed the jail and secured the man's release; Baker called for the North West Mounted Police.

Major Sam Steele brought seventy-seven NWMP men and officers with him, built a small post near Galbraith's Ferry and quickly negotiated an end to the "crisis." He then left the territory, but grateful locals changed the name of the settlement to Fort Steele. The fort was not then or ever legitimately graced with a stockade like the one that now surrounds the tourist re-creation, enclosing a few renovated buildings from the original town, buildings moved from other pioneer towns nearby, and reconstructions based on what existed at the turn of the century.

Now in a modern September, the actors who in summer play nineteenth-century roles have hung up their costumes, and the wide grassy spaces within the stockade are all but empty of tourists. Though a bus tour is on the grounds, by judicious positioning, I can hide them behind frame buildings and log barns and look down deserted streets I people from my own imagination. Then an American in a bright pink shirt appears on the staircase that leads to the restaurant and hollers across the grass, "We're over here. We're having lunch here." Like cockroaches emerging when the light is turned off, bus tourists pop out of doorways and scuttle for food. "Looks all right," says one, wheezing up the stairs towards the cafeteria. "Makes a change from McDonalds." He orders a hot dog and a Coke.

The line slows, stops. An American at the front of the line berates the cashier, who politely regrets that he cannot give back American change. "We won't come back here," snorts the tourist. "We'll go to Hawaii." The cashier manages a fixed smile. "Who *is* he?" asks another tourist, embarrassed. "Is he one of our group?"

Outside, two motorcyclists in neck-to-toe bright red and white leathers stroll hand in hand across the grass. Their bike, in the parking lot, is red and white as well, right down to the Alberta licence plates.

Fort Steele lies at the confluence of the St. Mary, Wild Horse and Kootenay rivers, below the westernmost peaks of the Rocky Mountains. The wide flat valley that brackets the Kootenay River to the north is part of the Rocky Mountain Trench. On the map, the trench is a sinuous slash between the Rockies and the succeeding chains of mountains to the west, reaching more than 850 miles from Montana to the Yukon. From here north almost 150 miles, river marshes and benchland forests provide homes and resting places for ducks, geese and swans, beaver and muskrat, deer and elk.

I turn off at the mill town of Canal Flats and sit looking out over a marshy slough, pondering how little human ambitions change. A low ridge, little more than a mile wide, divides the Kootenay from the Columbia river here. A century ago, an English adventurer euphoniously named William Adolph Baillie-Grohman devised a scheme to join the rivers by canal, draining the waters of the south-flowing Kootenay into the north-flowing Columbia. One could thus, he suggested, end the floods that yearly inundated the flats that flanked the Kootenay River downstream at Creston and create safe, fertile, and permanent farmland there.

No philanthropist, Baillie-Grohman envisioned great riches flowing to him and those wise enough to invest in his canal project. One of those dreamers, by turns bombastic and visionary, common on the frontier of nineteenth-century North America, Baillie-Grohman drew word pictures of a fine colony thriving on the farmland thus created. The colony would, of course, be British to the bone: other races need not apply to breathe the pure Kootenay air of the settlement. Syndicates were formed and investors inveigled. The project suffered through quarrels and law courts, shots in the night, land grants and leases, protests and retractions, Baillie-Grohman viewed as either a hero or a teller of tall tales. In the end, the project was reduced to a narrow canal to link the rivers at the flats. But the government decreed that, to protect the rights of existing farmers and settlers, the locks on the canal must be closed during the very months that the syndicate required them open to keep the Creston flats from flooding.

Baillie-Grohman liked to call himself and others trying to make their fortunes in the western colony Busted Britishers. With his project busted too, he went home to England, where he wrote books and gave lectures filled with inventive tales of his own derring and almost-do in the Canadian wild west.

No one calls B.C. Hydro "busted." When the provincial power corporation looked greedily at this same narrow neck of land in the 1970s, and talked about reversing the Kootenay into the Columbia to produce more hydro-electric power, people in the valley took them very seriously indeed. Opposition was immediate and effective: the plan was halted. Yet every few years, whispers of it resurface, buoyed by calculations of how much power could be produced and sold at a profit to the Americans. Somnolent in the sunshine, watching ducks paddle in the slough, I can only hope the promoters always fail.

The highway follows the shore of Columbia Lake now, the headwaters of the mighty Columbia River system, then swings around the Dutch Creek hoodoos, pinnacles sculpted by thousands of years of wind and rain—or, if you prefer, part of the skeleton of a giant fish that once moved along the Rocky Mountain Trench. It died at Canal Flats; one-half of its ribs formed these hoodoos, the other half hoodoos near Fort Steele.

The warm lakes and mountain beauty of the wide valley that stretches north from here for fifty miles have attracted many Albertans, who flee the harsh prairie weather for the milder playground of the trench. I turn away from the resorts, condominiums, cabins and houses that cluster on the mountain slopes and beside lakes Columbia and Windermere, and take a road through scrub brush and logged-off hills above Windermere Lake. Just at the outskirts of the town of Invermere, I almost drive off the road. Yes, a dozen eight-foot-tall ostriches *are* rubbernecking over a backyard fence.

These gangly creatures are the future for Jim and Karen King. Jim goes behind the strands of wire to show off Big John, the 350-pound, eight-foot prize cock? rooster? stallion? of the flock. "They can be quite friendly," he reassures me as he ruffles Big John's glossy dark brown feathers. "Of course, they are very curious and they peck a lot to investigate," and Big John lowers his head to Jim's. "That can take getting used to." But the King kids are only a little wary, and the cat walks unconcerned around the corral. When the birds arrived, the Kings were the most popular kids in school: no one else had ever even seen a live ostrich. Things have calmed down a little now and everyone has their ostrich chores. "The kids feed and water them," says Jim, "and I say hello to them once a day." Karen grins. "Oh, come on, you look at them a lot more than that!"

Forget llamas, forget Norwegian fjord horses, forget, if you hadn't already, silver fox farms. Ostriches are the wave of the future. Jim and Karen sold their house, bought some land for their new ostrich ranch, built a new house and acquired their flock of twelve birds, all in the space of six months. Now they talk about ostrich ranching with the fervour of complete converts. In their house, the *Ostrich News: Heartbeat of the Ratite Industry* vies for space with arrangements of ostrich feathers and huge, hollow ostrich eggs. Jim waxes enthusiastic about the potential. The ruby-red meat, similar to beef but low in cholesterol and fat, high in protein, will soon be in great demand. Already, the few ostrich butchers that exist get twenty dollars a pound for the meat. The leather, soft, durable, made distinctive by its little feather holes, can be cobbled into upmarket cowboy boots that sell for six to seven hundred dollars a pair, or made into briefcases, purses or belts. The feathers retain their magnetic attraction for dust despite repeated washings: General Motors uses them on their new cars, says Jim. The eggs—well, if you were very hungry, you could eat a five-pound egg, equivalent to two dozen chicken eggs, and use the shell for a lampshade, a vase, a whole panoply of crafty household items.

Getting into the ostrich-ranching business isn't cheap. A good breeding pair or trio (the females get shortchanged, as usual) can cost forty thousand dollars, and a proven six-year-old producing pair could set you back sixty-five thousand. On the other hand, the average ostrich in captivity matures in two to three years and lives to be fifty to seventy-five. As befits a valuable beast, most of these birds are micro-chipped, with a little chip implanted behind the neck, its ten letters and five numbers readable by scanner, to guard against inbreeding. The Kings plan to raise their birds to maturity, then sell seven and keep five as their ranch herd.

I leave, bemused. Could I ever learn to love a bird three feet taller than me, with bony runner's legs and knobbly knees, with a burly body and a snaky neck that ends in a head all beak and haughty eyes, a bird that likes to peck just to show he cares? I think I'll have to seek my fortune elsewhere.

North again, the highway follows the terraces above the valley where the channels of the Columbia River twist through the wetlands, below the Douglas fir forests on the first slopes of the mountains. A west wind is hustling through the valley, ruffling the surface of the sloughs and flattening the cat-tails. White Charolais cattle lie, sleepy, in green pastures that front the fir trees and the rhomboid shape of Steamboat Mountain. Ducks, too distant to be clearly identified, float among the reeds, and a kingfisher flashes away from a log bridge across the river, two parallel boards angled over round logs. Overhead, a pair of magpies try out their various voices from the top of a river poplar, then swing away, their long tails propped on the wind.

At Radium Hot Springs, Our Lady Queen of Peace Shrine and Stations of the Cross, built in the 1970s as a tourist attraction, has been sold. Across the gravel road from the shrine, three trailers—daddy, mummy and baby-sized—are parked next to a ramshackle log building, and burly, wooden, chain-sawed men and women line stolidly up in front of a gift shop. But there is no sign of Rolf, the fluorescent-haired (some days green, some days orange) chain-saw carver. Someone says Rolf has closed his business for the winter and gone up the mountain to work on his tree-thinning contract. Someone else conjectures that he has flown back down to South America, where he likes to visit remote Indian tribes, or hitch a ride to Antarctica with whichever navy is making the long trip south.

The Great Green Toad and Bufo, in the seventeenth year of their assumed lives, lurk underground in the Parks Canada building near Radium. Bufo, officially known as Kootenay National Park naturalist Larry Halverson, guides me through the maze to the office he and the GGT share: "It's easy: it's a government building, so you just go round in circles." The toad himself, chief park naturalist Ian Jack, and Bufo (small guffaw here for naturalists' Latin joke) were born of the river, the only known specimens of the monstrous Columbia River Toad, a beast suspected in a multitude of cattle and chicken kidnappings.

Ian has been at Kootenay for twenty-four years; the GGT expedition was born shortly after Larry arrived at Radium eighteen years ago. "We decided we would drift a section of the river every once in a while, where it's still semi-wild," recalls Ian. "Even people in our own field had trouble just relaxing. When people caught on, that they didn't have to paddle like hell, that they could just drift, climb up on the terraces, they had a real relaxing weekend." Now the GGT is an annual expedition, recognizable by its toady cry, "How deep is the water there? Knee-deep, knee-deep, knee-deep."

No one suggests that the toads have trouble relaxing. Larry was so enraptured by his five children that he took to bringing their photographs to work, filling each coffee break with new pictorial displays and cute stories. Ian watched for a while; one day, he brought in photographs of the cattle he raises north of Radium, and, bestowing on each beast a cute name, he embarked on stories of their latest accomplishments. Larry leaves his pictures at home these days.

Then there was the time that open season was declared on ravens, and city folk down in Vancouver expressed their environmentalist dismay. The Columbia Valley had a surfeit of ravens at that time. Larry and Ian wrote straight-faced letters to the editors of the Vancouver papers, encouraging people to shoot ravens and including such things as a recipe for cooking the birds: "Put the raven in a pot with water and a rock. Boil. When you can stick your fork into the rock, the raven is done."

The jokes and the GGT expedition are expressions of Ian's and Larry's delight in the Columbia Valley. "This valley is so incredible," says Larry. "You have winter sports, skiing and cross-country and mountaineering and skating. Some years, the ice on the lake is so clear, you can see the fish below. You can take the kids tobogganning, and build a fire on the river. In the summer, you can canoe down to a cafe in the next town for supper, or just go floating down the river." The valley below, the mountains above: after eighteen years, he can still be surprised by the variety and the beauty of the terrain, the flora, the fauna. "Yesterday, I was working on a goat survey by helicopter. We came across a lynx at seventy-two hundred feet. That's very unusual. Here, every day can be different."

That feeling for the valley is also expressed in their battle to preserve it. When B.C. Hydro planned its Kootenay River diversion, Ian helped lead an army against the plan. "We had no trouble organizing people.

We had forty different agencies in there. Now, the wetlands may be designated as a wildlife management area," which would protect them from development, "and we've had a commitment from Hydro that they are going to remove their flood reserve. The key now is some kind of good plan for the valley."

Incomers have always seen the potential of the valley; for many, recognizing that potential means development and change. "There are always wheeler dealers who want to come in and do this, that or the other thing. Some of them want to make the whole valley into a golf course." He smiles. "They're a challenge. It wouldn't take us long to get enough people out to put an end to that kind of nonsense."

At Radium, most of the tourist traffic veers into the Rockies, Banff and Lake Louise. The road I follow up the valley skirts tiny communities that lie, barely glimpsed, between the river and the road. Just south of Spillimacheen, population sixty-eight, Art Galbraith has hung his flannel shirt on his runner beans and digs carrots in the autumn warmth.

The last time I saw Art, he was the resident river rat on the Great Green Toad expedition, floating with the current in a yellow rubber dinghy, a fringed yellow lawn umbrella shading his head, tootling on a harmonica. Art's grandfather came south up the valley from the mountain passes more than a hundred years ago. The firs grew thickly then, and he couldn't see clearly the lake that sparkles a few hundred yards from where we stand. But he knew he had come home. "The valley opens up right here," says Art. "You can see why he chose it."

Art's mother was born here ninety-two years ago; Art was born here in 1921. "When I was thirteen, fourteen, fifteen, we'd go out into the mountains to saw logs, out in the dark in the morning and back in the dark at night. Me and another kid were up at the lake one time. We corralled a wild cow, put the calf away, milked the cow. You had to look after yourself then." Different from kids now, his face says.

Art worked as a logger, a sawmiller, a miner. The last job he had, as a foreman on the national park trail crew, was the best. "I travelled all over the mountains. I try to tell people, but it's hard to explain. It's so beautiful." The rest of the crew would be eager to get back to warm beds, hot showers, and TV. "I'd get up there, and I didn't want to come back."

Though he is officially retired now, Art still cuts Christmas trees every year and sends them off to Calgary. "I've done that for thirty years. It doesn't seem right till I do that." And he still goes trapping down on the river every spring. He makes water sets for beaver in April or May, when the ice breaks up, canoeing half a mile away from the beaver houses so the little ones won't get caught. "I set deep, eighteen inches or so, so I catch the big ones. The small ones, when they climb out of the water, the small ones don't get their paws down so deep. And I put rocks in the traps, to make sure when the beaver get caught, they drown right away."

Art looks across the garden, towards the river. "You got to catch so much, otherwise you lose your trapline. The government takes your line away. But, you know, now I'd just as soon just go out on the river and watch things." He starts digging carrots again, then looks up at the mountains. "I'll be right here until I die."

The road climbs northward and the mountain rock walls close in upon the river. But, as I drive north, if I turn my head, I see what Art's grandfather saw: the green and widening valley, flashes of blue lake and turquoise river, pale marshes rising into fertile benchland, and the green-black silhouettes of the mountain firs.

CHAPTER 18

On the Tourist Trail

JJ Where the Kicking Horse flows into the Columbia at the city of Golden, the Rocky Mountain Trench highway
meets the Trans-Canada. For the first time since I left the Okanagan,
motels sprout *No Vacancy* signs, their rooms filled with European,
Japanese and North American tourists doing the Banff-Jasper-Radium
circle through the Rockies.

It's just above freezing when I wake in the morning, and the car
groans reluctantly into life. But bright sunlight soon floods over the
mountains. Two young elk stand unconcerned beside the highway east
of Golden; a few minutes farther on, backlit water curtains over a wide
arc of rock. A flagwoman bundled in down jacket and woolly scarf
waves traffic past the inevitable road construction. Last week, a television crew came to film this traffic on what they labelled the most
dangerous stretch of road in Canada. At first, it seems just the usual
British Columbia highway of cliff-hugging curves and long hills, but I
soon realize that the traffic combination here makes this road more
frightening than more perilous back roads. Heading up a long hill, I am
the sandwich filling between a dauntingly slow mobile home with
Quebec licence plates and an empty Alberta fourteen-wheeler, whose
driver, eager to get home, considers two feet a safe following distance.

I escape from the traffic at Field, a town of two hundred, once a major
railway construction camp, now the headquarters of Yoho National
Park. At the Siding Cafe, a woman whose husband works for Parks
Canada moves along a bench at the communal table to make room,
herding her two children with her. After coffee, she'll deliver the kids
to a bus that will take them up into the mountains, to Lake O'Hara, with

a group of parks old-timers, who'll show them around and tell them about the birds, the animals, the rocks and the other wonders of the mountains. She would like to go along, but no private vehicles are allowed on the road to the lake, and the bus was full before she got a chance to sign up. So she'll wander down to Golden and amuse herself in town for the day.

A man in Parks Canada uniform demonstrates with his hands how he ran his truck into the ditch up by the bridge the other day. The truck jack-knifed, front wheels down in the ditch, trailer hitch high-centred and the horse trailer with two horses aboard angled back down onto the road. He unloaded the horses and tethered them, jacked up the front wheels of the truck alternately, putting boards under them to hold them steady, then finally inched the truck back out onto the road. "I wasn't going to call for help—especially not from you," he tells his coffee buddy, knowing that long months of merciless teasing would have been the price of help.

"What about that guy who locked himself in the toilet the other day?" asks one of the coffee group. The Parks Canada man laughs. He was headed for coffee when he saw a truck parked outside the biffy, engine running. He thought maybe he should check, but coffee was a greater lure. Half an hour later, the truck was still there. "That man was there from ten to nine till after ten o'clock. He said he was about ready to tear the sinks off the wall to make a fire." He grins. It will be a long time before the kidding stops on this story.

Back on the highway, traffic continues to build: long-distance haulers and gravel trucks, mobile homes, rental cars, motorbikes. Some turn north on the road to Takakkaw Falls, where water spills almost thirteen hundred feet from a high valley into a lower one. In the parking lot, the vehicles are almost all white rental cars and mobile homes from Calgary and Vancouver. Two young Germans in serious hiking shorts stop to don heavy boots and packs, and are preceded up the trail by a mini-vanload of camera-festooned Japanese in bright shirts and running shoes, wearing tags that say, more or less, "If lost, return to Jalpak Tours." Behind them come a young couple from Calgary, she in tights and ballet slippers, he in ragged high-top runners; a trio of Europeans in knickerbockers and down jackets; and a man of unidentifiable origin in a shabby suit and tie. In line, we march along the short path to the falls, agree they are worth of their name (which means "it is magnificent"), take pictures, turn about, and march back to the parking lot.

Back towards Golden, campers tow cars, cars tow trailers, long-haul truckers hunch over their wheels impatiently, paving trucks trundle gravel to road repairs. Albertans in Oldsmobiles tailgate each other at eighty miles an hour on the straights, then slow down to twenty astraddle the double yellow line round the sharp curves. We form a slow-moving parade down a long hill, first gear all the way, first a double-trailered gas tanker with air brakes chuffing, then what looks like an old milk truck converted to camper van and painted sunshine yellow, three white rental cars, and a car cowboy from Medicine Hat, pushing his old boat of a Plymouth along two feet from my back bumper. He can't go past the parade, but he seems determined to go under, through, or over.

Enough. Just east of Golden, a gravel road leads to the back country.

On the old Golden-Donald road, all is quiet, not even a shambling bear pausing to stick a curious paw into the old tin cans at the town dump. Someone has parked two fraying lawn chairs in front of a rickety camper levered up on blocks beside the road. In one man's yard, the rusting remains of every car he's ever owned lie at odd angles in the long grass. The breeze stirs the topmost leaves of the aspens, turning gold now, curious horses poke soft noses through the roadside fences, and cows lie heavily in the shade of the trees. Near a junction, a moustached man whose belly rounds his T-shirt wields a lazy paintbrush on the fence at the community hall, just up from the "Ma" and "Pa" outhouses. I raise a hand. He waves the paintbrush. Eventually, I run out of gravel road and must descend to the Trans-Canada once more.

Unbelievably, the road is almost empty. It snakes westward towards the boundary of Glacier National Park and the blue-white glaciers and jagged peaks of the Columbia Mountains. Missing meals has become a habit on this trip; my back road detour took me away from the restaurants of Golden. I break one of my primary travel rules: *never* eat at a major tourist stop on the Trans-Canada Highway, especially if it advertises seating for bus tours. Especially if it's the only restaurant on a long stretch of highway.

In the self-serve cafeteria behind the fancy lodge lobby, tired hot dogs turn on greasy spikes. The special, homemade chicken soup, comes with half an inch of fat floating on top, and a small glass of milk costs a dollar. An overweight, whey-faced table clearer looks at my disgruntled face, at the fat I have ladled into a saucer, and says, tiredly, "It's hard when you get a thousand people a day through here." Taking a coffee break, the bus girls complain bitterly about the shifts they are working at the end of the four-month-long tourist season, and a bus boy takes desultory swipes at a dirty table with a greyish rag. I finish my meal quickly.

At Revelstoke, where a short stretch of the Columbia River joins Lake Revelstoke, reservoir for a hydro dam, to Upper Arrow Lake, I find an almost-perfect motel, just blocks from the river, away from the highway traffic but close enough to the train tracks to hear the deep horns that sound the end of a railway era. Back in the days of steam, everyone who came to Revelstoke came by train: workmen and prime ministers, kings and housewives. But no more. Except for tourist specials, no passenger train now travels the tracks through what was born as a railway town. I walk across an old one-lane bridge, boards under my feet, cars jouncing past on the metal mesh deck. Below the bridge, the Columbia River flows, the first route through this region for native people and for white explorers and settlers. Just to the north, a train chugs past on the railway tracks: Revelstoke was founded with the coming of those tracks in 1885. North again, the new Trans-Canada Highway bridge crosses the river, speeding travellers on their way to somewhere else. My random musings on history are interrupted by the manifestation of another historical fact: I am near what the natives called SkExi-kentEn, "the mosquito place." Scratching, I turn back to town.

This land near the river is Lower Town, once known as Farwell. In the early 1880s, Arthur Stanhope Farwell, government and railway surveyor, guessed that the CPR tracks would cross the river here and applied to the provincial government for a land grant along the river. He laid out a townsite, and waited for the sound of train whistles and the clinking of money. But no one holds the CPR to ransom, then or now. The company refused to pay Farwell's price for the land, and laid its tracks and built its station on higher ground. The Canadian government proceeded to grant land to other claimants; the overlapping provincial and federal grants left the townsite in a litigious stew, and held back town development until 1898, when the claims were finally sorted out.

Many of the houses and stores built near the railway station once the property dispute was settled still grace Revelstoke's downtown. In the early dusk cast by the surrounding mountains, I walk past neat, restored houses, with gingerbread trim and roofs steeply angled to shed the heavy snow that falls here, along the cobbled streets of downtown where ornate metal lampposts stand before the restored fronts of square, uncompromising post-Victorian commercial buildings. Above the town, the peaks of the surrounding mountains catch the last rays of the September sun.

Ruby Nobbs has lived in a small, neat house, three blocks from downtown, for most of her life. Her father, a railway worker in Scotland, came to Revelstoke in 1905, drawn by advertisements for railway workers. He went back to Scotland in 1906, to ask his childhood sweetheart to marry him, then returned to Revelstoke and bought this house for her. "The CPR had told the people of Donald [eighty miles east]," Ruby explains, "that Donald was going to be the permanent divisional point, so they had gone ahead and built substantial homes instead of just shacks and log huts. When the CPR decided they were going to move the divisional point to Revelstoke, there was consternation among the people of Donald. To pacify them, the CPR agreed to move their buildings here. This was one house that was moved."

Ruby's family moved to a bigger house across the street when she was a young child, in 1916. When she got married in 1929, she and her husband bought back the little house. She has lived here ever since.

For decades, Ruby lived the railway. Her father, Jock Rutherford, was a locomotive engineer; for forty-three years, he drove the steam trains west to Kamloops and east to Field. "My mother used to say she never knew when dad went to work in the winter whether he would be home the day after tomorrow or the week after next. There were snow slides in the winter, mud slides in the spring." When a railroader went out he never knew when he'd be coming back.

They called Jock "the Royal Engineer" because he had driven trains that took dukes and duchesses, kings and queens, through the mountains. Jock didn't talk much about his work; what the family learned, they learned from other kids' dads. Jock did talk about one accident, when boulders the size of the dining room table rolled down a mountainside, and the engine tilted precariously but righted itself; nine cars were tumbled down into the fast-flowing river by the slide. "I suppose they released the steam right away," says Ruby. "They usually did, to safeguard the engine."

Ruby was just a young child when she first rode on a steam train. "In those days, it was the coaches where you could push the windows up, so you'd get all the coal dust in your face. We liked to go east, because when you went east, it was an oil burner, so you didn't get the dust and cinders. My mother always had bananas and oranges and ice wafers, real treats to sort of keep the kids occupied."

Not all the memories are good ones. Just two years and three months after Ruby married in 1929, her husband was killed in a train accident. "His son was born six days after he was killed," she says, still emotional after all these years. "It was kind of a rough haul through the Depression. But either you give up or you pick yourself up and go on." Ruby picked herself up. Ten years later, she married Wilfred Nobbs.

She worked as a schoolteacher, then as manager of a bowling alley she and her husband bought. Time dragged when she retired in 1981, so she "worked like a Trojan" at the museum, got involved in a greenbelt committee for the town, and worked for restoration of Revelstoke's historic downtown. "Revelstoke is as old as Vancouver," she notes, "but look at the size of Vancouver. That's part of the reason we have so many heritage buildings in the old town. In most places as old as Revelstoke, the old frame buildings have been torn down and replaced by modern structures. Here, they haven't been." Ruby gives full marks to local businesspeople and the town council, who worked valiantly to restore the old buildings. Now Ruby is at work on a history of Revelstoke, using material she unearthed while writing a newspaper column on local history.

Her heart remains with the now-absent passenger trains. On November 7, 1985, the centenary of the driving of the last spike on the CPR, Ruby was invited to a re-enactment of the famous event. Her son took her down to the railway station before seven in the morning. "I was just standing there, talking, when I heard the steam engine coming along the tracks. I wouldn't have believed it would have had such an effect on me," and the tears are close now, just remembering. "I can't explain— but to look into the dim, breaking day and see this huge steam locomotive coming towards you, its headlight on, puffing out steam and smoke from the smokestack. There was something alive about that steam engine, throbbing there. I was just overwhelmed by it."

At dinner, the waitress gives the couple at the next table a minitour of Revelstoke. Looking for action? The best bet would be the Hug 'n Slug, the local name for the hotel beer parlour where cowboy wannabes hang out. "One minute they're hugging, next minute, they're slugging," the waitress explains.

Someone has big plans for a new ski resort, but the waitress emphatically disapproves. "I sure hope they don't. We're doing just fine the way we are. If I want to live in a busy place, I'll move to one." The couple asks her about bears, and she tells them about the bear that treed a golfer the other morning. "He was sitting up there throwing his golf clubs at the bear," and I grin at the picture of a terrified golfer scampering up a tree, but remembering to take his golf bag with him. "They came and tranquilized the bear and took it away. Don't worry about bears, though. They only come down when the kokanee spawn."

I fall asleep to the sound of train horns and wake to a sunny day. I had planned to continue on the Trans-Canada, through the Shuswap Lakes country to Kamloops and home. But the Trans-Canada oppresses me with its loaded trucks, speed jockeys, signposted viewpoints, sullen waitresses and tired tourists. Three hundred rental houseboats now ply the Shuswap Lakes. On what is probably the last summery weekend of the year, they may all be on the water and people will crowd onto the beaches with barbecues and loud radios. I turn south again, to follow less frequented routes.

Only a car or two shares the thirty miles of winding pavement south from Revelstoke to Shelter Bay. Near the dock where the ferry carries traffic across Upper Arrow Lake, a convoy of army trucks trundles north, ten trucks on the road, a further ten trucks marshalled by the side of the road, another group on the ferry itself. Baseball cap mania strikes here too: even the army drivers are wearing them. On the twenty-minute ride across the lake, tourists from Ontario ask about the best route to take back to the Okanagan, but are dubious about the mountain routes through the Slocan to Kaslo and back along the southern highway. They are entranced by the scenery, but not quite ready to dare narrow mountain roads.

Beside the road from Nakusp to the ferry that crosses back over Arrow Lake, osprey nests are perched atop the crossbars of hydro poles, but the ospreys have gone south for the winter. At the dock, a lone ferry crewman methodically unloads and stows life jackets on the small cable ferry, ignoring the waiting line of traffic. When departure time arrives, the crossbar by the dock lifts and the crewman turns his back. Passengers are expected to know how to get their vehicles aboard and into whichever line seems convenient.

On the far side of the lake, westward again from the ferry dock, the road curves and climbs rapidly through cedar, spruce and pine. At the Spruce Grove cafe, just beyond the Monashee summit, two logging truck drivers drink coffee and trade truck talk. The first time one of them tried to make it up one of the logging roads that leads off this highway, he stuck fast in the mud and had to be hauled out. "There was one guy in the snow, he was barefooting it, he wouldn't put no chains on, the other guys had two and a half chains, but he made it, he knew the road."

They talk about other places they have worked. "I worked Fort Nelson," up on the Alaska Highway, says the second driver. "You should see the riff-raff there. Guys that are broke, they're going to work double shift and pay off all their bills in a month. But they get nothing but grief." Making a living, dealing with isolation: constants of a small-town life.

The road winds down into the dry hills and irrigated fields of the Okanagan Valley. Signs of the city appear: a subdivision with the "best of rural living," name brand furniture for less, luxury adult condominiums, car dealers, four-lane roads, fried chicken, traffic. I cross the valley quickly and head west from Vernon, past new retirement communities filling with prairie and Ontario people tired of winters that are too long and snow that is too deep, drawn by the dry climate here and the promise of a lifestyle that is city, but not *too* city.

Away from Vernon, the traffic thins again, but for once I am caught by the rhythm of the road and do not dawdle. Gone are the enclosing chains of mountains; the dry country stretches ahead, scattered lakes, spreading pines, rounded hills repeating towards the western sun. I had planned to spend the night in Kamloops, but fly past the advertisements for tourist services, next six miles, past the cloverleaves and flashing neon signs.

Half the traffic flows away along the four-lane, limited-access Coquihalla Highway, an hour shorter to the coast than the older routes. The Trans-Canada twists west, between wind-sculpted hills, cutting along the bench above the sunlit flash of the Thompson River, between the irrigated hayfields and the grey green rabbitbush that spots the ridged slopes. Above the road still curve the shattered wooden flumes that once carried water from the Deadman River to the doomed colony of Walhachin. Picture them now, these gentleman English farmers, lured to the west by a promise of bounteous orchards and rich soils, arriving to this arid, barren country. They tried, in the best of British tradition, building flumes to bring water to the orchards they planted in the poor and scanty soil. In the traditions of their class, they held the Walhachin hunt, balanced teacups at afternoon tea, and danced to the notes of a grand piano. But the land, more suited to cattle grazing than to fruit growing, gave them little to work with. It must have been with a sense of guilty relief that the young men welcomed the First World

War and the chance to return to England, to fight for their country. Without them, the colony wavered and dwindled. By the 1920s, all the colonists had fled. Today, only the remains of the flumes and a few broken-backed apple trees on the bench above the river testify to their efforts.

Near five o'clock, I reach Ashcroft, down on the Thompson between the tracks of Canadian National and Canadian Pacific rail lines. I could stay at the town's one hotel, but the bridge beside the hotel is noisily under construction, bridge timbers are piled in the hotel parking lot, and the pub is filled with road crews. Tonight, I do not want an evening alone in an anonymous motel room, two chairs, three lamps, a printed red and gold bedspread on a printed orange carpet, or the curious glances of people in a cafe or bar. For the first time in my life, I opt for a night at an expensive dude ranch. It would be nice to go horseback riding through the sagebrush, in the evening light.

Expensive duding is, of course, not that simple. Guests are invited on a morning ride and an afternoon ride, but not an evening ride. One cannot go off and ride by oneself. Out of alternatives, I check in anyway, planning on riding in the morning. The afternoon ride straggles back in, city people, some of whom have been spending their holidays here for years. No one speaks directly to me unless I speak to them first: city reserve is back. When we do talk, their first question is a city question: "What do you do?" In the morning, the men have donned their spotless polka-dot neckerchiefs and the checkered shirts they wear just once a year, and are talking horse talk. "I know they probably laugh at me here," confides one Fraser Valley man, "but the horse I have at home, I treat her like a pet."

They are nice enough people, but after a month of the easy acceptance usually awarded by small-town people, making conversation about jobs and cars and city life is too difficult. And the idea of a nose-to-tail, walk-here, canter-there, gallop-now ride now seems absurd. After breakfast, I leave.

The dry hills give way to cliffs and canyons that narrow down towards the Fraser River. Ponderosa pine and rabbitbush disappear; firs and spruce clothe the ever-steepening mountains, and streams dash down the rocks. I swing down into Hope, the Fraser Valley, and the road home.

CHAPTER 19

Winter: Riske Creek

)) Everyone I talk to this week thinks I'm crazy. "You're driving *up there*? Alone? There's snow up there. It's cold. The roads will be closed. It's not safe. You're not even," said with incredulity, "going skiing."

Half these people have snuffling colds that have lasted for two weeks in the wettest Victoria November on record. On Vancouver Island and in the Fraser Valley, basements have flooded, hillsides capsized into back yards, creeks and rivers overflowed onto roads. I have seen the sun twice, briefly, in the last ten days, between renewed onslaughts of the daily deluge. White whirling snow, clear midnight skies, cold sunny days, and frost-fringed forests sound infinitely attractive. I am not Going Skiing, Going to a Conference, or Going Crazy. I am, simply, going north in winter.

A bumptious December wind roughens the sea between the island and the mainland, and a sonorous announcement from ferry crew warns passengers not to try to slalom down to the car deck on the rolling heaving ferry until the ship has docked. On shore, the radio gives forth a new rainfall warning for the Fraser Valley: up to half an inch of rain expected, with winds ranging to sixty miles an hour. In the valley, water spins up from truck wheels, stands in the fields, gurgles in the ditches. Eastward, the rain pelts down onto water-logged snow that clings to the roofs of saddle-backed barns and spots the spongy farm fields.

Rain persists northwards into the Fraser Canyon, melting the grubby piles of snow scraped to the roadside by snowploughs. I have snow tires, tire chains, a new heavy-duty battery, lock de-icer, windshield scrapers, a snow brush, a shovel, a down sleeping bag, a down coat, two pairs of gloves, a scarf, and a woolly hat. The only thing I don't have is winter. A warm front has swept down across southwestern British Columbia, and temperatures halfway up the province rise well above freezing.

At Spuzzum, where the Fraser River runs white and turbulent between high, narrow canyon walls, a buck-toothed waitress with a devastating smile serves soup and pie at a cafe warmed by a log fire burning in a cast-iron stove. The Drivers' Den, at the back of the cafe, contains a special truckers' table, complete with chair-level phone. An extended family heading home from the valley, Christmas tree bouncing in the back of their station wagon, argues over which part of the canyon highway is the scariest, while Dad drags the kids away from the video games and pool table they have discovered in the darkened bar next door. An unhappy man wanders back and forth from the washrooms, toting mops and wrenches.

Outside, the rain eases. Huge empty trucks thunder past, spraying up gritty water from the road, or, loaded, grind slowly up the hills. Patches of blue appear in the sky at the head of the canyon, and the strong piny smell of the dry country fills the air. For thousands of years, this natural boundary has marked the end of the native coastal Salish territory, based on the riches of ocean and rain forest, and the beginning of the interior Salish society, nomadic, based on this less bountiful land. For me, it is the beginning of the hinterland, and no matter how many times I drive this route, the transition has the power to surprise and enchant: rain and fir and cedar and abrupt black mountainsides, then, suddenly, the warm red bark of Ponderosa pines, ridged hills, and the golden grass of the interior dry lands. Light changes in the winter coastal sky are subtle, almost undetectable. Here, as the dusk creeps west in the short December day, golden light floods through a break in the clouds and awakens the extraordinary colours of the landscape: straw-gold grass, deep blue shading to black of the distant mountains, blue and grey and pearl of the shifting sky.

I stop for the night at Clinton, a few short side streets that run a block or two off the highway. Years ago, Clinton gained a tough-guy reputation when local cowboys undertook to explain politely to a motorcycle gang that their black-leathered, uncouth selves were unwelcome in this Cariboo town. The gang left, the cowboys went home— or, more likely, to the bar. The new, big log barn of a bar is peopled tonight only by a scattering of cowboys and Indians. Beside the highway, which doubles as main street, ranch hands have built a nativity scene, complete with Cariboo hay bales, next to a billboard advertising the Clinton rodeo. Warm yellow lights glow behind net curtains in the stately white frame houses that front the street, and strings of multicoloured Christmas lights frame the teddy bear and tinsel windows of the Sears Catalogue Office and Jacquie's Gingerbread House Gifts.

Winter is finally here: a snow-laden wind howls up the dark street, and slick ice makes walking treacherous. Visible through the windows of the Clinton Vi_l___ Sen__rs _ome, residents knit, play cards and watch television. A sign in the window of the general store announces that the grade nine class wants to earn money for a field trip by shovelling snow. At the Cariboo Lodge, homemade shepherd's pie is the dinner special. The owner worries at an out-of-kilter furnace, and offers three extra blankets, just in case.

In the morning, a piebald sky hangs over the highway. Just a few minutes north, the patchwork is replaced by leaden grey, and horizontal snow drives furiously south. Then the snow is as suddenly gone, and the sky clears to brilliant blue. Though this isn't the cusp of winter/ spring known locally as dogshit season, it might as well be: melting piles of grubby snow reveal nothing attractive.

The Kamloops radio station announcer states confidently that Highway 20 west from Williams Lake to Bella Coola, the road I plan to take, is closed because of avalanches. I doubt it: from Williams Lake west for two hundred miles, the highway runs through plateau, and I don't know where an avalanche would come from. For a moment, I feel the mixture of tolerant amusement and less tolerant anger the small-town resident experiences every time the big city gets it wrong again. At Williams Lake, my suspicions are confirmed: the highway is open west to the mountains, closed through the mountain passes to the coast.

The road climbs a long hill through the slim straight jackpines, then cuts down sharply from the irrigated benchlands of the Fraser River to the Sheep Creek Bridge. Across the bridge, west of the Fraser, east of the Coast Mountains, lies the Chilcotin, a vast, upside-down, right-angled triangle of plateau drained by the Chilcotin River and its tributaries.

As far as is possible in these days of satellite television and easy air travel, the Chilcotin is still frontier. The descendants of the original settlers, the Chilcotin Indians, make up more than half of the people of this open, rolling land, with its jackpine forests and turquoise rivers and lakes. They share the land with the settlers of this century, stubborn individualists, ranchers, guides, loners of one variety or another, who look askance at rules and regulations, schedules and traffic lights.

No traffic lights exist in the three hundred miles from Williams Lake to Bella Coola, and the biggest town en route is Alexis Creek, population 120. Most names on the map are "blink and miss it": a general store that houses a post office, liquor agency, video rental, gas station; a few houses with signs advertising carpentry, well-drilling, machinery repair. The glaring yellow Quonset hut of a general store announces that I have reached the first of these communities: Riske Creek, population 75.

At the Chilcotin Lodge, RCMP Constable Cece Grinder is drinking a Coke and going over the events of the day with a new police recruit. Cece grew up at Anaham, a Chilcotin Indian village up the road. Like most men and boys on the reserve, he worked on neighbouring ranches, bringing in the hay, riding out into the hills to check on the wild horses. He remembers boyhood winters. "There was lots of snow in years past, not like this," he gestures out the window at the meagre snowfall on the ground. "The best entertainment was using old car hoods for sleds, see if you could make that big jump." He smiles, remembering hay rides, sleigh rides, weekend dances. Now, as then, each reserve holds a hockey tournament in the winter, players on the ice from morning till dark— and on, if the rink has lights.

For the past ten years, Cece has been a police officer, working as liaison between the detachment in Williams Lake, most of its members white and from eastern Canada, and the Chilcotin people. "It's different here," he says of the necessity for his job, "because there are more natives than whites in the Chilcotin. My role is teaching the regular RCMP about our culture and background. Sometimes, it's fun. Sometimes, it's not fun. But every day is different."

He was in the office a few nights ago when the detachment got a call from one of the reserves. "Good thing I was there," and in his voice is the good-natured scorn of many a Chilcotin man, white or native, for the townies. "They didn't have a clue how to get there."

Today, Cece took the new man down the back roads from Williams Lake through ranching and logging country, for a look at one small piece of the far-flung territory the detachment covers. I ask the new man what he thinks, but he's still in shock over the size of the region and the roads that edge through it; he just shakes his head.

In a rare lull after Cece leaves, Sadie Garland sits down for a brief break before the next clutch of logging truck drivers comes in for coffee and truck talk. Sadie was born in Williams Lake, grew up in Merritt and Alberta. When her father died, her mother moved the family back to her old home, the Toosey Reserve just along from Riske Creek. Sadie was old enough by then for a job cooking and cleaning at a lodge deep in the wilderness of the coast mountains, a job she loved. "Everybody was family there." She moved to Alberta again, then back to Toosey with her three children, who are now six, eight and ten.

To support herself and her family, she needed a job, and jobs are scarce in the Chilcotin. Though she feels lucky to have this one at the hotel, it keeps her away from her kids from noon to 8:00 P.M. every day. "They're real good. They know I have to work," she says, regretfully. "They do the vacuuming and the dishes." But she misses them and looks forward to the time when she can get weekends off.

Outside, Sandie Bardua looks doubtfully and with some antagonism at a pile of logs that need chain-sawing to stove size. Solid, blonde, energetic, enthusiastic, Sandie has owned and run this lodge for fourteen years, but that hasn't taught her to like chain saws. Fifteen years ago, Sandie was looking for something away from the city, different from her bookkeeping job. "I wanted maybe a hobby farm. Then I saw an ad for this place in the Vancouver paper, and it sounded so appealing. We"—Sandie, her husband, and their year-old-son—"came up and looked at it and said, 'No way.'" The lodge, then, had rooms for rent, but no restaurant or separate suite for the owner. Heat was supplied by a relic of an old wood furnace in the basement that took about two pieces of wood at a time; water supply was erratic. The family went home. But the more Sandie thought about living in the Chilcotin, the more attractive it sounded.

The family moved north. The appeal quickly palled on her husband, who went back south, but Sandie stayed with her young son, Robbie. "I'm a real pioneer," she says now. "I love a challenge. I don't look at a problem as being a bad thing. It's learning." Maybe sometimes a little more learning than she wanted. That first winter, the wife of one of the road workers who were staying at the lodge decided to help by cleaning out the fireplace. She put the ashes in a cardboard box, put the box on the back step. At three in the morning, Sandie was woken by a crackling somewhere outside. Drowsily, she peered out the window —to see flames licking at the roof shingles. She grabbed Robbie and ran through the place, yelling. With no hoses available, the road workers formed a bucket brigade and saved the lodge.

Some of those workers are still her friends. "They looked after Robbie, kept the fires going, brought in wood. They were company." In the years following, Sandie expanded the lodge, with a new restaurant and living quarters for herself and Robbie. Good times, bad times, she loved the Chilcotin. But now she feels it's time for a change. Robbie needs to be in town for his last year of high school, taking part in extracurricular activities instead of riding the school bus two hours a day. And Sandie is ready to move on. "I'm just not used to being in one place for this long. I came for one year. When I came here, someone said I should plant trees, but I said I'd never see them grow." She shrugs and smiles. In fourteen years, the trees would have grown tall.

In the morning, a faint bar of pale light marks the distant horizon as I crunch down through the snow under the stars to the Riske Creek store. Noreen McDonald swings her battered, muddy school bus through the frozen ruts and levers open the door. Every school day of the year, Noreen wakes at 3:00 A.M. when her husband gets up to start his twelve-hour day driving a logging truck. She listens for a moment before she falls back asleep: if the logging trucks are speeding up the hill outside her house, the weather is clear. If they growl slowly up, she knows it has rained or snowed overnight, and the roads will be treacherous. Armed with this knowledge, she leaves at ten to seven, her own two children still padding sleepily around the house.

December is the darkest month, the days shortest. Dawn creeps towards us as we make the first circuit of the bus route, picking up high-school students. Clad in jeans and sweatshirt, a tall, slim, gum-chewing brunette with blue eyes that shade to hazel in some lights, Noreen manhandles the door open at each stop, and the teenagers, under-eager, straggle aboard. Down the highway first, then off the side road to Toosey, then back to the highway, where mothers wait at side roads, engines pluming exhaust in the cold air, to make sure the bus arrives to pick up their offspring. On another side road, Noreen meets a second bus that will take the high–school students to school in Williams Lake.

Now she backtracks, retracing her route. The younger children pile on, all flying arms and legs and giggles. "I sure know when it's Christmas time," Noreen sighs. "All that sugar, all that excitement. And I can smell the Japanese oranges on the bus." She is matter-of-fact about driving: the bigger the vehicle the better. Trucks were her favourite childhood toy. Once, when her brother refused to give her a toy truck she wanted, she nailed his foot to the floor with a crowbar, right between the toes.

"Driving's never really scared me," she says. When it rains in the winter, the back roads get very icy by morning, and she has to climb down from the heated warmth of the bus and chain up. "I don't like to do that. I get wet and cold. So far this year, I've been pretty lucky. Someone has always come along to help me. The truckers are pretty good about that." Women are expected to do their job out here, but when help is offered, you'd be foolish to be too proud to accept.

Only once was Noreen terrified. "I went to take off from a stop, too fast. I touched the brakes and went sideways across the hill." She grins. "But it was okay. I stopped. If you get into trouble, you just drive it." We turn back down to Toosey, where a gaggle of kids charge aboard. "Is that kitty I gave you still okay?" Noreen asks one. She has known most of these kids since the day they were born. Half a dozen dogs come to see the children off, then ramble away, tumbling over each other. We head back for the highway and the elementary school behind the lodge. Once the children are dropped off, Noreen and I have coffee, promising to keep in touch.

~

Later, Noreen leaves a message, inviting me to breakfast the next morning, a Saturday. "I was so nervous the other day," she confides, "that I didn't say what I wanted to say about living here." In the morning, over eggs and bacon and gallons of coffee, she shows me some memories of her Chilcotin childhood that she has written out:

> *After we had our coffee this morning, I came home and fed the horses and I got to thinking just how much things have really changed, and all the extras that we have and people take for granted.*
>
> *I can remember when we were kids and we didn't have hot or cold running water. We would have to pack our water for baths etc. We didn't have a bathtub, so myself, Pat and Wesley (my brothers) heated our water and took turns bathing in a square washtub, which your arms and legs hung out of, because it was so small. I remember there was always a fight over who was going to bath first. I always wanted to go first, because I just knew the boys would pee in the water, and we all used the same water.*
>
> *Electricity was something we didn't have until I was a teen-ager. When we used to have Gordon and Vi Woods [old-timers from Meldrum Creek] come over to Riske Creek and play for dances at the hall, we used to have a light plant for*

power. I can remember getting ready to go to the dance with a light from a coal oil lamp that we used to carry from bedroom to bedroom. When we got to the dance, you could pretty well count on about 11.30 to midnight, halfway through a song, the light plant would go dead. A couple of guys would grab their siphon hose and a five-gallon can, go to someone's pickup and siphon some gas out, fill the light plant, and then we'd dance for a couple more hours.

Noreen's memories of growing up are a reminder of how close the Chilcotin is to pioneer days. White settlers began to filter into the Chilcotin early in the 1900s, but this is a vast land, and newcomers lived isolated lives, on ranches far apart. The road that connects Williams Lake to Bella Coola was completed only in 1953, by the people of the coast and Chilcotin who shrugged off a government decree that it couldn't be done and did it themselves. But for years, much of it was only a cart track, with spring mudholes you could lose your truck in. For those who live well off the highway, telephones are still luxuries, and power is supplied by diesel generators.

With Noreen and her husband Ed, I drive a few miles down the road to the house where she grew up and where her parents still live. Irene Jasper arrived in the Chilcotin in 1946, a war bride from Shropshire coming to her Canadian soldier husband's home. She was sick the entire six days at sea, and not very happy the next seven days by rail to Ashcroft. She took one look at the dry dusty hills, the shacks and the lonely cottages and "thought it was the last place God made." The trip by road to the isolated community of Meldrum Creek where she was to live made no better impression. Yet the beauties and the solitude of the Chilcotin grew on her. When she decided to end the marriage, she stayed here. She met and married Delmer Jasper and came to this homestead at Riske Creek. They had eight children, packed wood and water, and went to town twice a year. Her boys hauled snow in to melt for the old washing machine on the porch, and she made soap from lye and horse fat. "I wouldn't leave here now," she says with conviction.

Delmer Jasper sips coffee and listens to his wife's story. That someone could learn to love the Chilcotin comes as no surprise to him. His roots are here: he was born in 1925 at Meldrum Creek, son of a man who came into the country from Washington State in 1910 and of a part-Shuswap woman who grew up near Quesnel. The family moved to Riske Creek when he was seven, and he has lived here ever since. His life has been lived old-time Chilcotin style. "We went everywhere on horseback. I went to school through grade four and that was it. I started to work for the Gang Ranch when I was thirteen. I got five dollars a week, room and board, and my dad got ten. We had to work ten hours a day, and we got Sundays off." He pauses, remembering. "It was fun."

Some winters, the temperature dropped to sixty below. "I've cut a lot of wood, you know," he says. "You just kept that cross-cut saw going all the time. You had to keep a pile ahead in case of emergencies. There was so much frost in the air you could hardly see the sun, and the cows would freeze their tails and their ears off. You couldn't work fast enough to keep warm."

"If the power went off at thirty below now," Noreen asks, "what would people do?" She is not romantically nostalgic for the old days, but she is close enough to those days to understand that hardship bred both independence and a sense of interdependence that children today lack. Riske has all the services now: running water, power, telephone, satellite television with its dozens of channels. The road to town is paved and the trip fast, so locals don't hold the dances and parties that brought them together in the old days, or support local events. Everyone does the larger part of their shopping in Williams Lake; the Riske Creek store survives from small purchases of candy bars and cigarettes. The older kids go to school and hockey practice in Williams Lake. The adults find their entertainment in town or on the television screens in their own homes. Half the logging truck drivers and others who work in the area live in town. No wonder, Noreen says, that the local rodeo that Delmer and Irene started decades ago and that used to bring ten thousand dollars to the community coffers last year made a profit of seven dollars.

Back in the 1960s, people came to work at the little independent sawmills that dotted the country. "There were more people here in the sixties than there are now," says Delmer. "Then the big outfits took over and all the little mills went broke. People came in and ran up a lot of bills, then left the country." "People still do that now," smiles Irene: the Chilcotin lures many, but making a living is never easy. Delmer worked on ranches and in sawmills, then for the highways department for twenty years, then ranching again. "Everybody helped everybody," he says of the old days. "Now, if people do something for someone, they want to get paid. Maybe that's why we never got anywhere." He smiles; he is content with the way his life has been. "I have no idea of moving anywhere else." Noreen shakes her head. "It's hard enough," she says, "to get him into town."

CHAPTER 20

Tatla, Tatlayoko

JJ Westward, deeper into the Chilcotin, the jackpine forests that have edged the road give way to the Chilcotin River bottom lands. Aspens and willow hang shaggy with hoarfrost; rough-coated horses poke their muzzles over log corral fences. A coyote, grey on white snow, trots across an empty field towards the turquoise river that flows, shallow, between gravel banks heavy with snow. Near Alexis Creek, cattle crowd into winter feed lots, and a loader manoeuvres a loaf-shaped hay bale into place. Lunchtime, and a dozen logging trucks loaded with pine poles are parked, engines running, at the hotel.

Now the first snowy peaks of the Coast Mountains thrust above the pines. A ridge of blue sky rides above dark clouds shovelled down upon the peaks. Five days ago, a storm dumped between three and six feet of snow from here west through the mountains. It lies deep and sparkling along the fences and in the fields, figure eights and long parabolas carved on its surface by snowmobiles that have ventured between the wide-spaced houses and through the trees.

A hundred and twenty miles out from Williams Lake, the pavement ends, but the surface now beneath the tires is flat and frozen hard. Small signs half-buried in snow point intriguingly to hidden lakes, but ploughs have left great banks of snow across the access roads. Exactly half-way between the Cariboo and the coast, I reach Tatla, unincorporated, population twenty-four.

The first buildings of Tatla appear between the snowbanks: a ranch house and barns across from winter feedlots filled with brown and white cattle, an inn, a post office, a carpenter's shop, the store and gas station, the community hall. Ahead, already almost out of town, lie the health building with the nurses' office and residence, a restaurant and laundromat, half a dozen houses. Out of sight is the rest of the community: the school and church, the baseball diamond and the gymkhana grounds.

The Graham Inn has been the social centre of Tatla since it was the Big House, the nucleus of the ranch Bob Graham founded back in 1901. For years now, it has served as restaurant, lodging place and drop-in centre for the west Chilcotin: if you don't find your friends eating homemade pie and drinking coffee here, you will certainly find news of their doings. Bruno Krawzik whips the dirty dishes off the tables and talks about how he landed in Tatla. He was working as a cook in Banff and looking around for a restaurant he could buy when he saw an ad for the Graham Inn in a real–estate catalogue. It wasn't really what he and his wife Jutta were looking for. "But if you have ever looked for a used car, you know what it's like. You look at so many, you don't know what you're seeing." Not long after, the Krawziks were mildly puzzled owners of the inn.

His marriage succumbed to the pressures of the business or the times, or to the stresses that cause relationships anywhere to crack. Now ex-wife Jutta, remarried to the Tatla carpenter, lives across the driveway, runs the Tatla post office, and helps out in the inn from time to time.

"I wouldn't run a restaurant again," Bruno proclaims. "It's too much work." He works almost every day, early morning to late evening, then gets woken up again by travellers who can't or won't read the hand-lettered "We don't sell gas" sign on the door. Yet in many ways, running the inn suits him: he cooks the food if no one else is on hand to do so, moves from table to table chatting, never alighting anywhere for long, rings up the bills at the cash registers, laughs with the regulars who drop in every time they pass through Tatla.

I sit next to the roaring fire at one of the brown arborite and metal tables centred by plastic flowers in old syrup bottles. Years of cowboy boots, gumboots, hiking boots, have worn the lino to a uniform pale grey, thinner in front of the cash register and the self-serve, all-you-can-drink-for-seventy-five-cents Chilcotin coffee pots. The bookcases that flank the fireplace are stuffed with old scientific texts, science fiction novels and the occasional local classic. On one of his passes through the room, Bruno taps a book left lying on my table: *Introductory Nuclear Physics*. "Do you know how much carbon 14 decays in your body every day?" he asks. An avid reader of science and science fiction, he accompanies my munching of bratwurst with graphic descriptions of nuclear decay and radiation. At forty, with close-cropped hair, stern glasses, and bundled energy barely contained, he looks like he would be more at home hunched over test tubes than over dirty dishes.

Five minutes walking after dinner takes me beyond the reach of Tatla's lights, the smell of wood smoke, the occasional roar of an engine or burst of conversation carried on the still night air. Out here, the only sounds are my boots crunching in the snow and the distant bawling of cattle. The world seems lit by stars, for the full moon is spent and the last quarter set or not yet risen, the sky preternaturally clear. I pick out the Milky Way, the Big Dipper, the Little Dipper, and renew my resolution to study astronomy. Bruno probably has a book.

But not tonight. I go past the hay-laden pickup truck in the parking lot, past the pay phone at the foot of the stairs where a timber cruiser phones his girlfriend in the city, past the wet snowboots in the hallway and the soggy clothing hung over the door of the communal bathroom, to my room. For a while, I sit in the raggedy armchair and look out through the cracked window over the lake towards the mountains. Then I climb up into the big high bed with its old-fashioned wooden headboard, and snuggle down under the quilt.

In the morning, Bruno presents The Fruit Plate: cantaloupe, honey-dew, watermelon, green grapes, red grapes, kiwi, grapefruit, orange, pineapple, pomegranate, and a strawberry, all fresh. "You don't like pineapple? Why didn't you say you didn't like pineapple? This man doesn't like watermelon, so I don't give him any." At Bruno's, you'd better clean your plate.

The watermelon hater, dark, moustached, leanly good-looking, is the owner of the pickup truck with the hay bales in the back. Steve Richberg has snowshoed out five miles to his truck from the wilderness traplines and horse ranch he and his wife Roma run, and made it down to Tatla. A neighbouring rancher—well, a rancher from up across the river and a couple of ranges of hills away, which is neighbouring by Chilcotin definition—wanted to reclaim some cows that had wandered onto Steve and Roma's property. They shared the cost of getting the road ploughed out, but the cat driver broke the bridge five miles out, then crashed through again trying to extricate his machine. So, for the rest of the winter, Steve and Roma will be on snowshoes or snowmobiles for the five miles from the bridge to home.

In the best Chilcotin tradition, Steve has come out looking for horses, some prize mares he thinks the wild studs stole for their harem. He rode out to look for them and snowshoed out into the hills, but he couldn't track them down. Now, he's come to Tatla to go flying with the German ranchers down the road who are looking for some cattle of their own that are strayed or lost.

Steve grew up in Toronto, quit school at sixteen and went north, working in the mines till he could no longer stomach the "rednecks" he worked with. A wilderness man at heart, he travelled a trapline with an Indian trapper. "That's when I found out that I loved trapping." He came to the Peace River country, and bought a trapline from an old Indian whose sons preferred living in town. He moved on down to the Chilcotin, just looking around, and met Roma, the young widow of a Chilcotin old-timer she met and married when she came up here for a summer job. "She lent me a horse and pointed me in the right direction," he recalls of his first Chilcotin wanderings. "Then I ended up working for her. Then we shacked up and then we got married. Winters do that to you sometimes." He smiles, self-mocking. Chilcotin men aren't supposed to sound romantic.

Steve is scornful of people who think trappers can't be environmentalists, of city people who think they know anything about trapping and the wilderness. "Even when lynx were eight hundred dollars, we took maybe three. When I came in, we trapped the beaver hard, because they were overpopulated and weak and diseased. Then we left them alone for three years. I want these animals to be there forever." He gets involved in any battle to protect wildlife habitat against destruction by logging or development. And he does habitat mapping for the provincial fish and wildlife service, for who knows these regions better than a man who rides, walks or snowshoes them every day of his life? "I've almost died out there," he says. "You break a snowshoe in the deep snow, go through the ice . . . well, hypothermia's the main danger."

He and/or Roma come in to town every Friday or every second Friday, for mail and news and supplies. In the summer, Steve or Roma sometimes work as forest service lookouts, or on recreational campsite maintenance, or Roma cooks for guide-outfitters in the fall, just to earn a little precious cash to build up their stock of horses. But mostly they stay where they like it best, in the wilderness, in the woods.

In a mobile home above a little lake west of town, Joy Graham opens a photo album filled with snapshots of the old days, and shows me pictures of Tatla pioneers. Back in the 1930s, when you couldn't get work down on the coast, Joy and her sister answered an ad in the paper for two girls to come and work on a ranch. "We never thought we'd get the jobs, but we did. I got the inside work and she got the outside work." Both sisters happily became part of a Chilcotin tradition, one that endures to the present: girls from the city come up to cook or clean on a ranch, and marry the rancher's son. Joy married Bill Graham, son of Tatla pioneer Bob Graham, and lived at the Big House on the Graham Ranch.

Joy points out the pictures of the people she knew back then, posing dramatically at picnics, standing with sweeps and stackers at haying time, taking the cattle down the lake on the ice in early spring. "We'd sprinkle hay on the ice to get them to go down to the end of the lake, and turn them out to feed on the sidehills. Not so many rules and regulations then. Now, you have to get permission to turn your cattle out, and the earliest you can is about May fifteenth."

One picture shows Joy with her sister, examining fur pelts. The two did a little fur trading back then, exchanging groceries at the Graham store for squirrel and coyote and the occasional mink or marten skin brought in by Chilcotin Indians or the rare white trapper.

The Grahams sold the ranch in the early seventies; the sale marked the passing of one Chilcotin era and the beginning of a new and not entirely welcome time. The ranch was sold, as are many Chilcotin ranches these days, to Germans. Joy has few good memories of the sale or of the court case that followed. Like many a Chilcotin old-timer, she's dubious about the German invasion. "You can't tell them a thing. They don't know ranching and they won't listen. They don't have the right sense for being around these animals." She stops, distressed because she doesn't really like characterizing people this way. "Maybe I'm wrong. But I think the basic reason [the Germans don't fit into the traditional Chilcotin] is that they are interested in the dollar more than the life-style." Then she chuckles, amused by the idea of ranchers being mainly interested in dollars.

"I know," I start, "the only time you make money . . .," and Joy finishes the oft-heard comment, "is when you sell the ranch."

Joy is not alone in her opinions. In the old days, when you crossed the Fraser, you left the pursuit of the almighty dollar behind. The Chilcotin was about riding the range looking for horses, telling stories on soft starry nights, mud and mosquitoes and making do. The corpo-

rate Germans with their four-hundred-dollar cowboy boots and han-
kering after instant cowboy status, their FAX machines and their private
planes, are viewed with wry amusement—and often resentment. Yet
Joy will always love the Chilcotin. "When it was snowing, I got Thomas,
that's my youngest grandson, to help me dig some of the paths out.
Pretty soon, he stopped, and he looked all the way around. Then he said
to me, 'Isn't it beautiful?'"

I go back to the centre of town through snow and sunshine. In his
workshop, cigarette smoke curls up from under Jack Henneveld's
creased and sawdusty cowboy hat and filters down through his unruly
grey blonde beard. A cabinet maker, Jack arrived at Tatla by an unlikely
route. Born in Holland, he escaped early to Spain and lived for a while
on Majorca. Then he crewed for a German boat owner, sailing across
the Atlantic to the West Indies and staying in the Caribbean for three
years. The boat owner bought a resort at remote Chilko Lake, and asked
Henneveld if he would come along and do some work there. "Yah, yah,
I thought," says Jack, his Dutch accent still strong, "I'll come up for three
months. Oh, man, it was so cold up here after Majorca and the West
Indies. But I'm still here." Sometimes he works up at the resort, sometimes he works down here, making cabinets, door harps, picture frames,
chess tables, whatever people want. He thinks Tatla is just the right size.
"Williams Lake, Bella Coola, they've got too many people. What are
there here? Twenty, twenty-two people?" Everyone here tells me this is
a good size for a town—though when I commented on how well
everyone seems to get on, even ex-spouses living in each other's pockets, someone guffawed and said, "Sure, now. Come back after three
months of winter and see. By then, we're at each other's throats."

Beverley Butler is cooking at the Graham Inn today. "I was fifteen
when I first saw this country," says Beverley. "I came with my foster
mother to Tatlayoko [near Tatla], and I loved it. I worked in the strawberry patch to earn the money to come back the next year. I got into
Williams Lake alone, and the stage to Bella Coola was gone, and I just
stood there bawling."

Someone rescued her, as Chilcotin people will, and she ended up
cooking at the Graham Ranch for a gang of twenty-two. "I didn't know
anything. The first morning, a man came in, and he asked me, 'Haven't
you started breakfast yet?' I didn't know what to do. He showed me how
to get the fire lit, and off I went." She, too, met the son of a pioneer rancher,
and they fell madly in love, the way only seventeen-year-olds can. But

the early years of her life, moved from one foster family to another, had not prepared her for another fact of Chilcotin life: hard times and hard work build strong women, and her mother-in-law was one of the strongest. "She lived a hundred yards away. She'd show up at five in the morning and tell us to get out of bed," Beverley proffers as one example of the way her mother-in-law tried to keep control of her son.

But Beverley endured, and learned to stand up for herself: she wasn't going to be forced away from the country and the husband she loved. Hunting, fishing, haying, anything outdoors, enthralled her. She was more than willing to do ranch work to earn needed money. "We were poor," she says flatly. She takes pride in how well she can do rough physical work. "I did tree-planting for three years when I was fifty," she says, "and I was one of the best. I could outplant the younger ones."

She and her husband had three children, including a daughter who got married this past summer. "Her and her dad rode horseback in their wedding clothes to church." Just as the horses reached the church, "a tour of Japanese came along in their bus. They all jumped out and started taking pictures." And you know another myth about how the pioneers live on the last frontier has been born.

Everyone tells you the Chilcotin is a wonderful place to raise kids— until they reach high-school age. No high school exists between Williams Lake and Bella Coola. If teenagers live beyond school-bus distance, they have two choices: correspondence lessons, or living in the school dormitory in Williams Lake. Neither is a good choice. Correspondence cuts students off from the resources a school can offer. But growing up on a ranch or in a tiny community where you know everyone and everyone knows you does not prepare a fourteen- or fifteen-year-old to tackle the city alone. Williams Lake can be a tough town, with the same patterns of drug and alcohol abuse and random street violence common to much bigger cities.

"It was awful," says Beverley, of the time her two older children spent in the dormitory in Williams Lake. "There was no supervision, not even as much as the parents would have given." She will never forget the fear-filled evening when she could not get in touch with her daughter at the dormitory, and no one seemed to know or care where she was. Her fear was soundly based. The daughter had, without her knowledge, been given drugs by people she trusted, then dumped at the dormitory to fend for herself. Her daughter recovered; her son got through the difficulties he faced in town. But Beverley's third child, a daughter now fifteen, studies at a table beside me: she works at the inn part-time as a waitress, and takes correspondence courses right here at home.

Two relief nurses working this week at the health unit down the road come in for enormous pieces of pie and fresh strawberry shortcake before they leave Tatla. In a cheerful West Indian blended with English blended with Canadian accent, Ruby explains that she stays on the nursing relief list so that she can move from place to place, never settling in one place for long. In many isolated British Columbia communities, the health nurse is the only health professional available, on call twenty-four hours a day. "We do colds, to murder, to suicide, anything that happens," says Ruby.

Kathy, the other nurse, spent five days here; last week, she worked at Atlin, far north between the Yukon and the Alaska Panhandle; next week, she'll be at the Anaham Chilcotin reserve, down the road from Tatla. Her home is the family ranch at Fraser Lake, west of Prince George, but she likes to see the country, so she travels around the province, working as a relief nurse.

Tatla Lake is snugged almost up against the Coast Mountains, just fifty miles from Mount Waddington, the highest peak in the range. Eighteen-sixties Victoria businessman Alfred Waddington noted how deeply into the mountains Bute Inlet cut from the Strait of Georgia, and conceived a scheme to rival the government's Cariboo Road. Waddington's route, by sea to the head of the inlet and overland through the Chilcotin to the Cariboo, was almost two hundred land miles shorter than the Cariboo Road. Waddington is best remembered for precipitating the short-lived Chilcotin War, when Chilcotin natives killed fourteen of his roadbuilders, who had intruded, without permission, on native territory.

Neither his contemporaries nor later commentators have been kind to Alfred: Sir John A. Macdonald called him a "respectable old fool" and later historians have categorized him as an incredible and unrealistic optimist, suggesting that Mount Waddington might have been better named for someone with more solid accomplishments. Perhaps they failed to recognize in him the prototype of the Chilcotin dreamer, albeit without the Chilcotin practicality that often sees those dreams through.

The next day, half a dozen of those practical and latter-day dreamers are at the Graham Inn, sorting through sacks of stone-ground flour, huge blocks of mozzarella cheese, and pails of natural peanut butter, all labelled for the Tatlayoko Co-op. One of them explains that this is not a real co-operative, but a loose assemblage of people who twice a year order natural foods in bulk from a Vancouver wholesaler. Most are in their thirties or forties; most have moved here in the last ten years, to live in the mountains away from what they perceive as the depersonalizing rush of the city.

Jean moved here eight years ago, with her husband and daughters, to a "sheep and coyotes" ranch sixteen miles north of the highway, an hour and a half or three days travel in, depending on the weather and the state of the roads. Spring is the worst season: at breakup, the famous Chilcotin gumbo forms and swallows vehicles whole. The road is best in winter—except after snows like last week's, the heaviest Jean has seen. She and her family came here from the American midwest, escaping what she terms the three p's: pollution, politics and population, and finding in the process a fourth, peace.

Jean has to meet someone up the road half an hour ago, Chilcotin time; she dashes off. Sally, Sandy, and Roma settle into chairs at the inn for more cups of the ever-flowing coffee. All three live south of Tatla, in or near the community of Tatlayoko Lake. Sandy Hart, dark, bearded, with an open, handsome face, runs a hay ranch off the Tatlayoko road, but spends much of his time as a consultant on land use and water resources. "Consulting doesn't have to be based in the city," he notes. His work takes him throughout the Cariboo-Chilcotin and along the central coast. He and his family came here from Quebec ten years ago, seeking a place in the mountains, "but on the dry side," away from the heavy rains that close in the western slopes of the mountains through half the year.

Sally Mueller and Roma Shaughnessy live on ranches a mile or two apart, not far from the Tatlayoko post office. Roma and her family are the most recent arrivals, in the Chilcotin just two and a half years. "We came from the Lower Mainland. We were just burned out." They worried they would not be able to find enough work here to finance their new lives, but Roma's husband makes do as a welder and carpenter and she works several days a week in the health clinic. "I'd never regret moving, even if we'd failed," she says. "Now, I feel I could go anywhere, do anything."

Most important to her is the sense of family and close community she feels around her. "Soon after we got here, I spun out on the ice and wrecked our only vehicle." It was thirty below, and her husband was away. "We had offers of six vehicles by the next day. And everyone watches out for your kids." Very few events carry an adults-only sign: the children are included in parties, dances, skating.

"The kids talk, not about the TV show they saw last night, but about the bear they saw on the road and did you hear the coyotes last night?" Sally seconds the thought. Light-brown hair falling straight to her shoulders, Sally looks the part of a sixties back-to-the-lander—and that's what she and her husband were. They moved to British Columbia from the United States in 1970, then came to the Chilcotin five years later to fulfill a long-held dream. Not long after Sally met her husband, she told him she had always dreamt of going to live in the Canadian wilderness. He dug out a map and booklet he had treasured when he was ten years old. On the map, at the end of Chilko Lake, he had drawn a little cabin, the place where he wanted one day to live.

Their place at Tatlayoko is not far from that cabin on the map. They raised three children here; the kids went off to school, to university, to jobs. "But if they could find a mate who would live here, find work here," says Sally, "they would be back. They were glad to go when they went, but they love it here."

As I drive along the ice-rutted road between piled snowbanks the twenty miles south to Tatlayoko, I feel again that anticipation that comes when you return to a place of special beauty and contentment. Over the last hill, and before me lie blue-black vaulting mountains that descend abruptly to the valley floor. Crooked fences dance through snowy meadows, ending where the trees begin. Past the little community of Tatlayoko, the lake lies, icy, turquoise, long and narrow, disappearing in the distance between the mountains. From its southern end the Homathko River flows, a short path only to tidewater at Bute Inlet; the warm wind that blows today, melting the ice on the puddles in the road, is a sea breeze.

Fran Haynes knows the sense of peace that this valley inspires. She moved from the Fraser Valley to Williams Lake "with four kiddies" in 1965, and worked waiting tables and behind a hotel desk. Harry Haynes likes to kid that he picked Fran up in the bar, but in fact, he found her working at the Famous, the Williams Lake eatery where Chilcotin people used to gather. "I came out here. I liked it. I stayed," is Fran's brief summary of events. "When I come over that last hill and see the valley, I know I'm home." Motherly, Fran serves coffee and cookies, then goes back to her knitting and television, leaving Harry to tell Chilcotin stories—which, everyone knows, is what he likes to do best.

With his weathered face, work shirt, jeans, and red-white-and-blue suspenders, Harry looks like the Chilcotin old-timer he is. In 1929, when he was seventeen, with "a notion that I'd like to be a cowboy," he came up from the coast on the "old P, G and E" railway, arriving at Williams Lake just before Christmas. He ran into a Chilcotin rancher in town for his Christmas mail, and went back home with him, to work as a cowboy. The next year, his mothers and brothers came up to the Chilcotin. "She came up in an old Hudson Essex touring car. From Redstone [thirty miles east of Tatla], it was just two ruts, a wagon road, and you had to cut trees to put on the road to get through the mudholes."

That didn't scare off Harry's Mum. She and Harry's younger brother pre-empted 160 acres at Tatlayoko, and by 1937, Harry had five quarter-sections of his own down here by the lake. "I had no machinery at first, so I worked for the neighbours at haying time, so I could use their machinery when we were done at their place."

Like any rancher I've ever met, Harry tells you right away that there's no money in ranching, unless you build the place up and sell it to someone who wants to be a cowboy more than he wants to be rich. "I had an old Holstein milk cow, and when she calved, all but one came out Hereford—the bulls threw strong to their own colour. That was a good cross. They were all good heavy milkers. But I didn't have enough cattle and I couldn't make a living from the ranch." Harry spent two full years and eight consecutive summers on the coast, "working my butt off," while his brother fed the cattle and looked after the ranch. "People would tell me they couldn't find work on the coast, but I never had any trouble. I worked in sawmills, logging, shipyards, anything I could find. I used to hit the railway tracks, go to warehouses all along the tracks and ask them if they had any work. I'd ask forty places if I had to. One year, I worked at two shipyards. Finished the shift at one and walked across the road to the other. I was tight— God, I was tight. I wouldn't spend any money at all if I didn't have to." That didn't sit too well with his first wife. "I got home and wanted to get rested up and she wanted to go partying." Harry came back to Tatlayoko with a nest egg and worked the ranch until he sold it a year or two ago. "I got thirty acres and this house left, and it's mine until I die. Then it goes back to the ranch."

Every Wednesday, Harry and Fran head into Tatla, hauling the mail to the post office there and picking up mail for Tatlayoko. When they get home, Fran puts on the coffee and sets out the cookies, and all of Tatlayoko drops by the post office in their house for mail and chat. "When we had a CB," says Fran, "our handle was Coffeehouse. The ladies talk birthday parties and weddings and babies, and the men talk politics."

The Hayneses used to have the only phone for miles, a radiophone in a booth beside the house. People came to use it, then wrote their charges down in the honour book Fran shows me now. Just this fall, Tatlayoko got wired: three-party lines installed throughout the valley. It brings to mind the day just twelve years ago when electricity surged in through the new power lines.

That was a community effort. The locals threw five hundred dollars each into the pot, to show the government they were serious. They formed a power commission and got a government grant, then cut poles and peeled them, put in the auger holes, hired a backhoe to dig pole holes, hired a contractor to come in and string the wire. When the job was done, everyone went into Tatla for a celebration banquet at the community hall.

One last cup of coffee, and I go back out onto the icy road, back down to the head of the lake, where I sit for a few minutes, looking out over the water and regretting that icy conditions and an inadequate car won't let me drive the lakeside road that leads ever higher into the mountains. I turn about, and climb the hill that takes me away from Tatlayoko.

Back at the highway, I consider: west through the mountains and down the Big Hill to the ocean inlet at Bella Coola, or back through the Chilcotin to the Cariboo. The road to Bella Coola is open again, the avalanches that thundered down the mountains a week ago cleared away. I can get in—but another snowfall is expected, and I may not be able to get back out. Reluctantly, I turn east.

At Lee's Corners, halfway back to Williams Lake, I stop at the general store. On a whim, I ask what the road to the Nemaiah Valley, reputedly one of the most beautiful places in the Chilcotin, is like. "You know people down there?" asks the woman behind the counter. "No." "You alone? I wouldn't go. You got anywhere to stay?" "No. Just thought I'd go in, take a look, come back out." "I wouldn't. Road might be okay. Might not. You know, that woman who died up in the pass to Bella Coola last week, she asked and they told her not to go. She went anyway," words spoken in that tone that says you have every right to be a damn fool if you want to.

I don't want to. Instead, I take the road out of the Chilcotin with a curious sense, not of regret, but of promise, that the next time I come here, there will still be new back roads to explore, places to discover, and stories I have not heard.

CHAPTER 21

The Lonely Road

)) The road from Williams Lake has led me north again, through a landscape familiar from last spring but subtly changed by winter. Morning in Prince George, five degrees above zero Fahrenheit, and fog hangs thick over the city, obliterating the outside world. I climb up from the bowl where the city huddles, through the sulphur-tinged pulp mill smell and ghostly grey landscape. At the bowl's rim, the fog abruptly vanishes, and bright sunshine glitters off frosty trees and piled snow.

Truckers call this highway east from Prince George to the Rocky Mountains the loneliest stretch of road in the country: a hundred and twenty miles without a village, gas station, or, until recently, a truck stop. The old British Columbia story of road, river and rail takes a twist here. When the railway builders laid their steel tracks west from the Rockies in the early years of this century, they followed the twists of the Fraser, so sinuous in this stretch it flows twice its crow's-flight length. As each railhead was established between 1910 and 1914, a community followed: railway men, loggers, sawmill workers, and their families. From then till the 1960s, these mill towns flourished, dependent on the railway for passage to and from the outside world. About twenty-five years ago, a large corporation bought out most of the small mills and closed them down. As everywhere, the railway cut back service. No employment, no transportation: the towns slowly dwindled. Then the roadbuilders came through in 1972, linking Prince George and McBride, at the foot of the Rockies. They built high on the benchland where nobody lived; twenty years later, still no one lives along the road.

In the morning sunshine, the long sweep of road stretches ahead, tails off behind. In twenty miles, one car, three trailer-trucks, one pickup, pass, heading west arrow-straight through a Lilliputian landscape of logged, replanted spruce forest. Then the highway curves, twists, rises. The snow-capped Rockies emerge from cloud and forest to the northeast, the Cariboo mountains to the southeast. A car tilted deep into the roadside ditch testifies that winter conditions on this highway can be treacherous. Moose tracks mark the increasingly deep snow. Ahead, logging roads spiral to the tops of clear-cut hills. Along the twists and turns of the road, country music from Prince George radio swells and fades into static: a twangy "Frosty the Snowman," followed by "You can't stop a woman when she's out of control."

A highways sign just outside Prince George warns travellers that they won't be able to get gas or food until they reach McBride. But the highways department reckoned without the persistence of Gary Cowell, who worked for four years to get the permits necessary to open the only cafe along this lonely stretch of road. Ninety minutes out from the city, a regulation blue-and-white sign announces the presence of the Dome Diner. I have been told that Gary has been refused permission to hang out a sign until he complies precisely with regulations on proper access. But then, blue and white signs aren't that difficult to create, and bureaucrats are unlikely to travel this road in winter.

The Dome Diner is housed in a raw new pressed-board building on a cat-cleared parking lot, with a sign proudly pointing to the privy. Inside, Gary serves up short-order hamburgers, hot dogs and pie twenty-four hours a day. If he can't get someone else to spell him off, he mans the diner through the night himself, catching a nap on top of the freezer at quiet times. For the hundred or so Dome Creek residents who live down by the river, well off the highway, the diner has quickly become a new social centre, somewhere outside of home that's always open. In Dome Creek, you don't phone your neighbour for a chat, since only a half-dozen homes have radiophones and no regular phone lines reach down to the village from the highway. For truckers driving the cold and lonely night shift through uncertain winter weather, it has become an obligatory stop, the only place for hot coffee and a break between Prince George and McBride.

Karen Birch, Gary's wife, comes in from her silversmithing shop down on the flat, where she has been wrestling with power problems and a balky heater. It's hard to say how many young Americans came to British Columbia in the late sixties and early seventies to homestead in the Chilcotin, start co-operative farms in the Kootenays and on Vancouver Island, drop out from civilization along lonely roads like this one, harder still to guess how many stayed away from the cities. Karen stayed: she came up from Colorado in 1970 and moved into the vestigial community of Bend, across the river, where half a dozen Americans, a group from Montreal, and some people from Prince George had taken over cabins deserted by homesteaders who tried their luck here after the railway came through. She squatted in an empty cabin for two years, then bought the place. One clear day, Gary, who was living in Prince George, came canoeing down the river, and tied up at Bend. He played poker with the people of Bend far into the night, trying all the while to persuade someone to act as bowman for him through the grand canyon of the Fraser just downstream. Finally, Karen agreed. "I've never been in a canoe," she told him. "You teach me, and I'll go." She smiles. "After that, he parked his canoe at my doorstep and never left." The two married, had a daughter and moved across the river to Dome Creek. Gary worked as a contract logger for years, but found he had to drive farther and farther from home as the forest companies moved deeper and deeper into the mountains. When travel to and from work took four hours each way, he quit and the Dome Diner was born.

The diner still looks makeshift, but Karen says it's a great improvement over opening week last August. "We had a great rush of customers when the guy was sanding the walls, and everybody and everything got covered with dust." She's already a little regretful about the day when an inside washroom will replace the one-holer outside. "You've got to have a little fun," she says, as she takes a picture of me seated in the privy.

Myra Hooker drinks coffee at the wobbly picnic table that tends to upend when too many people sit on one side. Myra, daughter of a pioneer school teacher and a North West Mounted Police man, came to Dome Creek from Creston forty years ago. Her husband Glen operated a sawmill down by the river, and the two of them ran a ranch and trapped and guided through the mountains. Their sons run the ranch now, but Glen still rides his snowmobile along the trapline, setting and checking his traps. Waiting for him to come in from the line, Myra talks about Dome Creek in winter, about the basket supper when the women bring and the men buy, to raise money for the children's Christmas presents, and about the traditional school Christmas concert that the students are rehearsing.

Myra and Karen remember the days when the back-to-the-landers met the old-timers of Dome Creek. "Once you guys realized we were serious [about farming and living here], we were pretty much accepted," says Karen. Myra recalls changing the seating around in the community hall, so the two groups would mingle instead of sitting along opposite walls.

Glen Hooker arrives, the ear flaps of his warm hat loose under the fur-lined hood of his parka. "I think I seen a fisher between here and the dump," he announces, pouring himself a cup of coffee. Then he produces little brown vials of the scents he uses to attract animals to his traps and passes them around. I identify the licorice smell of anise. "They'll go miles for that," says Glen. Everyone sniffs and nods; we all know people like that.

Glen's father rode to the end of steel here at Dome Creek in 1912, when they were building the bridge that shouldn't have been. At Dome Creek, the railway was to cross from the south to the north bank of the river. One day in 1912, the captain of a steamer headed upriver lurched into the riverbank, halted by the low beam of a new bridge edging out across the current. The contractors had been told by the government that their railway bridge must be high enough to allow river traffic to pass underneath. But Dome Creek is a long way from Victoria and even farther from Ottawa, and the railway builders had no objection to a monopoly of freight traffic along the river. By the time the government tried to enforce their ruling on the bridge's height, the bridge spanned the river and the rail crews were moving west. And that was the end of steamboat traffic on the upper Fraser.

Glen was born here in 1922. He guided and trapped for his dad from the time he was fourteen, and started work in the bush when he was fifteen, felling trees with a crosscut saw. "In them days, we skied to school, over the top of the railway fences, the snow was so deep. The winters were colder then. Lots of time it was forty below, down to sixty below. But it didn't seem bad, because it was dry. When I went down to Vancouver, I froze to death."

Glen is laconic about the changes that have taken place in the woods since he was young. "There was very little logging around here when I was growing up. All summer, they might cut 13 million feet. Now, they cut that in two weeks," is his one comment.

The area public health nurse drops by for a coffee on her way to Prince George, and the talk switches, for some reason, to tetanus shots. Myra remembers her last shot, after a beaver chewed her hand. Someone asked Myra if it was an unprovoked attack. "I said, 'I shot him. I think he was very provoked.'"

Glen, Myra and the health nurse leave, and Karen sits down for a chat about winter on this Yellowhead Highway. A few years ago, she hit a patch of black ice and rolled her car. Cargo she was carrying shifted forward and hit her on the neck. "I had 49 percent spinal cord damage. I was the thickness of a piece of paper away from being a quadriplegic." But she shrugs off the suggestion that the accident could have scared her away from Dome Creek. "I watch it on the ice now, and I've got real good tires." Twice a year, she heads for town, and hits the case-lot sales at the big supermarkets in Prince George to buy staples for the next six months. For incidentals, she drives in the opposite direction, to McBride. There, "you can hit every store in town and be back out in an hour."

Yesterday, people warned me not to venture down the slippery, curving hill to Dome Creek. But the sanding truck made its rounds this morning, and the hill is safe. I spiral down through frosted trees and moose meadows, past a partridge so unmoving it looks like a lump of dirt on the road. Across the railway tracks and beyond the snow-covered meadows of a picturesque farm lie the Dome Creek community hall and school. A tiny shack in front of the hall advertises that this is the Dome Creek library. For years, this little building was a peripatetic post office, hauled from one end of the community to the other as different people took on the postmaster job. Then the reigning postmaster moved the office into his own home, and the shack was anchored by the community hall, complete with a stack of donated paperbacks and books from the library at McBride.

Across the road, a teacher kicks a big, sandy-haired dog out from his favourite lair under the table, and the school children abandon the posters they are painting for the school Christmas pageant and crowd around to talk about life in Dome Creek. One hates it here and hankers for the big community she came from—the three-hundred-strong Kootenay village of Riondel—but most delight in Dome Creek and its surroundings. Two of the bigger children toss a complaisant third between them, to show how little and how light he is. "My brother's so light," says one, "that we have to fill his pockets full of snow and rocks so he doesn't blow off the railway bridge" where the railway crosses to the north side of the river at Dome Creek. Invention? "No," an adult informant considers, "the wind really howls through there sometimes."

Before the Fraser starts to freeze up, the boys can cross the river by boat. Later in winter, a solid ice bridge forms, and they can walk across on the ice. This time of year, their mother walks them across the railway bridge, meets them after school to walk them home. They don't really like walking on the narrow bridge; the railing on the only stepout is gone, and you don't hear the trains until they are almost on top of you. But they want to come to school, and that's the only way. The problem may be solved next year, says the older brother. If two more kids move away from Dome Creek, the school will have to close and everyone will be working at correspondence lessons, the way he and his brother did grades one and two. And pretty soon, the problem will be solved for this year. For three years, he says, "the ice got solid on December tenth." Today is the tenth of December.

Back up on the bench, the mountains hem in the highway on all sides, and the midafternoon sun disappears behind the snowy peaks. Even less traffic breaks the monotony of the icy blacktop, just a long-distance truck or two whistling past the rare highway signs, draped in black plastic, that point to parks or wilderness areas closed for the winter. As darkness gathers, I reach a widening valley and catch my first glimpse of the Fraser. Farm fields edge the highway and houses are set behind gates and fences. Signs point to a bed and breakfast house and to cross-country ski trails, and side roads slash across fields lightly covered with snow. A small collection of houses, most of them new, stand between the river and the road, near the sawmill that sustains McBride.

At dinner, Marilyn Wheeler talks about her life in this town of six hundred people. Though she came to Saskatchewan in 1955, she still speaks with her native English accent; she and her husband, John, arrived in McBride in 1958, taught at the local school, and ran a sheep farm. The first woman president of the area farmers' institute, she got serious about local politics about ten years ago, and has been a director on the regional board, representing the six thousand square miles from Dome Creek south to Valemount, ever since. "I knew it was no good sitting around bitching about things. I might as well get involved."

She, Matthew, and her other son John, who wanders in at the coffee stage, team-tell McBride stories, one filling in when the other runs out of steam. Whiteouts of blowing snow that obscure everything on the road, black ice, hills so slippery that the big trucks can only sit and spin their wheels: the Wheelers know the hazards of winter driving. They tell about one trucker, crossing a bridge at the bottom of a hill, who looked out to see his tandem riding beside him, broadside across the bridge.

Marilyn asks John about replacing the headlight that was broken by a moose horn. What moose horn? The Wheelers exchange amused glances. Marilyn and John were driving to to an all-candidates meeting at election time last month; John was looking at the local paper when Marilyn shouted, "There's a moose!"

John screws up an imaginary ball of paper and flicks it high into the air. "The newspaper went like that. The guy in the car coming the other way didn't see the moose at all till the last minute. He started to turn. Mum slammed on the brakes." The other car rolled past, and Marilyn skimmed by on the road shoulder, accelerating past the moose, just catching its horn on her headlight.

They stopped and got out, went over to see how the people in the other car were doing. Said the driver's wife, "We didn't expect any moose. In Vanderhoof, we shot them all."

Marilyn understands why some people turn tail and run from small towns. "One of the questions I always ask when we interview for a position here is whether the person will like living in a fishbowl. Often, people hate the thought that everyone knows more about their business than they do. You can't live in a place like this without great stress. Either you decide to like it, or you leave. I love every minute of it. I rather like the fact that people care."

Next morning in the coffee shop, I eavesdrop on the coffee ladies, some of the half-dozen retired women who meet every morning to drink coffee, swap stories, and give support through any crises that may occur in their lives. Madge and Kay and Elizabeth make it in this morning over the icy roads. "We meet here and the men have coffee at Snoopy's—and isn't that appropriate?" asks Madge, tartly. Madge and Kay worked together at the hospital, cooking, cleaning, and doing laundry, until they retired in the late seventies. At eighty-five, Elizabeth is the doyenne of the group. A pioneer in the valley, she still does volunteer work at the library and the hospital.

"McBride's a lovely little place," announces Madge. "When you're sick or when there's a death in the family, everybody pulls together. They all just treat you wonderful. I was having problems yesterday, getting the ice off my car, and I wanted to go for coffee. Somebody came along and finished cleaning the ice off for me. The other day, the mayor said to me, 'Madge, any time you want to go to town and it's icy, you just phone me and I'll come and get you.'" We chuckle over the idea of the mayor of Vancouver making a similar offer. Last Sunday, the proprietor of the local Stedman's five-and-dime variety store declared seniors' day, offered a seniors' discount, picked up all the seniors, brought them to the store for their shopping, and took them home again.

Outside, the snow drifts gently down. Idling cars send exhaust plumes into the air as bundled-up drivers dash into the post office to pick up their mail. I pull back out onto the road, and enter the final miles of this winter odyssey.

Full Circle

)) East of McBride, snow blows horizontal in the wind, sweeping in dusty devils across the highway. A patchy grey sky shifts above the mountains, their peaks revealed and obscured by high-flying curtains of snow. Though widely spaced homes break the cold monotony of icy fields, this stretch of road seems, ironically, far lonelier than yesterday's unbroken forests. The hiss of tires on the pavement shivers the silence; the radio feeds only static into the air. The great extent of this northern wilderness is borne in on me, and I feel a sudden longing for the comfort that comes from being with an old friend. I think of the elderly women in McBride, years spent working together, laughing together, relying on each other in times of trouble, and of a time not long past when friendship and interdependence were the lone bulwarks against the wilderness.

That kind of interdependence is what Lily Hill found when she moved to this country seventeen years ago. Lily and her husband, Claude, run the white, blue-trimmed general store at Dunster, a tiny community off the main road, on the railway line, across the river. "Claude came here hunting in 1962, and he just loved the area," says Lily, as she serves someone at the post office in the corner of the store, then moves back behind the other counter. "We got married, and he wanted to come back here so bad, we bought the store."

Lily was not convinced at first that rural, isolated Dunster could replace the urban Vancouver she had lived in for years. "I wasn't burning my bridges." But a few years in Dunster changed her mind. "It's the people. Out here, we still need each other." She serves two small girls who venture in from the school next door. "Yes, your mum phoned," she tells one who has forgotten her lunch and needs her mother's approval to put a store-bought lunch on the family tab. Then she trades a few words with a bearded man in a stocking cap who stands by the post office wicket, carefully composing a letter that will go out in today's mail. Mondays, Wednesdays and Fridays, Dunster people gather to check their mail, exchange news about farms and families, and shake their heads over the terrible weather this winter.

Back out on the highway, I turn southwest through the fading remnants of Tete Jaune Cache, once a major settlement but now just a few houses and a highways yard, and onto the last long leg of my journeys through small-town British Columbia. Two hours down the road, as the light fades from the short day, an unofficial flagman holds up his hand to stop the few cars and trucks on the road. The truck drivers climb down from their rigs and walk up the road, hands in pockets, baseball caps pushed to the back of their heads, nodding and pointing. One comes back down the line, to say that a truck driver swerved to miss a deer and jack-knifed his cab and trailer into the ditch. The road is narrow, the ditches close on either side, and the drivers of two heavy-duty tow trucks are trying, with little success and much advice, to drag the trailer back onto the road. Twilight bears down and temperatures drop. Finally, the tow-truck drivers unhook and beckon the waiting traffic past. At the town of Clearwater, I stop, to spend just one more night in the shadow of the mountains.

Morning and south again, away from deep snow and spruce to almost bare hills and Ponderosa pine. By midafternoon, I am on the old road from Kamloops to Merritt. Now that a four-lane expressway speeds people south towards Vancouver, few drivers choose this road that snakes, snow-covered, through rolling hills, past small lakes grey in the dusk, and isolated lights in farmhouse windows. The road curls past the long stretch of Nicola Lake, dark water and pale ice, and I arrive in Merritt ten months after I saw it last.

At the motel, Opie Oppenheimer's works, in vivid dry country shades of purple and orange, blue and green, are on display. Down at the Legion on main street, Carol Tessier, Christmas festive in a silky red blouse, remembers me, signs me into the register at the door, invites me to pull up a chair at the table where she sits with the other volunteers who put on a baron-of-beef lunch every Saturday. Husband Alf is out of town, up on the Coquihalla highway where he is ploughing snow this winter, where he plans to spend Christmas and New Year's Day, making double time and a half, doing what he loves best: working. Carol shows me a photo of Alf in Santa Claus garb for a children's Christmas party: with his roly-poly figure and white beard and hair, he hardly needs a disguise.

Looking younger and more vulnerable out of her RCMP uniform and in civilian clothes, Judy Dempsey comes in for a Saturday-afternoon beer. Husband John, twice Judy's size and a born entertainer, sits down at the other end of the table. He knows every joke in the world, and tells them well. He starts off on a shaggy-dog story about his father. "Is he serious?" I ask Judy. She nods. She's wrong.

Legion members drift in, adding on one table, then another. Wayne buys a round, Ken buys a round, John buys a round. People talk about how slippery it was on the town streets today, cars sliding into snow banks, but no real damage done, and about the strange things happening around town lately as the days grow shorter and winter tensions begin to build. Kidding leapfrogs back and forth across the table. Under the general din, Judy invites me to go along to the Canada Cafe for the Chinese smorgasbord. We slip out into the winter night, and cross the street for deep-fried prawns, sweet and sour boneless pork, and chow mein. Everyone knows everyone; even I recognize faces from the last time I was here. After dinner, we walk over a block or two to the Grand Hotel, where the local helicopter pilot and his band are playing country and western music. John and Judy like to sit at the bar, but all the stools are occupied tonight, so we find a table near the wall. Friends come by for a hug or a handshake, music twangs out over the small dance floor, and cigarette smoke hangs heavy over the tables.

Then it's time for me to go. Judy writes down her address, and tells me to keep in touch. She gives instructions, too: straight down this street, then up past the Coldwater, back to the Legion where my car is parked. "That way, you won't have to walk past the pool hall."

Frost is once more welded to my windshield under a starry sky. The Merritt streets are empty, the Red Top Cafe closed. I drive up the hill and climb into bed, thinking of the places I have visited, the stories I have heard, and the people I have met over the last year. Back in my city life, I will remember the welcome and the easy friendliness that so many people offered me. I envy those people their closeness, their ability to live at a less competitive pace, and their strong determination to create and preserve a way of life against increasing odds. I will miss the unending variety and the beauty of the lakes and streams, the hills and valleys and mountains, the skies crowded with stars, and the unbroken fields of snow that are the companions of those who live in rural areas. And I know I will return again and again to the comforts of small-town British Columbia.